LOUISE BOURGEOIS
MEMORY AND ARCHITECTURE

LOUISE
BOURGEOIS

MEMORY AND ARCHITECTURE

MUSEO NACIONAL CENTRO DE ARTE REINA SOFÍA, MADRID

NOVEMBER 16, 1999–FEBRUARY 14, 2000

FRONTICEPIECE: The Bourgeois family house and the tapestry
workshop in Choisy-le-Roi, France, ca. 1914

After sixty years as an artist, Louise Bourgeois has become a special case in the history of art, a case which unites the legend of her strong personality, her frank attitude to social conventions that threaten to sterilize art, and her works, which despite their singularity and nature, very in keeping with Bourgeois' own vital vicissitude, never deplete their power to become universal imaginings of the human soul.

The title the organizers of this great retrospective exhibition in the Museo Nacional Centro de Arte Reina Sofía have chosen, *Louise Bourgeois: Memory and architecture*, synthesizes the meaning of this artist's work better than any other statement. "All my inspiration comes from my childhood, from my education in France, from a specific moment in my life...", Bourgeois has admitted. And the metaphorical reconstruction of this past has given her work the profound space where the tightest and best plaited fabric of thinking and feeling is to be found, a reconstruction that has also been a therapeutic way for her to exorcise the ghosts of her memory at the same time.

On the other hand, Bourgeois has stated that "architecture has to be an object of our memory", and that "memory is a form of architecture". That is why her work, above all her sculptures, can be seen as an attempt to build a house, the house of fear, desire and hope for life. This is what our childhood home also represents for all of us. That sentimental preference that cold reason has not been able to erase is transmitted as an obsession from Bourgeois' sculptures, drawings, paintings, engravings and installations.

This current exhibition is a momentous event celebrating the artistic dedication of a whole life to creations with a perturbing character that conserve the magnetism of darkness and the abyss that rise up from the well of emotion. This has most likely been the most immediate source from which Bourgeois's work flows. Someone once said that Louise Bourgeois sculpts emotion, and the general public will be able to see how her works of art communicate this intimate flow and allow it to perform.

Mariano Rajoy Brey
Minister of Education and Culture

The house is a sign of life. Everything inside fights against the empire of gravity. The walls, the pillars, the dimensions, the spaces, all bear witness to a resistance against collapse, an endurance. The house is the right angle's kingdom, but that geometry can be concealed without anything falling down and without there being any risk for the mass which would plunge to the ground without the support of the blind lines due to its own weight. This balance was founded by Louise Bourgeois with one of the most representative icons of her art, the *Femmes Maisons*, in which a house is supported by a woman's fragile legs, one of the most eloquent images of the woman's condition this century which the Franco-American artist has filled with her life and her work. It is a privilege for the Museo Nacional Centro de Arte Reina Sofía to present Bourgeois' work in an exhibition that combines the harmonizing effort of the artist, patently obvious in many of her creations, with the stimulated thought of those who have conceived the exhibition as it is and those who have collaborated in the catalogue with their essays.

The exhibition in the galleries of the Reina Sofía Museum takes us on a journey through nearly six decades of creation, specifically designed as if memory itself were taking us back in time, in which childhood and memories, art and life, affection and eroticism, vulnerability and strength, balance and the threat of collapse all interweave, like knots in the same tapestry. Bourgeois' work is a sublimation of all these knots that has led her to be the renowned artist she is today and, no doubt, the one who has most influence among younger generations of artists. The eighty-two works of art in this exhibition reveal the enormous emotional charge Bourgeois gives her creations. On the whole they are based on schematic and primary shapes with an obvious constructive concept, a model of structure that is essential for any construction, whether it be memory or a house. The biographical and confessional aspect of these works of art is no less important. This theme recurs again and again in a hundred versions of figures and renderings, in series (*Femmes Maisons, Cells, Spiders*, etc.) which continue one after another, like links of the artist's firm loyalty to herself. It is difficult to speak of others when speaking about Bourgeois, as it is not easy to find the same affiliation to such tenacity; in fact, her independent and rebel spirit is contrary to grouping artists together by tendencies, and to aesthetic affinities. Bourgeois stands as a figure on her own, unique for her audacity.

As I mentioned above, in *Femmes Maisons* the women's legs always support the "house" halves of these "woman-house" beings, whose other half is the union of a woman's body and a house. These legs are the image of frailty, but also of strength, as they express the cheerful framework of our journey through life. Louise Bourgeois has made her vital journey to a creativity based on variation and repetition, and has converted her world of obsessions into a unique image of a world of freedom that affects everything most intimate and where there is no place for any trickery.

Louise Bourgeois has shown her generosity in the same radical way in everything concerning the organisation of this exhibition in our Museum. Thanks to her help the project of the organizers, Danielle Tilkin and Jerry Gorovoy, has come to a happy conclusion, and from here we would like to convey all our admiration and our gratitude. We would also like to thank the above mentioned organizers for the enormous task they have undertaken, in all aspects, as well as express our appreciation of the essential contributions that Joseph Helfenstein, Beatriz Colomina, Christiane Terrisse, Lynne Cooke, Mieke Bal and Jennifer Bloomer have made to the catalogue. Finally, we are very grateful to those who have loaned the works of art, as without their collaboration this exhibition would not have been able to take place.

José Guirao Cabrera
Director of the MNCARS

Acknowledgments

We would like to express our gratitude to those persons and institutions who through their help and collaboration have made this exhibition possible.

TO THE LENDERS FOR THEIR GENEROSITY:

Guy & Nora Lee Barton

Carnegie Museum of Art, Pittsburgh

Centro Andaluz de Arte Contemporaneo. Junta de Andalucia

Centre Georges Pompidou, Musée National d'Art Moderne/Centre de Création Industrielle, Paris

Daros Collection, Switzerland

Frances Dittmer

Galerie Lelong, Zurich

Karsten Greve

Agnes Gund

Ellen Kern

Kunstmuseum Bern

Lucy Lippard

Frank Millman, C Project, Miami Beach

Musée d'Art Contemporain de Montreal

The Museum of Modern Art, New York

Museum of New Mexico, Museum of Fine Arts

Ivan Wirth
Sammlung Hauser & Wirth, St. Gallen, Switzerland

Ginny Williams

The Ginny Williams Family Foundation

and those who chose to remain anonymous.

TO THE PERSONS WHO ENCOURAGED THE PROJECT FROM ITS BEGINNING:

Richard Armstrong

Marie-Laure Bernadac

Geneviève Bréerette

Chus Burés

John Cheim

Alicia Chillida

Carmen Gimenez

Marussa Gravagnuolo

José Guirao

Christine Lahoud

Soledad Lorenzo

Richard Marshall

Howard Read

Janine Ronsmans

Robert Storr

Pandora Tabatabai Asbaghi

As well as the galleries Cheim & Read in New York, Karsten Greve in Cologne, Pièce Unique in Paris and Soledad Lorenzo in Madrid.

TO THE FOLLOWING COLLABORATORS IN NEW YORK:

Wendy Williams, Louise Bourgeois Studio

More Specialized Transportation

Our very special thanks to the writers to the catalogue, and to Louise Bourgeois whose strength and vitality has been a source of inspiration to us all.

Contents

There's No Place Like Home

JERRY GOROVOY AND DANIELLE TILKIN

A place where there isn't trouble. Do you suppose there is such a place, Toto? There must be.
It is not a place you can get to by boat, or train, it's far, far away, behind the moon, beyond the rain.

DOROTHY, *The Wizard of Oz* (1939)

I was in effect a runaway girl. I was a runaway girl who turned out alright.

LOUISE BOURGEOIS

IN REAL ESTATE, the saying goes, the three most important things are location, location, location. The runaway girl knows this too because who you are depends on where you are. "Every time I moved I hoped again." Bourgeois says, "Rue de Seine, rue Roger Collard, avenue d'Orléans, rue Mazarine, the back of the store, hotel Montalembert, hotel des Grands Augustins." But yet, "Nothing did it. 63 Park Avenue, 333 East 41st, 142 East 18th, 335 West 22nd, 347 West 20th, 518 Van Duzer, 475 Dean. Broken promises. I paid my dues, I can leave: intoxication."[1] Escape becomes euphoric. Intoxicated by the journey, her suitcase may have appeared to be packed full of hope, but in truth what she carried was the heavy luggage of the demons of the past. Her survival strategy for dealing with this past? To build, yet again, new structures to house her fears.

Bourgeois' awareness of this process is quite explicit: "A work of art is a solution to the problem of the terrified artist. What is the shape of the problem?" Her answer is found in architectural metaphors. "It is a logical elaboration, constructed like a building, stone by stone.... As the architectural consciousness of the shape mounts, the psychological consciousness of the fear diminishes...."[2] And it is in this "balancing act between architecture, as an equivalent of understanding, and the fear," where one replaces the other "in the artist's consciousness," that Bourgeois' art has dwelled.

Following this logic then, we can understand how architecture does not appear in her work only as a representation, but as a methodology, a way of building a new life.

In this sense Louise Bourgeois has been on a journey inspired by architecture for six decades, from the early realistic drawings of interiors she made upon her arrival in New York City in the late 1930s, to the plaster *Lairs* of the 1960s, and the *Cells* and recent commissioned works for architectural settings of the 1990s. In her figurative work she has drawn, painted, printed, and sculpted everything from skyscrapers, courthouses, tenements, greenhouses, and glasshouses to labyrinths, sanatoriums, towers, nests, and the very image of houses she has lived in over the years. Yet architectural elements have also appeared in her work in the form of pillars, caryatids, doors, windows, rooms, staircases, and passages. And in her anthropomorphic works, such as the *Femmes Maisons*, the relationships between inner vital functions of the body–respiration, digestion, coordination, and locomotion–have been given architectural equivalents in space. In her world, eyes and orifices have become windows and mirrors, while human figures are sculpted for niches, hang from ceilings, hide behind staircases, and live in the *Cells*.

Like the young runaway Dorothy Gale from Kansas who appeared in the American popular imagination in

1939, a year after Bourgeois arrived in New York City, Bourgeois has been on a journey to alleviate a core experience of abandonment. At the outbreak of World War I, her father enlisted in the army. Her mother dragged the young Louise from military camp to military camp in an attempt to be close to her husband.

Thus the family was without a consistently present father figure during the early years of her life. After the war, when he finally did return, her mother became critically ill with the Spanish flu, and it was Bourgeois' responsibility to be her mother's nurse until she died in 1932.

Exacerbating the fracturing of the family and furthering Bourgeois' experience of loss and chaos, in 1922 her father hired the young Englishwoman Sadie Gordon Richmond to serve as governess to Bourgeois and her siblings. Hired to be a teacher and surrogate mother, Sadie then became the father's mistress. The result was that the family home became a cell harboring a mixture of loss and fear where the mother (who was sick), the father (who was constantly absent as he traveled around looking for tapestries and womanizing), and their children all lived and worked under the same roof with the father's mistress/children's governess. As Bourgeois so aptly put it, "How is it that in a middle-class family a mistress was a standard piece of furniture?"[3] One can sense how architectural walls, passageways, and rooms thus functioned to hide and protect the duplicity and odd "furniture" that riddled the house. For Bourgeois, there were two intruders in the house: Sadie coming for her father and death coming for her mother.

In this sense, like Dorothy in *The Wizard of Oz,* the young Bourgeois was knocked into the unconscious by the force of a chaotic childhood. Although it was a window shutter let loose by the oncoming tornado that knocked Dorothy out, it is the very material of memory and its architecture that Bourgeois has spent her lifetime wrestling with. As she puts it, the past is something she does not remember so much as construct through her artistic encounters in the present. "My works are a reconstruction of past events. The past has become tangible in them; but at the same time they are created in order to forget the past, to defeat it, to relive it and to make it possible for the past to be forgotten."[4] One senses in such a statement her ambivalence to the volatility of her childhood, a world where in fact "the walls begin to shake, the house to quake" in Dorothy's words. In this sense both runaway girls run from the past yet seek to reclaim and rebuild it.

Both are runaways for whom furniture and humans literally and metaphorically whirl about in a fury, turning one into the other. Each runaway's journey has served to transform the familiar, but estranged, black-and-white landscapes of their respective childhood traumas into vivid Technicolor lands where new geographies and new spatial relations construct the ability to return home. In the land of Oz, everyday objects such as ruby slippers, buckets of water, broomsticks, and falling houses are infused with supernatural powers, while, over the course of her career, Bourgeois has turned such common materials as wood, wire, latex, marble, and paper into magical evocations of house and home that healed the psyche. And while Dorothy

FIGURE 3. The Bourgeois family home in Antony, France, ca. 1932

skipped along the yellow brick road accompanied in her quest by the scarecrow (who was seeking brains), the tin man (who needed a heart), and the lion (in need of courage) (Figure 2), Bourgeois' journey has been to reconnect with such fractured aspects of her own unconscious. As the runaway, she has had to confront matters of the heart (emotion connected to the father) and brain (her mother's intellect).

And with great relevancy to the present collection of critical essays, it is via a rational journey into architectural structures and themes that Bourgeois has been able to reconstitute, relive, and control the dramas of her dysfunctional childhood family, creating her own ideal family unit in the present. Architecture has been an active means for working through memory; for attaining self-knowledge and protection; for succeeding at seduction, survival, and escape. To find her equilibrium, she has sought to repair and reconcile human relationships by putting them on a grid or creating an elaborate sculptural set in which to control them. In this sense architecture is the rationalist side of Bourgeois, a daughter of Descartes. For her, geometry is util-

itarian in nature. With direct access to the unconscious via the gift of sublimation, Bourgeois has been able to give tangible form to her fears in order to exorcise them. Art is a rational process of working through the fear. Her exploration of architectural themes and principles therefore reflects an architecture that is in an active state of "being." This is an architecture in which, as Gaston Bachelard put it in *The Poetics of Space,* "The house shelters daydreaming, the house protects the dreamer, the house allows one to dream in peace..." so that "our memories of former dwelling-places are relived as daydreams... these dwelling-places of the past remain in us for all time... and if the house is a bit elaborate, if it has a cellar and a garret, nooks and corridors, our memories have refuges that are all the more delineated."[5] Whether delineated through art or a trip to Oz, the trick for both Dorothy and Bourgeois has

FIGURE 4. Louise Bourgeois country house in Easton, Connecticut, 1940

been to discover the click of the ruby slippers that leads them through memory back toward home. Indeed, these runaways know that "there's no place like home," particularly that home or "architectural consciousness" that one has built over a lifetime of art.

NOTES

1. Louise Bourgeois, diary entry, January 14, 1999. Louise Bourgeois Archive.

2. Louise Bourgeois in a conversation with Jerry Gorovoy, 1999. Louise Bourgeois Archive.

3. Louise Bourgeois, *Partial Recall* (videotape). New York: Museum of Modern Art, 1983.

4. Louise Bourgeois, diary entry, 1996. Louise Bourgeois Archive.

5. Gaston Bachelard, *The Poetics of Space,* trans. Maria Jolas (Boston: Beacon Press, 1994), 6–8.

Louise Bourgeois:
Architecture as a Study in Memory

JOSEF HELFENSTEIN

LOUISE BOURGEOIS' work has frequently been considered from the point of view of the autobiographical content that is encoded in it, with reference to the artist's obsessive analysis of her childhood. There is a long tradition in art history, which I will not go into,[1] that limits the discussion of women artists' work to emotion, autobiography, and the antirational. In this essay, I shall examine a basic feature of Bourgeois' work that stands in opposition to such one-sided interpretation: the significance of structure, order, and rational composition within her work.

Louise Bourgeois' parents (her mother was from Aubusson) had a business, first in Choisy-le-Roi, then in Antony near Paris, selling and restoring historical Gobelins tapestries (Figure 6). From the age of ten, Louise learned to complete the designs on the 18th- and 19th-century Gobelins. Later, upon entering the Lycée, she chose the mathematical track, which was an unusual decision for a girl. After receiving her baccalaureate in 1932, she briefly studied mathematics and geometry at the Sorbonne. In 1936, she began to attend several art schools and workshops in Paris and, at the same time, studied art history at the Ecole du Louvre in order to serve as a docent to English tourists. Most important for her was her apprenticeship in 1938 with Fernand Léger, who taught her for free because of her knowledge of English (Léger, like many other artists, lived largely by teaching students from overseas). It was Léger who turned her interest in geometry and mathematics into a passion for sculpture. By the fall of 1938, when she moved to New York with the art historian Robert Goldwater, her interest in structure, order, and methodical procedure was fully developed.

Louise Bourgeois was twenty-seven years old when she arrived in New York. The American city with its

FIGURE 6. Joséphine Bourgeois at the tapestry gallery, 174 Boulevard Saint–Germain, Paris, ca. 1911

extreme spatial experiences–skyscrapers, street canyons, human beings disappearing into cars, elevators, subway shafts–was absolutely new for the young woman coming from the capital of the 19th century. The shock of these experiences reinforced what was to become an enduring interest of hers: the relation of human beings to their environment.[2] Changes in her family–for instance, she and Robert Goldwater

FIGURE 5. *Portrait of Jean-Louis*, 1947

| 19

adopted a son in 1938, and in 1940 and 1941 she gave birth to two sons—intensified her sensitivity to rooms and to what happens inside houses. The stifling quality of rooms is a recurrent theme in her paintings and etchings. Her *Femme Maison* paintings of the years 1945 to 1947 forcibly combine the female body with a house. This allegory shows the drastic reduction of women to their domestic functions and the prisonlike quality inherent in this division of social roles.

Such is the first manifestation of a fundamental trait of Bourgeois' work: a tendency toward drastic concision, even hermeticism, that is downright aggressive in what it excludes. Architecture becomes the symbol of this experience of the hermetic. On the one hand, it exudes a sense of contact phobia and the feeling of exclusion, and on the other, of intimacy confined to the point of autism (Figure 7). In this context, nothing corresponds more clearly to the basic American constellation of cold Puritanism and uninhibited pioneer spirit than the skyscraper.[3] The most spectacular examples of this architecture were only a few years old when Bourgeois arrived in New York.[4]

BODY AND ARCHITECTURE

The tendency to reduce relations, emotions, and persons to basic figures which frequently correspond to images of architecture and dwellings, or are pictured through the relation of figures in a space, dominates the work of the 1940s. In 1947, Bourgeois published a book with a sequence of etchings and short texts under the title *He Disappeared into Complete Silence* (Plates 4 and 5). The parabolic short stories deal with loneliness and failed relationships. The partly macabre content is communicated with merciless brevity in concise, rudimentary language, from which any sign of the author's emotional involvement has been removed.

This tone of would-be unemotional detachment points to a basic characteristic of Louise Bourgeois' art: the principle of contradiction, i.e., of the marked (though hidden) connection of opposites. For her use of unemotional language conceals states of extreme concern and vulnerability. Bourgeois' use of language thus demonstrates her method of using rational logic to force the chaotic urgency of emotions into a new form and thus to neutralize them.

The relation of etching to text in *He Disappeared Into Complete Silence* seems ambivalent, or at least haphazard.[5] For instance, in the images architectural representations, towers, and grids predominate. There are skyscrapers with elevator shafts, water towers, and cell-

FIGURE 7. *Untitled (Self-Portrait)*, 1943. Saint-Louis Art Museum.

like bare rooms, and moments where windmills, antennae, cranelike constructions, and ladders have replaced people. It is a cold, mechanical world whose atmosphere is comparable to the emotional tones found in Franz Kafka's texts—in other words, a world that is a mixture of frozen anxiety laced with the sensation of anonymous, silent death.[6]

In 1949 and 1950 in the Peridot Gallery in New York, Louise Bourgeois had her first exhibitions of the sculptures she had worked on since the mid-1940s. These are pole-shaped figures, forms as reminiscent of African tribal art and Indian totem poles as of skyscrapers. Some of these standing sculptures pick up the *Femme Maison* motif but in a different form. *Portrait of Jean-Louis* (Plate 7) shows the seamless combination of two different realities: a lower body with pelvis and legs, which, in the upper part of the sculpture, turns without transition into a repetitive highrise structure. The artist later commented on this object—one of her most famous works—as follows: "I wanted my son to be as beautiful as the skyscrapers here in New York."[7] The form of *Dagger Child* (Plate 12) seems even more inspired by Manhattan's architecture. The sculpture has a striking resemblance to one of the most famous Art Deco giants of the New York skyline, the Chrysler Building (Figure 8). At its completion in 1930, it was for only a short time the highest building in the world—some thirty meters higher than the Eiffel Tower of Louise Bourgeois' Parisian past.[8] William von Alen, the Chrysler Building's architect, went to a Beaux-Arts Ball in 1931 dressed as his own

FIGURE 9. The Beaux-Arts Ball, New York City, 1931 (center: W. Van Allen as the Chrysler Building)

building (Figure 9). He thus anticipated Bourgeois' allegorical combination of human figure and high-rise architecture.

The first generation of *Personnages*, as Bourgeois calls her standing sculptures, seem monolithic. Their marked verticality suggests self-assertion. Their frontality both demands dialogue and creates an atmosphere of defense. At the same time, the fragile bases of these sculptures point toward vulnerability and instability. Bourgeois has called this the "fragility of verticality."[9] Her statement addresses problems of rootedness and immobility, but also of the potential danger of the collapse of order and rational structure.

ADDITION AS SCULPTURAL PRINCIPLE

At the beginning of the 1950s, the compact vertical figures give way to sculptures that are assembled from several sawed or planed parts, for example *Mortise* (1950) (Plate 19), *Memling Dawn* (1951) (Plate 21), *Femme Volage* (1951), *Spiral Woman* (1951–52) (Plate 22), and *Red Fragmented Figure* (1953). The support for most of these figures is a metal rod which can be seen as analogous to the steel frame of skyscrapers. Bourgeois' method of threading layers of uniform pieces of wood is contradictory: on the one hand, it is an act of spearing, while on the other, it is an imitation of children's games such as threading wooden balls on wires in order to learn how to count. To spear and quantify as elementary expressions of control is, as it were, the sculptural

FIGURE 8. Chrysler Building, New York

metaphor for the methodical use of reason as a weapon in taking possession of the world. In terms of psychodynamics, this additive action–this repetitive structure or layering of the same elements–is ambiguous. On the one hand, it is an act of soothing, but, on the other

FIGURE 10. Segmented sculptures, ca. 1950

hand, it is an expression of *aporia* and compulsion. The law of physical economy represented here seems to correspond to the expression of psychic energy. And so the methodical consistency with which Bourgeois works becomes clear. Structure and materials stand entirely in the service of the idea. Form is as much an expression of method as of a figurative imagination. Bourgeois' procedures demonstrate her attempt to

reduce problems to basic constellations in order to make them comprehensible,[10] revealing a methodical logic that does honor to her spiritual predecessors, the French philosopher and mathematician René Descartes (1596–1650) and Blaise Pascal (1623–1662). Descartes is considered one of the founders of modern epistemology, whose logic is based on an ideal of mathematical laws. He is known for laying down the rule, or critical weapon, of all philosophical investigation: his *méthode du doute*. Pascal's best-known writings are *L'esprit géométrique*, a treatise on the philosophy of mathematics. Louise Bourgeois, who after 1932 studied mathematics and philosophy, if only briefly, is well acquainted with the work of both thinkers.[11]

The *Personnages*, in other words, the monolithic and assembled vertical figures from the early 1950s, manifest a fundamental–and intentionally unresolved–contradiction between rigorous compulsion toward form and an utter lack of interest in it (Figure 10). Obviously, the *emotional* power of the object, its fetishistic component, is stronger for Bourgeois than is the notion of "form" as an aesthetic principle. For form comes into being at point zero, at the moment of the *tabula rasa*, when pressing, overwhelming emotions erupt. Here we see that Bourgeois has introduced a new dimension to modern sculpture. Her contribution is of decisive significance for the art of this century and would be inconceivable without the influence of both non-European tribal art and psychoanalysis.

The mid-1950s marks a caesura in Bourgeois' work. Around 1960 she began to use not only the vertical dimension of space, but more intensely, its breadth and depth. Habitat, as an existential metaphor, appears frequently and in many variations in her work. But now, as the title *Lair* shows, they are habitats relating to the animal world, in other words, cave- or nestlike haunts. It is important to emphasize that the form these objects take–earthbound and flat or suspended bag-shapes–is opposed to the "mathematical" verticality of the 1950s. They are rough, collapsed shapes that conjure associations ranging from animal excrement to primitive structures. Again we see how seductively Bourgeois fuses form and content. The *lair* is, after all, an ur-form of habitat corresponding to a raw, primitive sculptural state (Figure 12).

Out of new materials (plaster, latex, synthetics, bronze, and finally, toward the end of the sixties, marble) emerge new forms. In the mid-1960s, Bourgeois' sculptures were examined within the context of work by Eva Hesse and Bruce Nauman (although this does not mean that her extensive oeuvre was known in its entirety). In the second half of the 1960s, almost simultaneously with, but independent of, the discovery of her work by a younger generation of artists, we notice

FIGURE 11. *Molotov Cocktail,* 1968

another transformation in Bourgeois' art. It is related to the political movements and social changes of those years (student revolts, feminism, the anti–Vietnam War movement). In this context belong the series of objects such as *Molotov Cocktail* (1968) (Figure 11) or *Femme Pieu* (1970) (Plate 42) that are barely larger than a hand and

appear to be harmless. The crudeness of these objects and the roughness of their material express an emotional intensity that is the motor of Bourgeois' art. These objects are multilayered in effect. Their horizon of associations ranges from archaeological objects and fetishes to infamous symbols of contemporary warfare. Here the iconography of the 20th century is put into a particularly intense relationship to materials that are charged with animism. Such a utilization of opposites is, as I have argued above, characteristic of Bourgeois' entire oeuvre.

REPETITION

The "modern" reception of Bourgeois' oeuvre occurs in the second half of the 1960s. In this phase her work has been viewed as the predecessor of the generation of artistic trends then emerging, trends that contrast with, and reject, kinship with Abstract Expressionism. Within this context there was increasing reference to the autobiographical aspect of her work (due, in part, to that fact that many of her statements were published during the 1970s). Yet what is most striking about her work – formal reduction, emotional charge, repetition as structural principle – indicates that autobiography is actually incidental for the viewer (if not for the artist). By the end of the 1960s it had also become obvious that there was no strictly chronologically based stylistic development in this oeuvre. Instead of linear chronology (a structuring principle that had become more and more obsolete in the art of this century), we find variation and repetition. We find, as well, her method of side-stepping into different, often opposing materials while maintaining an obsessive continuity of themes and motives.

It will be argued here that repetition has a significance in the work of Bourgeois that goes far beyond its formal aspects. For instance, many motives and themes are taken up again and again over decades. Repetition here becomes the equivalent of emotional urgency. This principle also appears in the manner in which she insists on experimenting with such materials as plaster, latex, rubber, bronze, marble, and alabaster. In the drawings, a medium particularly suited to her self-reflexive method, repetition is especially prominent in the obsessive growth of forms and the *tapisserie*-style parallelism of the shading. In sum, the emotional intensity of Bourgeois' sculptures and drawings suggests that these are not objects that reference the external world. Instead, their power resides in the way that they refer primarily to themselves, or, to put it more philosophically, the way that they demonstrate and perform their own existence.

FLUID FORM

The principle of dismemberment that appears frequently in her work also points in the direction of the obsessional and to a psychodynamic symbolism of the working process. The manner in which she uses dismemberment and bodily fragmentation is not about destruction, but, at a deeper level, is about a method of analyzing–of gathering and ordering–in preparation for the creation of a new synthesis. In other words, the reconstruction of the dissected whole is implicit. In this way, the method of spearing, or threading, separate parts is the equivalent of the inverse of dismemberment. And yet, cumulatively, this method of reparation has an element of menace, of devouring, to it. This is demonstrated in many sculptures and drawings, but most clearly, perhaps, in Bourgeois' first installation, *The Destruction of the Father* (1974) (Plate 44). This work also proves that, even under conditions of explosive emotional charge, the artist is by no means out of control, but works methodically. The principle of construction, by way of additive alignment, is combined with the sense of a horizontal dissolving of the sculpture, as appears for the first time in *Soft Landscape II* (1967) (Plate 34). The principle of dissolution, i.e., of solidifying and liquefying states, forces the object into a new union. Such a process is particularly impressive in the plaster sculpture *Labyrinthine Tower* (1962) (Plate 26) where the form gradually transforms from a geometric shape into an organic one. What occurs then that the viewer is given the impression of the tower collapsing into itself like a softened colossus. Here Bourgeois has yoked together ideas of solid construction and soft organ, of geometry and organic growth, and placed her material (plaster) in the service of the fusion of such a dualism. The spiral form is a metaphor both for Bourgeois' procedure (i.e. her insistent repetition) and for the manner in which her work spirals around itself.[12]

Bourgeois' use of language and writing, too, is indicative of her methodical procedure. Many drawings have writing on the back, some on both sides. In the *Insomnia* series (1994–1995)–which numbers over two-hundred sheets–the written notes and reflections play an important part. This preponderance of private notes has various consequences. It demonstrates Bourgeois' need to reflect, to control, and to objectify psychological processes. However the resulting order is subjective, hence hermetic. In order for the viewer to take in her imagery, he or she must engage in self-abandonment simultaneous with overidentification (with Bourgeois), resulting in almost torturous exercises in time-consuming decipherment. Bourgeois' use of personal notation in her drawings is therapeutic or, as the artist has called it, an exorcism. It is based on the psychoanalytical method of curing neuroses through verbal formulation. Another effect of the private notations is to underline the diaristic nature of the work, which is of interest here because the basic feature of diaries is, in fact, repetition. "Only repetition gives physical reality to experience," as Bourgeois has said.

SCULPTURE AS ARCHITECTURE
THAT CAN BE ENTERED

The end of the 1970s brought the first clear signs of a lasting interest in Louise Bourgeois' work. In the course of a few years, the artist became the center of the New York art scene. In 1982, the Museum of Modern Art organized the first extensive retrospective. Demand for her work and institutional offers of one-woman shows increased by leaps and bounds. By the end of the 1980s, Bourgeois was one of the stars of the international art scene.

The installation *Articulated Lair* (1986) (Plates 52 and 53) marked the emergence of a new, important direction in her oeuvre. *Articulated Lair* is an installation of variable form made of metal screens which can be entered and exited through two small door-openings. Inside, a small stool is placed on the floor. Baglike or tube-shaped black rubber objects are suspended in front of the screens. The overall effect is another demonstration of the violent fusion of opposites that characterizes Bourgeois' work, in this instance, of the organic and the mechanically prefabricated.

Here, sculpture becomes architecture by way of becoming a structure one can enter. Yet *Articulated Lair* is a radically nightmarish representation of what inhabiting a space can mean. The title points to the familiar monomaniacal metaphor of habitat, but this idea is reduced, with mathematical rigor, to the model of a basic constellation. "You can add or subtract. That's what 'articulated' means. So articulation is the symbol of a relationship that can change and improve."[13] In

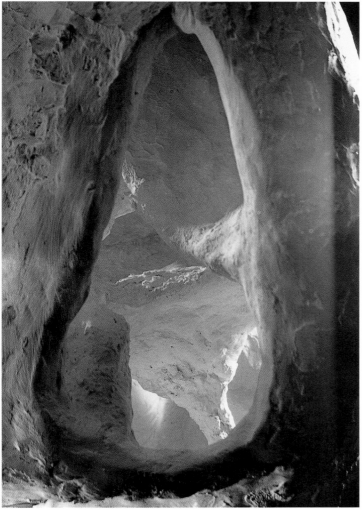

FIGURE 12. *Fée Couturière*, 1963 (detail)

Articulated Lair, the visitors' emotions become the content of the sculpture. Reactions oscillate between feeling trapped, or feeling homeless and vulnerable. In general, *Articulated Lair* creates an unsatisfied need for protection.

The expansion of the idea of sculpture that is begun in *Articulated Lair* is developed further in Bourgeois'

1992 installation *Precious Liquids* (Plates 62 and 63). Here she returns to the principle of fluid form as the expression of psychological processes that have been transferred to associations with bodily fluids.[14] The installation can, again, be entered. It has the character of a subterranean space from the beginnings of industrialization.

The principle form Bourgeois' work has taken in the 1990s, beginning in 1991, is that of the *Cells*. These installations appear to be harsh studies in memory. The outer skin consists of doors from abandoned factories and demolished houses that have been arranged in circles, spirals, or rectangles. Here it is as if the viewer were thrust into an interior space constructed from Bourgeois' past, complete with metal beds, tables, chairs, glasses, pieces of clothing, blankets, statuettes, and other objects. The use of mirrors reflects the mute eloquence of these rooms that are drenched in the melancholy of things past. Embroidered in red thread on white cushions, mottoes like *"Je t'aime"* or "Pain is the Ransom of Formalism" create an atmosphere of vulnerability and tension that is pregnant with emotion. The objects seem to be materializations of emotions turned outward. The overall effect is one of claustrophobia. The artist has explained that the title *Cells* refers to the history of political movements and actual architecture, as well as to microbiology: "Communist cells, prison cells and biological cells."[15] Later, Bourgeois commented on the phenomenon of the larger assemblies splitting into ever more numerous parts: "The cells represent the closed-in space. Is there any communication between them? Are they closed or open? They can describe either a person or a biological cell, they make us very conscious of limits."[16]

The walls assembled in a precariously provisional arrangement, as in a slum, hide their content as much as they expose it. This is even more explicit in the *Cells*, each of whose outer skin is a giant cage into which one enters as if into a prison, a prison bathed in the residue of the past. The materials used for the outer skin of the *Cells*, such as the doors and cages, are obsolete objects that have been stripped of their original use. Bourgeois is passionately interested in these cast-off symbols of an abandoned history. And New York, the epitome of the dynamic, self-regenerating metropolis with its warehouses and dumps, is the ideal storehouse for this passion. Bourgeois uses America's omnipresent symbols of waste—its landscape of rubbish—not for the purpose of recycling such waste, but rather for its association with the passing of history, of the past.[17] Thus the artist becomes an archaeologist of industrial society at the end of the 20th-century, commenting on the manner in which it discards and replaces its resources and instruments at an ever-increasing pace.

With the *Cells*, Louise Bourgeois has enacted habitat as a place of revelation; a shock of confrontation with the past. The sheer reality of the architectonic installation, complete with nostalgic inventory, has banished the last vestiges of "representation"—a concept which here seems like a ghost of times long past. Nevertheless, the reality of the *Cells* is based on memory, a formulation of memory that remains hermetically tied to a subject: "The architecture has to be an object of your memory," says Bourgeois. "When you summon, when you conjure the memory, in order to make it clearer, you pile up the associations the way you pile up bricks to build an edifice. Memory itself is a form of architecture."[18]

1. One of the most famous examples is the American artist Georgia O'Keeffe, who, although twenty-four years older than Bourgeois, is in many respects her contemporary. From her first show in 1917 on, O'Keeffe's work was celebrated by her American colleagues and art critics as an example of feminine, emotional art, rooted in the experience of nature and completely untouched by the rationalism of the European avant-garde.

2. Lucy Lippard, "Louise Bourgeois: From the Inside Out," *Artforum*, vol. 13 (March 1975): 27.

3. Cf. Louise Bourgeois: "I have nothing against puritans because I had escaped from a French promiscuity, and thus Puritanism did not make me suffer." In Alain Kirili, "The Passion for Sculpture. A Conversation with Louise Bourgeois," *Arts Magazine* (March 1989): 69ff. In the same conversation Bourgeois comments on her phase of *mal du pays*, of homesickness, after her arrival in New York.

4. The most famous skyscrapers in Manhattan were completed in the second half of the 1920s and the beginning of the 1930s. The Great Depression put a stop to the development of high-rise architecture in New York and other American cities after 1931.

5. Cf. Deborah Wye's comment in Deborah Wye/Carol Smith, *The Prints of Louise Bourgeois* (New York: The Museum of Modern Art 1994), 72ff.

6. Cf. Louise Bourgeois: "This is about survival… about the will to survive," in Wye/Smith (1994), 72.

7. *Louise Bourgeois: Blue Days and Pink Days* (exhibition catalogue), ed. Jerry Gorovoy and Pandora Tabatabai Asbaghi (Milan: Fondazione Prada 1997), 108.

8. Even today, the Chrysler Building (height 319 m), together with the somewhat higher Empire State Building (1931), is among the most famous skyscrapers of the world. The top of the building is modeled on the shape of the Chrysler automobile's hood.

9. Kirili (1989), 70.

10. "I mean solid geometry as a symbol for emotional security. Euclidean or other kinds of geometry are closed systems where relations can be anticipated and are eternal. It comes naturally to me to express emotions through relations between geometrical elements, in two dimensions or three dimensions." Louise Bourgeois in conversation with Susi Block, in *Art Journal*, Vol. 34, No. 4 (Summer 1976): 372.

11. In a later conversation about her working method, Louise Bourgeois said, "it is not deductive, it is intuitive" and compared it to Pascal's method. Cf. "Louise Bourgeois, An Interview with Donald Kuspit," (New York: Elizabeth Avedon Editions/Vintage Contemporary Artists (a division of Random House, 1988), 29. For Pascal, cf. also Paulo Herkenhoff, "La Finesse de Pascal and the Refusal of Renunciation," in *Louise Bourgeois* (exhibition catalogue), (Chicago: The Arts Club of Chicago, 1997/1998), 5ff; Robert Storr, "Arachne on 20th Street," in *Louise Bourgeois: Homesickness* (exhibition catalogue) (Yokohama: Yokohama Museum of Art, 1997/1998), 131ff, see also 132; 136.

12. Cf. Kuspit, *An Interview with Louise Bourgeois*, 1988, 45: "I am involved in a kind of spiral, a spiral motion of motivation."

13. Bourgeois in Rainer Crone, Petrus Graf Schaesberg, *Louise Bourgeois. The Secret of the Cells* (Munich/London/New York: Prestel, 1998), 13.

14. "Intense emotions become physically liquid – a precious liquid." Louise Bourgeois in Gorovoy/Asbaghi 1997, 206.

15. Ibid., 216.

16. Louise Bourgeois in Gorovoy/Asbaghi, 221.

17. Cf. Kuspit, *An Interview with Louise Bourgeois,* 38.

18. Louise Bourgeois in a conversation with the author, New York, March 31, 1999.

The Architecture of Trauma

BEATRIZ COLOMINA

Art is the experiencing – or rather – the re-experiencing of trauma.[1]

I cannot get out of the house. I want to. I have to. I would like to. I was planning to, but I gave up at the last minute.[2]

LOUISE BOURGEOIS

I.

"BAUDELAIRE," writes Walter Benjamin, "speaks of a duel in which the artist, just before being beaten, screams in fright. This duel is the creative process itself."[3] Benjamin could have been writing about Louise Bourgeois, who says, "At the beginning there is panic, and there is an absolute survival instinct to put order around you in order to escape the panic."[4] But if, for Baudelaire, the figure of shock is connected to the experience of life in the metropolis, for Bourgeois, shock is connected to domestic spaces. To escape the panic, she reconstructs these spaces, reconstructs them precisely to get rid of them.

All of Bourgeois' work is rooted in memories of spaces she once inhabited, from the houses of her childhood – in Paris, Aubusson, Choisy, Antony – to the multiple apartments she lived in New York City, the country house in Easton, Connecticut, her studio in Brooklyn, and the brownstone on West 20th street where she continues to live today. Houses figure prominently in her stories, in the innumerable interviews, the diaries, photographs, drawings, sculptures, and even titles of her work. The result is that we know, intimately, where she has lived, more intimately, in fact, than is common with artists (except, symptomatically, in the case of architects). Bourgeois describes herself as "a collector of spaces and memories,"[5] and offers us countless lyrical recollections of spaces going back to her early years.

Aubusson was the town where my mother and grandmother spent their childhood. It was founded in the 16th century by tapestry makers . . . because of the special chemical qualities found in the Creuze River. . . . Tannin poured into the water from upstream and wool washed in it was particularly receptive to the dyeing agents. . . . My grandmother had her own atelier . . . She had married a granite-cutter because that was the men's work. (Creuzemen were famous all over Europe for their stone cutting. . . . All the window lintels in town were carved by hand from the granite from the countryside.)[6]

If all of Bourgeois' work is concerned with the physical locations of her memories, these spaces are all domestic and all associated with trauma. Aubusson, for example, is where the family moved during the war, to a house where Bourgeois' mother and grandmother had a tapestry atelier opposite the Creuze river and the local slaughterhouse. Bourgeois recalls the sound of war coming into the house, invading the very space that was meant to be a refuge from the war:

I remember the soldiers used to come back from the front in the night. There were whole trains full of people who were wounded at the front and you would hear them in the night. . . . I was in Aubusson because my parents had packed us away to live in the mountains so that we wouldn't be so near the front, but you could hear the wounded all the time.[7]

The war also starts a lifelong sense of dislocation. When her father volunteers for military service at the outbreak of World War I, the young Louise is repeatedly taken to

FIGURE 13. *Cell (Choisy)*, 1990–93. Ydessa Hendeles Art Foundation.

29

the front by her mother, who anxiously follows her husband from camp to camp. "I remember her nervousness," she says, "and I remember my pain at the time."[8] The father is wounded. (Figure 14) Then wounded again. The disruption of the house becomes a disruption of the body, and a new form of dislocation as Louise travels from hospital to hospital, enveloped by the disturbing sight of fragmented bodies. House, war, slaughterhouse become indistinguishable. The sound of war becomes the sound of her mother crying, as her father returns one more time to the battle, a sound she will "always remember."[9]

FIGURE 14. Louis Bourgeois with nurses at the front, ca. 1916

Bourgeois' lyrical descriptions of domestic life effortlessly slide into descriptions of traumatic events. The artworks emerge out of this slippage between lyrical narrative and traumatic experience. After the war, for example, the family moves to the outskirts of Paris, to a property in Antony that again includes a house and a tapestry atelier and gardens that are separated by the banks of a river (the Bièvre) that had the necessary tannin for dyeing tapestries. Once again, Bourgeois offers us an extraordinary description of the site, entangled with a description of the tapestry repair work that was done in her home:

> First the tapestry had to be cleaned in the Bièvre with a special unadulterated blue soap from Marseilles. On the river bank was the public wash house where the women came to do the laundry. There were rocks lining the bank that they would use as washboard. When the tapestries were brought to the river for washing, the workers had a special wooden box to kneel in, placed on the rocks, each with a pile of straw or a cushion to protect their knees. The wet wool would be so heavy that men would have to help the women as they held the tapestry in the water. Then it would be spread out to dry in the open air, reverse side exposed to the sun. Once dry, the tapestry would be laid down and nailed in place on top of a large table, and the women would start the reweaving.... We all enjoyed planting things in that soil from the river. What grew well was boxwoods. When it rains they smell so sweet. And there were hawthorns, pink and white. And tamaris. There were asparagus beds... masses of peonies. Fruit trees... pear and apple trees... poplar trees.[10]

> There were all kinds of animals. There was a donkey, there was a pig. It was full of guinea hens... ducks, and families of rabbits. And all these animals. The point of it was to show that all animals can live together in peace and harmony.[11]

But soon the idyllic scene is disturbed. Bourgeois discovers, through the gossip of the women working on the tapestry, that her live-in English tutor, Sadie, is sleeping with her father. Bourgeois will return again and again to this primal scene of betrayal, sometimes suggesting that the rage provoked by that situation, which lasted a decade, is the motor of her work.

> The thing about Sadie is that she lived in the house. And she stayed for 10 years—the formative years of

my sister and myself.... The motivation for the work is a negative reaction against her. It shows that it is really the anger that makes the work.... Sadie, if you don't mind, was engaged to teach me English. I thought she was going to like me. Instead of which she betrayed me. Now you will ask me: How is that in a middle-class family this mistress was a standard piece of furniture? Well, the reason is that my mother *tolerated* it! And this is the mystery.[12]

Sadie is a part of the house, a piece of furniture in a house where furniture is not taken lightly. Her father "had a passion for fine furniture." Antique chairs, for example, were suspended from the ceiling in the attic, a display that Bourgeois regards as the origin of her hanging pieces.[13] What seems to be the major offence is that Sadie lived in the house, even in a complex household of workers and family members, symptomatically described by Bourgeois as floating body parts ("twenty-five *petites-mains*" working on the tapestry[14]). Sadie will have to be detached from the house, killed outside by the river, twisted like a tapestry. The twisting will be a means of revenge and a means of art, art as revenge:

> The spiral is important to me. It is a twist. As a child after washing the tapestries in the river, I would twist them with three others or more to wring the water out. Later I would dream of getting rid of my father's mistress. I would do it in my dreams by twisting her neck. The spiral—I love the spiral—represents control and freedom.[15]

The spiral exorcises the out-of-control domestic situation of her parent's house. It becomes a dominant figure in her work. As she often says: "The spiral is an attempt at controlling the chaos."[16] The spiral is a means of establishing order, constructing a space that can be entered and yet there is no clear line between inside and outside. The spiral is a space that closes and opens at the same time, a space that progressively reveals itself.

Sadie is not the only piece of furniture turned into art. In a far more sanguine story, Bourgeois describes the dining table of her childhood as the site of her "first work of art... *une poupée de pain*"[17]:

I was drawn into art because it isolated me from difficult dinner conversations where my father would brag about how good and wonderful he was.... I took white bread, mixed it with spit and molded a figure of my father. When the figure was done, I started cutting off the limbs, with a knife. I see this as my first sculpture solution. It was right for the moment and helped me. It was an important experience and certainly determined my future direction.[18]

Une poupée de pain, a bread doll, a doll of pain. Bourgeois discovers art as therapy, at the age of eight, at the dinner table. It worked for the moment. It helped her. It determined her future direction, conceptually and formally. The connection between art, therapy, and domestic space will never leave her. No wonder she received an Honorary Award in 1943 for her tapestry work in "The Arts in Therapy," an exhibition that promoted artistic and craft activities as part of a rehabilitation program for those who were wounded in the war.[19] She had been practicing all her life.

For Bourgeois, art is always a form of therapy. It prevents the artist from going mad, from becoming a criminal. "To be an artist is a guarantee to your fellow humans that the wear and tear of living will not let you become a murderer."[20] And the way to avoid becoming a murderer in life is to become one in your work: "In my art, I am the murderer. I feel for the ordeal of the murderer, the man who has to live with his conscience."[21] If in life, Bourgeois sees herself as a victim, in art she regains control by selecting her victim.

In one sense, Louise Bourgeois becomes Louis Bourgeois, the father, who must be "liquidated" because he "liquidated" her.[22] Louis Bourgeois had a bad temper and was prone to exploding at the dinner table. These outbursts were such a common experience that Louise's mother kept a pile of saucers near him at the table, so he would break the crockery rather than yell at the children. Louise will often break things to make art. In fact, she will often break her own art. In a television documentary, *Chère Louise* (1995), Bourgeois breaks a piece of crockery as she recounts the story of her father's behavior at the dinner table, smashing it against the floor as if to demonstrate the sound, and smiles.[23]

II.

More than fifty years later, Bourgeois returns to the scene of her first crime, to the dining table that still haunts her, for one more murderous piece: *The Destruction of the Father* (sometimes titled *Le Repas du Soir (The Evening Meal)*, shown at 112 Greene Street in 1974 (Plate 44). Here, the primary materials will not be bread and spit, for Bourgeois will descend upon New York's Meat Market district and buy dozens of animal limbs in order to make the piece out of actual flesh.

> I went down to the Washington Meat Market on Ninth Avenue and got lamb shoulders, chicken legs and cast them all in soft plaster. I pushed them down into it, then turned the mold over, opened it, threw away the meat and cast the form in latex.... I built it here in my house. It is a very murderous piece, an impulse that comes when one is under too much stress and one turns against those one loves most.[24]

Can we forget that Bourgeois lived across the street from a slaughterhouse during World War I? (Figure 15). And what to make of that photograph of her, in the basement of her brownstone on 20th Street, against a brick wall, her shadow merging with a big stain on the wall that suggests blood, below a straight line of animal limbs prepared for *The Destruction of the Father*, looking up to them? (Figure 16).

But more important than how the piece was done, and what it represents, is why it was made in the first place, the childhood trauma that triggered the piece (as if crime in art needed an explanation or justification) and how the therapy worked:

> Now the purpose of *The Destruction of the Father* was to exorcise the fear. And after it was shown ... I felt like a different person.... Now, I don't want to use the term *thérapeutique*, but an exorcism is a therapeutic venture. So the reason for making the piece was catharsis. What frightened me was that at the dinner table, my father would go on and on, showing off, aggrandizing himself. And the more he showed off, the smaller we felt. Suddenly there was a terrific tension, and we grabbed him – my brother, my sister, my mother – the three of us grabbed him and pulled him onto the table and pulled his legs

FIGURE 15. The slaughterhouse at La Villette, Paris (Photo by Eli Lotar)

and arms apart – dismembered him, right? And we were so successful in beating him up that we ate him up.... The recall was so strong, and it was such a lot of work, that I felt like a different person. I felt as if it had existed. It really changed me. That is the reason artists go on – it's not that they get better and better, but they are able to stand more.[25]

But how? By re-creating the spaces, the figures, and then mutilating them, dismembering them, cutting their parts out. And if the bodies are identified with the spaces, the spaces will also be cut, as when a guillotine passes right through an exact model of one of the houses of her childhood in *Cell (Choisy)* (1990–93) (Figure 13). Arms are sliced off. Rooms are cut in half. It is not that Bourgeois reproduces the houses in order to re-create them as presences, as places to inhabit. She reproduces them in order to liquidate them and

FIGURE 16. Louise Bourgeois posing with pieces for *The Destruction of the Father*, 1974

basement eating their lunch. And I had such revulsion, such revulsion. I had to do something about this unfortunate occurrence with legs.[26]

To get a job in a museum in those days you had to be amputated.... All of them were crippled in some way. It made a very big impression on me—I couldn't take it, again, I couldn't take it.[27]

The repetitions are not casual. Bourgeois says she was so revolted she could not eat. Yet, body parts dominate her work. In fact, they keep returning, even in edible form, at times arranged in banquets. In the artist's installation *Confrontation* (1978) (Figure 17), the biomorphic forms from the interior space of *The Destruction of the Father* are laid out on a long dining table. The performance piece *A Banquet/A Fashion Show of Body Parts* is then enacted around this table (Figure 41). The shapes laid out on the table like food are worn as clothing. Unable to eat (not by chance Bourgeois is a vegetarian), the multiple body parts are worn outside rather than consumed inside. Bodies are wrapped in body parts. Or rather, they form whole, new bodies. Bourgeois will happily wear one of the costumes from the performance as a new body while standing in public outside her brownstone in New York, and in the even more public space of the pages of *Vogue*.[28] (Figure 18)

consume them. Her sculpture starts at the dinner table with a wounded father who wounds his family and is cut into pieces. *The Destruction of the Father* returns to finish the bloody job that the original bread-and-spit sculpture began.

There have been other dining tables, other horrifying wounds. When she was eighteen, Bourgeois became a docent at the Louvre. She recalls her revulsion at all the crippled veterans eating lunch in the dining room of the museum, a revulsion at the act of dismemberment that her art will carry out again and again.

So I go downstairs and find a hell of people with amputated limbs, people who had been wounded in the war. If you are wounded in the war in France you are entitled to an official position. I'm talking seriously now. And I walk in and look and a leg is cut off or an arm is gone and they are all in that

FIGURE 17. *Confrontation*, 1978. Hamilton Gallery, New York
Solomon R. Guggenheim Museum, New York

FIGURE 18. Louise Bourgeois in the latex costume she created for the performance piece *A Banquet/A Fashion Show of Body Parts*, Hamilton Gallery, New York, 1978

> This is a sort of "show off." I am delighted to have all these, lets call them mammaries.... breasts. I made them big, and lots of them. And since I know men like that–they've told me so–I put that cloak on, and if you look at the expression on my face, you can see I am happy.[29]

Let us shift from the dining table to the bed with *Red Rooms* of 1994. Not such a big move since she has already told us that the bed and the dining table are the same thing. The dining table in *Confrontation* is also a "stretcher for transporting someone wounded or dead,"[30] and *The Destruction of the Father* "represents both a table and a bed."[31]

> When you come into a room, you see a table, but also, upstairs in the parents' room is the bed. Those two things count in one's erotic life: dinner table and bed. The table where your parents made you suffer. And the bed where you lie with your husband, where your children were born and you will die. Essentially, since they are about the same size, they are the same object.[32]

Red Rooms was inspired by the apartment Bourgeois lived in as an infant at 172 Boulevard Saint-Germain on the fourth floor, above the Café de Flore. Her parents' bedroom was decorated in the Directoire style, all in red. "There was red toile de Jouy on the walls, and the curtains had a red decorative motif with red silk lining. The rugs, which were never nailed to the floor so that they could be easily shaken out of the window, were red as well."[33] Echoing her parents' bedroom, Bourgeois designs two bloody rooms in 1994, *Red Room (Parents)* (Plates 68 and 69) and *Red Room (Child)* (Plate 67).

They are both labyrinthine, if not claustrophobic, spaces. You enter the *Parents* room through the narrow passage between two curved walls made out of old dark wooden doors until you are suddenly faced with an unexpected scene. The visitor is thrown into a domestic space. A double bed in the center is covered with a red hard surface, which turns it into a table. Soft red pillows are interrupted by a small white pillow embroidered with cursive red letters that say "*je t'aime.*" On the bed/table, a curiously shaped musical instrument case and the red caboose of a toy train on tracks are sinister, menacing presences. A large oval mirror at the foot of the bed witnesses the disconcerting scene.

The *Child* room is similarly set within a spiral made out of old doors, but a window has been cut in one so that visitors can see into the room before entering. The word "private" is written on the glass. Inside, nothing can be reconciled with the traditional domestic scene. And yet the space is filled with objects from Bourgeois' domestic world: spools of red and blue thread, red candles, gloves, kerosene lamps, red wax hands... An amputated hand is as domestic here as a typical piece of furniture.

In response to the traumatic architecture of her youth, Bourgeois comes up with another architecture. It is not a therapeutic architecture in the sense of spaces cleansed of horror but rather, an architecture of trauma that reenacts the horror, exposes it. The table and the bed are scenes of killing.[34] Meat is dismembered, blood flows:

> Red is the colour of blood
> Red is the colour of pain
> Red is the colour of violence
> Red is the colour of danger

Red is the colour of shame
Red is the colour of jealousy
Red is the colour of grudges
Red is the colour of blame.[35]

But more than anything, red is normal. Blood, pain, violence, danger, shame, jealousy, grudges, blame are basic facts of everyday life. Irritated with a television interviewer during the filming because he tells her that cutting "seems an act of violence in a lot of your work. You cut arms off, you cut heads off, you dismember." She snaps back: "Don't you cut your lunch when you are ready to eat it? Is that a crime? I am a vegetarian, but you're not a vegetarian, no, you have lamb chops over and over again."[36] Cutting, like the color red, is everywhere.

Working on a sculpture that will become *Rabbit* (1970), she starts to obsess about the fact that it does not touch the floor, that it has seemingly been cut by the table on which it sits (Figure 42). She feels the cut in her own body. She remembers the *lavandières* in France, whom she used to see as a child: "When they

FIGURE 19. The wash-house on the river Bièvre, Antony, France, ca. 1920

washed tapestries in the river, these girls knelt inside little boxes. You couldn't see their lower bodies; they looked as if they were cut in two (Figure 19). That gave me a fantastic pleasure because I myself wanted to cut them in two. I wanted to move from the passive to the active, since I experienced myself as cut in two."[37] Blouses hanging in a closet suddenly seem to be bodies cut in half. A fur wrap seems to have been cut.[38] All the

basic elements and activities of everyday life drip blood. Bourgeois' art simply echoes the nightmare of daily life:

I was working on a small sculpture about 15 inches high. I was sitting in the center of the table. I became uneasy, progressively anxious, terrified. The pain was physical, and yet it was so deep within the sculpture. What was wrong with the sculpture was what was wrong with me. Knowing what was wrong with the sculpture would enlighten me.... What crept in my mind was that the sculpture had nothing to stand on, no relation to the floor. One half of its being was cut off by the table. I had this feeling that I might be cut in half myself. There was this terrific, intense identification with the sculpture. I felt cut in two. I visualized the caryatid or a woman cut in two. I thought of the kitchen cleaver, and of the fear of the cleaver, which would cut me in half. I had an identification with an animal I put into the cooking pot. I had this tension around my waist and I relieved this fear of a little child. But I kept thinking, 'You are not a caryatid, you're not an animal, you're not passive. You're active. Don't let this happen to you. Just do it to someone else.' The compulsion subsided. I rebuilt the sculpture from the floor up.[39]

Bourgeois reconstructs not only the scenes of the childhood traumas that she says are at the root of the work, but the trauma of the creative act itself, which she feels in her own body, as amputation; that is, as physical, as well as psychological, trauma.

But why is she telling us all of this? Is this part of the lifetime "self-analysis" that she says her work amounts to?[40] And if so, what does it mean for the critic to listen to it? What is our role in this scene?

III.

Bourgeois stages a kind of lifelong performance-piece about the traumas of her childhood and the traumas of her art, constantly blurring the distinction between them. All the elements of her domestic drama: the table, dead animals, amputation... spin round and round. And we are hypnotized. What can the critic say that she has not said already and so much better? Bourgeois' work is almost always read in terms of her stories, her spins, in spite of her deep suspicion of artists' words, expressed repeatedly during interviews, to the point of anger:

> I don't really see why the artist should say anything, because the work is supposed to speak for itself. So whatever the artist says about it is like an apology, it is not necessary.... A work of art has nothing to do with the artist..., so I repeat that it is totally unnecessary to ask what I want to see in a piece.[41]

> The finished work is often a stranger to, and sometimes very much at odds with what the artist felt or wished to express when he began.... The artist who discusses the so-called meaning of her work is usually describing a literary side-issue.[42]

And yet she incessantly weaves stories around her work, with any excuse, in any form, from the diaries of her childhood– continued throughout the years, on paper and on tape– to her writings, her correspondence, the numerous interviews, the documentaries, videos, films... even to conversations with visitors, which she records carefully "so that I am sure life does not pass me by."[43] Her words move backwards and forwards, often repeating the same motifs, following the same thoughts, as if to take advantage of some leftover threads. But what is this continuous talk, if it is not, if it can not be–and how can one disagree with that–an explanation of the work?

Is it a protector, a prophylactic to prevent access to her real fears, the deeper fears that drive her work, the ones she won't tell us about, and why should she? (An interviewer pushing the limits is resisted: "Why in the world should I tell you about my demons, which are numerous, if you do not see it in the work?[44]) Or are the words themselves a form of therapy, reconstructing, like the sculptures, the scenes of the trauma in order to get rid of them?

> Everyday you have to abandon your past or accept it and then if you cannot accept it you become a sculptor.[45]

> You see, you have to do something about it. If your need is to refuse to abandon the past, then you have to re-create it.[46]

I am a woman without secrets. Simply because my life everyday is a liquidation of the past.[47]

The past is re-created not just as a three-dimensional reality but as stories. The point is: Bourgeois' words do not explain the work. They are part of the work. She constructs with her stories another reality, which has some of the same qualities of her sculpture or her drawings. It reproduces an experience that is above all spatial: "I am a prisoner of my memories. I have been a prisoner of my memories and my aim is to get rid of them."[48] The stories bring the tight space of memory out in the open, they reproduce that claustrophobic space.

And even if Bourgeois' writing and talking is in the open, it acts as a hiding space. Bourgeois quotes La Rochefoucault, who said: "Why do you talk so much? What is it that you have to hide?" and she goes on to say: "The purpose of words is often to hide things I want to have total recall and total control of the past."[49] The words protect by weaving a safer space. Talking, for Bourgeois is a form of tapestry, a textile. She names a print from 1948, where the words "Hand Weaving" are repeatedly rubber-stamped on the paper in a dense pattern as if knitted, *Weaving Word*. Weaving and talking are one. They collaborate to define a space, a safe house. Like the skeins of wool in her childhood houses, the words construct a refuge:

> The skeins of wool are a friendly refuge, like a web or a cocoon. The caterpillar gets the silk from his mouth, builds his cocoon and when it is completed he dies. The cocoon has exhausted the animal. I am the cocoon. I have no ego. I am my work.[50]

Bourgeois, like the caterpillar, weaves stories around herself to the point of exhaustion. Exasperated with the increasing number of interviews around the time of her participation in the Venice Biennale, she explodes: "All of you interviewers flock upon me like birds–to say what? My work is finished.... Finally, I have succeeded in totally exhausting myself. You people want me to do all the work."[51] Yet clearly she does want to do all the work, she wants to define every detail of her cocoon.

> What I am interested in and ferociously jealous of is my image–my scribble, the way I see things, the way I express things.[52]

I need my memories. They are my documents. I keep watch over them. They are my privacy, and I am intensely jealous of them.[53]

Bourgeois guards her stories. She is obsessed with documenting her account of the work and maintaining a particular tone. Her strategy is like that of another weaving insect that fascinates her, and that she identifies with, the spider: "The female spider has a bad reputation – a stinger, a killer. I rehabilitate her. If I have to rehabilitate her it is because I feel criticized."[54] Bourgeois' endless words are a spider's web that catches the critic, paralyzing it, gobbling it up, to the point that he/she becomes part of Bourgeois' body, liquidated, assimilated. Which doesn't mean that it is not without its pleasures for the critic:

The artist is a sadist and afraid of his own sadism, of inflicting death. Is it murder or suicide? It depends on how you feel. Think of the bird ensnared by the snake. Nobody has ever proved that the bird suffers from his fear. Who says that the bird doesn't enjoy it, that there is not a sexual thrill? That there is no ecstasy in death? That the bird dies fulfilled, as he's gobbled up.[55]

For their own pathological reasons, critics endlessly rehearse Bourgeois' pathology, embracing the therapeutic model she presents. The repetition of her stories is the key. They repeat what she repeats:

Repetition is very important. . . . I always have the feeling that whatever I say I have to repeat at least six times to make the other one understand. . . . I have to repeat, and repeat, and repeat. It is that important to me. I never tired of repeating. I am used to it. It is how I handle fear.[56]

It is the repetition, the back and forth between interconnected stories that constructs the web, the almost irresistible space of her work. A seductive space in which classical art criticism, happily meets its death.

Repetition is the artist's substitute for therapy: "The truth is that Freud did nothing for artists, or for the artist's problem, the artist's torment. . . . That's why artists repeat themselves – because they have no access to a cure."[57] Each work, each repetition "alleviates momentarily a state of pain," like a "sedative," but one

that "doesn't last very long."[58] So you need another one, and then another. Art as addiction:

I am an addictive type of person and the only way to stop addiction is to become addicted to something else, something less harmful.[59]

Bourgeois' whole obsession with architecture has to be understood in precisely these terms. Even moving house is an addictive substitute for therapy:

Intoxication, Intoxication, Intoxication, Intoxication, that crashes after 2 hours or 1 hour. The joy of being alive, of understanding, revelation!, of success, followed by a certain confusion and a certain fear, fear of what. Everytime I moved I hoped again. Rue de Seine, rue Roger Collard, avenue d'Orleans, rue Mazarine, the back of the store, hotel Montalembert, hotel des Grands Augustins. Nothing did it. 63 Park, 333 E 41, 142 E 18, 335 W 22, 347 W 20, 518 Van Duzer,

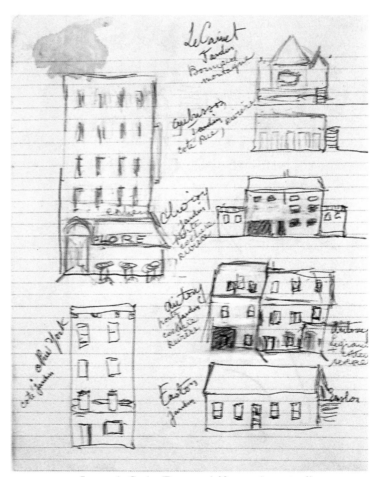

FIGURE 20. *Insomnia Series* (Bourgeois' houses), 1994–95
Daros Collection, Switzerland

475 Dean. Broken promises. I paid my dues. I can leave: intoxication.[60] (Figure 20)

Whether Bourgeois' work is therapeutic or not is impossible to judge. What can be said is that she stages her work as a therapeutic scene, and her words are an integral part of that performance. Even her repeated attempts to make a distinction between her words and the work is part of the work itself, part of the construction of a therapeutic scene. The real question then is not Bourgeois' pathology, but the particular space she constructs between the objects and the words.

IV.

Bourgeois constantly rebuilds a world (people, spaces, furniture, colors, materials) and labels it "traumatic." The scene she constructs as she reconstructs and narrates is that of homesickness, in the double sense of mourning for a lost home and the sickness of the home itself.[61] What Bourgeois carefully constructs is therefore an architecture of homesickness that traces a complex movement between attachment and detachment; reparation and destruction. A clue to this complex operation is offered by her first sculptural work exhibited in New York in 1949 and 1950 at the Peridot gallery, where over thirty *personnages* – thin tall painted wooden pieces – were scattered around the gallery space. When Pierre Matisse and Marcel Duchamp came by the gallery, Bourgeois explained to them that the work was "simply a manifestation of 'homesickness.'" A statement they listened to, absorbed and then, "look[ed] at each other and understood."[62]

Once again, the words participate in the work. Bourgeois elaborates a precise explanation and interpretation. She tells interviewer after interviewer that the key to the pieces is that she had just moved to a new apartment in the "Stuyvesant Folly" (142 East 18th Street) and that she was using the roof as her studio and as an escape from the house (Figure 21). Access to the unconfined space of the roof allowed the tall figures to emerge. They grow in her roof like plants, or like the skyscrapers of the city, long tall houses with windows as eyes that, Bourgeois says, reconstruct the family she had left behind in France.

Suddenly I had this huge sky space to myself and I began doing these standing figures. A friend asked me what I was doing. I told him, "I feel so lonely that I am rebuilding these people around me. I run away from them because I couldn't stand them, and as soon as I'm away from them I rebuild them.[63]

FIGURE 21. Louise Bourgeois working on her sculptures on the roof of Stuyvesant Folly, ca. 1944

Bourgeois reconstructs the people she had amputated herself from. She misses them, as if suffering some kind of phantom pain. She rebuilds them as prostheses, like the canes she had used in her childhood hikes (Figure 22), like the cane her older sister Henriette, who had a stiff knee, always used: "She had in effect a wooden leg (Figure 23). This bothers me very much, because her demeanor when she walked was very special. On top of that she used a cane and when I was little this impressed me as a kind of threatening and

FIGURE 22. Louise with her father and mother (from *Child Abuse*, project in *Artforum*, December 1982)

unfortunate event."[64] Bourgeois even made a "portable brother–a pole with hand-shaped indentations serving as handles, you could carry around" and "[keep] close by."[65] The figures are unstable on their own, they lack feet. Bourgeois complains about the bases she was forced to build to protect the floor of the art gallery. The bases "betrayed" the pieces: "It is a period without feet... because things during that period were not grounded. They expressed a great fragility and uncertainty.... If I pushed them they would have fallen. And this was self-expression. They had a literal relation to the ground."[66] The *Personnages* don't stand on their own because they are part of her body, vital attachments that may be "threatening and unfortunate" but allow her to survive. She carried the *Personnages* around, from the roof, to her apartment, to the country house in Easton, as if bringing members of the household to keep her company, even photographing herself with them. In fact, one of the *Personnages*, *Portrait of C.Y.* (Plate 9), is not a relative of Bourgeois but a house-guest of hers in Easton who irritated her:

> She wanted my attention all day. Her presence was exhausting to me. Whenever I prepared a meal, she always said 'No thank you. I am not hungry.' ... This piece kept me from doing to her what I did to the sculpture.... I got to the point that I put the three children into the car, Robert and I drove back to New York and abandoned her in the house.[67]

In detaching herself from the house, she detaches herself from the guest, cuts the guest off, then reconstructs the figure, hammering nails into its head. Detachment leads to reattachment. These prosthetic figures have to be considered in terms of space rather than as discrete objects. They "need the room" as Bourgeois says,[68] they are part of the space, as is evident in many of the titles: *Figure Gazing at a House, Figures Holding Up a Beam, Figure Leaning Against a Door, Figure Who Enters a House, Statue for an Empty House, Figure Leaving Its House, Figure Carrying Away Its House*. As part of the space, they have to be reattached. These sculptures are environmental, they open Bourgeois up to an ongoing reflection on space,[69] a reflection on what it was to "abandon" her family house.[70]

The trauma of exile is primarily seen as homesickness, loss of ground. *The Blind Vigils* (1947–49) sculpture, later retitled *The Blind Leading the Blind* (Plate 8), is a response to the trauma of being investigated, along with Duchamp and Ozenfant, by the House Un-American Activities Committee. Bourgeois' defense was that she didn't know what "the men I was involved with were doing politically." The blindness that she claims as defense against McCarthy is the very blindness that

FIGURE 23. *Henriette*, 1985

FIGURE 24. Louise Bourgeois in 1966 with *The Blind Leading the Blind*, 1947–49. Collection Detroit Institute of Art

she had rehearsed all her life to deal with the traumas of her domestic scenes: "I had to be blind to the mistress who lived with us. I had to be blind to the pain of my mother, I had to be blind to the fact I was a little bit sadistic with my brother, I was blind to the fact that my sister slept with the man across the street."[71]

Homesickness results from abandoning the house and abandonment within the house. All the traumas are traumas of abandonment from the beginning, from birth:

> When I was born, they abandoned me flat. I was born on Christmas day; my mother was very apologetic and the doctor said: "Madame Bourgeois, really you are ruining my festivity." I mean who is born on Christmas Day? I was a pain in the ass when I was born. To all these people, they had their oysters and champagne and there I came.[72]

> When I was born my father and my mother were fighting like cats and dogs. And the country was preparing for war, and my father who wanted a son got me, and my sister had just died. Please let me breathe.[73]

Abandoning a house that abandoned her sets off a never-ending chain reaction of detachment and reattachment. It is not by chance that *The Blind Leading the Blind* was first a house, then she eliminated the house, leaving the double rod of red figures.

In a photograph of *The Blind Leading the Blind*, she appears inside the sculpture (Figure 24). What we see is Louise Bourgeois inhabiting a claustrophobic space. But she does not inhabit it in the sense of a figure within an enclosure, for she is part of the space, or rather, the work is part of her. Like another exile artist with whom she shares more than one obsession, Frederick Kiesler (Figure 25), she cannot separate herself from her own work. She wears it, she pets, she hugs it. As when standing in front of her house she wears the breast coat. Or when she carries *Fillette* "like a baby or a doll" to Mapplethorpe's studio.[74] Or when she strokes her sculptures as if in search of comfort, or to comfort them, during an interview.

v.

Bourgeois cannot separate her body from her sculpture. Sculpture is itself a body, with emotions, anxieties, fears, pains: Louise Bourgeois' body, a homesick body, a body that cannot separate itself from the house, a body always trapped by a house.

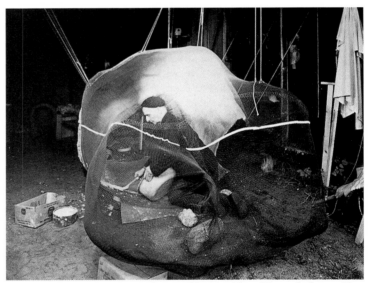

FIGURE 25. Frederick Kiesler working inside of *Bucephalus*, 1963

Femme Maison, the series of drawings from the 1940s depicting nude female bodies with houses as heads and upper bodies, is usually translated as "Woman-House" but it also means, literally, wife-house, housewife, a woman trapped in the house. The house is part

FIGURE 26. *Femme Maison*, 1947. Private Collection

the window are smiling."[78] Yet at other times she describes the character of the house as if it were a difficult person, for instance, severe.

Bourgeois will do drawings of all her houses. One drawing even assembles all the façades of all of the houses she has lived in on one page (Figure 20). If the drawings of houses are understood as self-portraits, this is a group portrait of all the different "Louise Bourgeois" through the years. Her life is visualized as a succession of architectures. Compressed into one image, they form a kind of neighborhood. It is not by chance that Bourgeois, who has now remained in one house for thirty-seven years, has continued to literally collect houses. One of them, in Staten Island, remains empty, but is repeatedly drawn. It is occupied only by being recorded, inserted into the artist's architectural genealogy.

But it is not just the drawings that are architectural. Her first work in sculpture already "needed" architecture so to speak. Not only did the *Personnages* grow from the roof of a house, Stuyvesant Folly, "the oldest apartment building in New York City,"[79] and were they moved around from house to house, but when finally exhibited they "needed the room, the six sides of the cube."[80] The space they occupy therefore is part of the sculpture. "I took hold of the gallery," she recalls, "of the space that was given to me and used it. Instead of displaying pieces, the space became part of the piece."[81] Architecture, for Bourgeois, is part of the sculpture, inseparable from it. "The show is a room. You prepare your pieces for the room, whether it is one piece or twelve."[82] The individual pieces are not as important as the way they relate to each other in a room, as members

of her body, it grows out of it. The little hands that pop out of the structure are, according to Bourgeois, screaming for help: "Please don't forget me. Come and fetch me. I hurt. I'm homesick.... Come, come and get me."[75] *Femme Maison*, she says, is a self-portrait.[76] (Figure 26) The house traps the woman, the anxious housewife that Bourgeois was in the 1940s but also today's Bourgeois. "I experience my whole house as a trap," she writes in her diary in 1980.[77]

If the *Femmes Maisons* are self-portraits, other works serve as family portraits in which, architecture and body again merge with each other. In *Easton House* (1946) – a drawing of her country house in Connecticut – every window is the face of a family member who inhabits the house: Louise, her husband, two of her children. She comments on this drawing as if it were a snapshot of the family rather than something she has produced: "I think we were happy there. All the faces in

FIGURE 27. Solo exhibition, Peridot Gallery, New York, 1950

of a family interacting with each other in a house, as "a group of people at a party."[83] (Figure 27)

Later, Bourgeois will feel the need to actually make architecture. Always dissatisfied with the space that an art gallery inevitably forces upon her sculpture, she prefers their original environment, such as the roof of Stuyvesant Folly; the "claustrophobic space" at the top of the stairs under the roof[84]; a closet in her apartment; or, against an outside wall in Easton (Figure 28). It is not just that the sculptures need the room, as did the *Personnages,* it is that the visitor needs to experience the space to experience the trauma: "When I began building the *Cells,* I wanted to create my own architec-

FIGURE 28. *Personnages* outside of country house, Easton, Connecticut, ca. 1947–49

ture, and not depend on the museum space, not have to adapt my scale to it. I wanted to constitute a real space which you could enter and walk around in."[85]

In the same way that Bourgeois had once left painting for sculpture because "she was not satisfied with its level of reality,"[86] she eventually leaves sculpture for

architecture. Bourgeois wants to reconstruct the spaces of trauma in order to reenact the trauma, to make it "tangible"; "to defeat it"; "to forget":

> My works are a reconstruction of past events. The past has become tangible in them; but at the same time they are created in order to forget the past, to defeat it, to relive it and make it possible for the past to be forgotten.[87]

Architecture for Bourgeois starts with the reconstruction of the scenes of domestic melodramas. As with the architect Adolf Loos, the house is the stage for the theater of family life. Whereas traditionally a work of art presents itself to a detached viewer as an object, Loos argued that the house is received as an environment, as a stage in which the viewer is already involved.[88] In 1903, in response to the overdesigned architecture of the Secession, Loos wrote:

> Try to describe how birth and death, the screams of pain for an aborted son, the death rattle of a dying mother, the last thoughts of a young woman who wishes to die... unfold and unravel in a room by Olbrich! Just an image: the young woman who has put herself to death. She is lying on the wooden floor. One of her hands still holds the smoking revolver. On the table a letter, the farewell letter. Is the room in which this is happening of good taste? Who will ask that? It is just a room![89]

Bourgeois wants the work of art to be like a house, an environment in which the viewer is completely involved. She wants the work to be architectural in the sense that architecture is a stage for the spectacle of daily life, the soap opera of the family. And while we are often pressed to think of Bourgeois as a victim of childhood trauma, of the patriarchal system, and so on, she is in complete control of her pathology, her performance. In that sense too, she is an architect, she leaves nothing to chance. She designs herself.

Even the famous photograph by Robert Mapplethorpe of Bourgeois carrying *Fillette* is, in many ways, her own construction. "Summoned," as she puts it, to his studio, she was "apprehensive" not so much about being photographed–as it is often said–but about leaving the house, her protection:

FIGURE 29. Louise Bourgeois photographed by Berenice Abbott in 1949

When Mapplethorpe approached us to make this portrait, I was a little apprehensive. Now, to be photographed is quite common, but you have to know how to be casual about it. You have to be ready for it. Instead of being photographed candidly in my own studio, I had to go to Mapplethorpe's studio. This is how it is with highly-professional photographers – it was the same with Scavullo and Avedon. They work on their own terms and operate from their own studio. It was up to us to go there. That gives me stress.[90]

She didn't want to leave the house but she had to. She is aware of the importance of a photograph and knows this is the way famous photographers work. She is an experienced sitter for such photographers, since her youth. Yet, she doesn't have a very high opinion of them. Indeed, she has to help them: "I think very little about photographers. Very seldom are they intelligent. You have to help them. When I went to pose for Berenice Abbott I was careful to [wear] my see-through dress (Figure 29). I put on my best clothes. I was trying to help the photographer. And I did the same thing for Mapplethorpe."[91] (Figure 30)

She wore her monkey coat: "I love monkey fur. It's a very long streaky thing, with a piece of white here and a piece of white there."[92] But at the last minute the hairy garment doesn't seem to offer sufficient protection. As

she leaves the house, she grabs her "doll," her "baby," *Fillette*, a two-foot-long, latex-over-plaster dildo: "I knew that I would get comfort from holding and rocking the piece."[93]

As architects always do with their buildings, Bourgeois constructs the photograph for the photographer. *Fillette* is a prop, as those used by the old photographers, something to support the figure. Except that here the support is itself a fragment of a figure, a body part, and the support it offers is psychological. Bourgeois is disturbed about leaving her house, so she takes with her something that protects her, yet needs itself to be protected: "The phallus is a subject of my tenderness. It's about vulnerability and protection. After all, I lived with four men, with my husband and three sons. I was the protector."[94]

FIGURE 30. Louise Bourgeois with *Fillette*, photographed by Robert Mapplethorpe in 1968

Bourgeois presents an image of her strength inside the image of her vulnerability and is very much in control of the tension between them. Control of her image in the media is control not only over her photographs but also over the words: "The purpose of words is often to hide things. I want to have total recall and total control of the past."[95] Even the manufacture of the work operates in the tension between hysteria and control. Take, for example, the technique of cutting that plays such a crucial role in so much of her work:

> Cutting – it means being in total control. Accepting the total control of whatever happens and it is quite aggressive and sometimes I wake up in the morning and I do not feel up to cutting. And I do not feel up to dealing with the machinery. Then I will draw, you have to be quite sure to operate mechanical tools, electric tools.... You certainly cannot be hysterical and use – if you want to keep all your fingers – and use power tools.[96]

Cutting is amputation. If sculpture is the body, we can say that it is constructed through amputation. In fact, the body is always amputated in Bourgeois' work. Take, for example, *Femme Maison*. The woman is not just trapped in the house. She is amputated by it – a relationship that becomes transparent in a later work, *J'y suis, j'y reste* (1990) (Figure 31), where an amputated foot in pink marble appears inside a glass house. If the work is all about control, architectural control, amputation is its guiding force.

FIGURE 31. *J'y suis, j'y reste*, 1990. Private Collection

A key aspect of this struggle for control is repetition. Bourgeois repeatedly tells us of her need to repeat, constantly reworking the same things in order to tame them:

> For a lifetime I have wanted to say the same thing. Inner consistency is the test of the artist. Repeated disappointment in its expression is what keeps him jumping.[97]

> So I wanted to do it again and again and again – the repetition of the person who is dissatisfied.[98]

> I have to repeat, and repeat and repeat. It is that important to me. I never tired of repeating, I am used to it. It is how I handle fear: I take it upon myself and become responsible for it.[99]

This endless repetition is fueled by a constant cycle of destruction and construction. In that too, she comes close to Loos, who argued in a 1926 lecture:

> Human works can be summed up in two actions: destruction and construction. And the bigger the destruction, the more human work is nothing other than destruction, the more it is truly human, natural and noble. [100]

For Bourgeois, the first gesture is always destructive. She prides herself on beginning to work always by destroying something, then rebuilding it, only to destroy it again, and so on. She sees herself in opposition to the family craft of repairing broken fabrics by privileging the destructive: "My mother was a restorer, she repaired broken things. I don't do that. I destroy things. I cannot go the straight line. I must destroy, rebuild, destroy again."[101] But by rebuilding what she breaks, she continues the family craft. She becomes a restorer of her own damage:

> Violence can be replaced by restoration.
> Fortunately, I come from that background where we repaired the damage on the tapestries and the idea of repairing has stayed with me.[102]

Indeed, Bourgeois thinks in terms of weaving. Space for Bourgeois is always textile. She repeatedly describes the fabrics her family worked on as having originally been a form of architecture. Tapestries are

FIGURE 32. Louise Bourgeois repairing a tapestry, 1998

Bourgeois' art likewise defines space with sensuous surfaces that wrap themselves around the viewer/visitor. The three-dimensional quality of her work develops directly out of the logic of fabrics:

> I, myself, have very long associations with tapestries. As children, we used them to hide in. This is one reason I expect them to be so three-dimensional – why I feel they must be such a height and weight and size that you can wrap yourself in them. Gobelins tapestries, out of fashion and discarded, were saved because in the colder climate of Aubusson, they were used to wrap animals in… protection for a cow giving birth, and as blankets for the horses…. My personal association with tapestry is for this reason, highly sculptural in terms of the three-dimensionality…. A tent is very important in my vocabulary – a form of textile sculpture to be entered – a form of collapsible architecture. In Africa, I remember the caravan blacks who wear clothes like tents and fold them around themselves, even sleep under them.[106]

understood as portable buildings or as the means to transform a building:

> Originally, tapestries were moving walls to use against the cold, and tents that were taken into battle to shelter the generals – a great luxury.[103]

> In the beginning tapestries were indispensable, they were actually movable walls, or partitions in the great halls of castles and manor houses, or the walls of tents. They were a flexible architecture.[104]

Yet again, the sensibility is very much that of Loos, who closely followed Gottfried Semper's mid-19th-century idea that architecture begins with portable, suspended textiles:

> The architect's general task is to provide a warm and livable space. Carpets are warm and livable. He decides for this reason to spread one carpet on the floor and to hang up four to form the four walls. But you cannot build a house out of carpets. Both the carpet on the floor and the tapestry on the wall require a structural frame to hold them in the correct place. To invent this frame is the architect's second task.[105]

The houses that Bourgeois constructs and lives in are also hiding places, places to seek shelter from the psychological elements. Their role is not unlike the long hair she use to wear at the time of the *Femme Maison* drawings (Figure 33), and can be seen growing out of the houses in the drawings (Figure 26). She says long hair comes in handy when you have something to hide: "Hair is simply protection women are wrapped in. Hair is like a caterpillar in a cocoon. But hair is more friendly in that the cocoon eliminates the subject."[107] Again this keeps Bourgeois close to Semper, who saw the prototype of the woven fabrics that defined the first architecture in the weaving of women's hair. Bourgeois is always constructing some kind of shelter. Eventually she removed her long hair. It would seem that she has nothing to hide.

VI.

Louise Bourgeois is clearly a figure in tune with contemporary culture. It is not just the women's movement or the recent return to an interest in biography in art history that has brought her back from the realm of

FIGURE 33. Louise Bourgeois in the studio of her apartment at 142 East 18th street, New York, ca. 1946

oblivion which she inhabited (she says, luckily) for many years. Rather, it is the current fascination with trauma, with the confessional, the voyeuristic mentality of the talk show. She is her own talk show, exemplifying today's radical confusion of any line between private and public:

> Whether a thing is private or public makes no difference to me. I wish I could make my private more public and by doing so, lose it.[108]

Bourgeois destroys the private by exposing it. Wounds are opened for inspection rather than closed. Vulnerability is to be flaunted rather than disguised:

> When I was at the Ecole des Beaux-Arts in Paris, we had a nude male model. One day he looked around and saw a woman student and suddenly he had an erection. I was shocked–then I thought, what a fantastic thing, to reveal your vulnerability, to be so publicly exposed! We are all vulnerable, in some way, and we are all male-female.[109]

To reveal in public your vulnerability; to expose yourself. This is what makes Bourgeois' work compelling today. It is not by chance that she did not tell the full story of her father and the mistress until the 1980s, while preparing a slide-show autobiography for her Museum of Modern Art exhibition in 1982.[110] The most private space can be most publicly exposed to a culture that lives for such painful revelations. On the one hand, she might seem to be a late-19th-century figure, echoing so clearly the sense of melodrama described by Adolf Loos. On the other hand, she is a thoroughly late-20th-century figure, totally resonant with a culture devoted to the soap opera and the talk show. The shyest personality, who rarely leaves her house, is infinitely attractive to a culture that wants to peer inside every building, every home.

This systematic destruction of the line between private and public is directly related to her idea of space, and the particular shapes she constructs. The labyrinth she favors is precisely the form that removes any simple line between inside and outside, private and public. The labyrinth allows everything to come out. It can expose the deepest core. Yet it can also be a place to hide. To radically undermine the difference between private and public is not simply to make an infinitely open space. Rather, it is to remove the difference between exposing yourself and hiding:

> The labyrinth has many meanings for me. It can hide me and no one can find me, and I can go out without anyone noticing. If I like my visitor the labyrinth becomes a means of seduction, what I call a tender trap.[111]

Bourgeois weaves her complex architectural lures out of words, drawings, paintings, sculptures, and installations. While flaunting everything, she can never be pinned down. She has nothing to hide yet remains hidden, forever seductive.

NOTES

1. Louise Bourgeois quoted in Jeremy Strick, "Sculpting Emotion," *Louise Bourgeois: The Personages* (Saint Louis: The Saint Louis Art Museum, 1994), 8.

2. "The View from the Bottom of the Well," a text from the 1960s first published in 1996 by Peter Blum Editions, New York. Reprinted in Louise Bourgeois, *Destruction of the Father, Reconstruction of the Father: Writings and Interviews 1923–1997*, ed. by Marie-Laure Bernadac and Hans-Ulrich Obrist (London: Violette Editions, 1998), 343.

3. Walter Benjamin, "On Some Motifs in Baudelaire," *Illuminations*, ed. Hannah Arendt (New York: Schocken Books, 1968), 163.

4. Bourgeois quoted in Marsha Pels, "Louise Bourgeois: A Search for Gravity," *Art International* (October 1979), 48.

5. Louise Bourgeois, "Collecting: An Unruly Passion," artist's review of the book *Collecting: An Unruly Passion* by Werner Muensterberger (1993) first published in *Artforum*, vol. 32, no. 10 (Summer 1994): 11. Reprinted in Louise Bourgeois, *Destruction of the Father, Reconstruction of the Father*, 276.

6. Louise Bourgeois, "A Memoir: Louise Bourgeois and Patricia Beckert," from a conversation recorded in the late 1970s, in *Destruction of the Father, Reconstruction of the Father*, 117.

7. Unpublished interview with Nena Dimitrijevic, 1994. (Louise Bourgeois Archive.)

8. "I was born at the outbreak of the 1914 war, and the first thing I knew is that my father was mobilized…it made my mother very nervous…unhappy. She started to follow my father from camp to camp, and my brother and sister were left home with my grandparents, and I was carried around by my mother to meet him in different places in Eastern France. I remember her nervousness, and I remember my pain at the time." Lynn Blumenthal and Kate Horsfield, "Louise Bourgeois," Video Data Bank, Art Institute Chicago, 1975.

9. "I was very young in 1917, but I always remember Maman crying when Papa went back after he was wounded for the second time." Louise Bourgeois, "Letters to Colette Richarme, 1937–1940," *Destruction of the Father*, 37.

10. Louise Bourgeois, "A Memoir: Louise Bourgeois and Patricia Beckert," *Destruction of the Father*, 121–122.

11. "Louise Bourgeois: Album," first published in 1994 by Peter Blum Editions, New York, and based on the 1983 film *Partial Recall*, Museum of Modern Art, New York. Reprinted in *Destruction of the Father*, 282.

12. Ibid., 283–284.

13. "There was a *grenier*, an attic with exposed beams. It was very large and very beautiful. My father had a passion for fine furniture. All the *sièges de bois* were hanging up there. It was very pure. No tapestries, just the wood itself. You would look up and see these armchairs hanging in very good order. The floor was bare. It was quite impressive. This is the origin of a lot of hanging pieces." Louise Bourgeois, "Self-Expression is Sacred and Fatal Statements," in Christiane Meyer-Thoss, *Louise Bourgeois, Konstruktionen für dein freien Fall/ Designing for Free Fall* (Zurich: Ammann verlag, 1992), 185.

14. Louise Bourgeois, speaking of *Cell (Choisy)* (1990–93), says: "This is the house were we lived and where the tapestry workshops occupied the second wing of the house here and there were twenty-five *petites-mains*, which worked on the tapestry." "Arena," edited transcript of interview with Bourgeois from the 1994 documentary film directed by Nigel Finch for Arena Films, London, and broadcast by BBC2, in *Destruction of the Father*, 257.

15. Louise Bourgeois in Paul Gardner, *Louise Bourgeois* (New York: Universe Publishing, 1994), 68.

16. Louise Bourgeois, "Self-Expression is Sacred and Fatal Statements," in Christiane Meyer-Thoss, *Louise Bourgeois*, 179. "The spiral is completely predictable. A knot is unpredictable." Louise Bourgeois, "Statements from Conversations with Robert Storr," in *Destruction of the Father*, 220.

17. "My first work of art was *une poupée de pain*." Louise Bourgeois in conversation with Jerry Gorovoy, 1996. (Louise Bourgeois Archive).

18. Jennifer Anne Luterman, *Louise Bourgeois: Interpreting the Maternal Body*, unpublished thesis, 1995. (Louise Bourgeois Archive).

19. Rainer Crone, Petrus Graf Schaesberg, *Louise Bourgeois: The Secret Life of the Cells* (Munich, London, New York: Prestel, 1998), 33.

20. Louise Bourgeois, "Select Diary Notes," 27 August 1984, *Destruction of the Father*, 131.

21. Louise Bourgeois, "Self-Expression is Sacred and Fatal Statements," in Christiane Meyer-Thoss, *Louise Bourgeois*, 195.

22. "It is, you see, an oral drama. The irritation was his continual verbal offense. So he was liquidated: the same way he liquidated his children." Louise Bourgeois, "Statements 1979," *Destruction of the Father*, 115.

23. *Chère Louise* (1995), documentary directed by Brigitte Cornand for Canal + .

24. Louise Bourgeois, "Statements 1979," *Destruction of the Father*, 115–116.

25. Louise Bourgeois, "Statements from an Interview with Donald Kuspit," first published in 1988 in *Louise Bourgeois* by Donald Kuspit. Reprinted in *Destruction of the Father*, 158.

26. Louise Bourgeois, "Taking Cover: Interview with Stuart Morgan," first published in January 1988 in *Artscribe*, reprinted in *Destruction of the Father*, 154.

27. Louise Bourgeois, "Interview with Douglas Maxwell," first published in a longer version in *Modern Painters*, vol. 6, no. 2 (Summer 1993), reprinted in *Destruction of the Father*, 244.

28. Ratcliff, Carter, "Louise Bourgeois," *Vogue*, vol. 170, no. 10, October 1980, 343–44, 375–77.

29. Interview by Bernard Marcadé for the film *Louise Bourgeois*, by Camille Guichard, Terra Luna Productions, Serie Mémoire / Centre Georges Pompidou, Paris 1993.

30. "*Confrontation* (1978) represents a long table surrounded by an oval of wooden boxes, which are really caskets. The table is a stretcher for transporting someone wounded or dead." Louise Bourgeois, "Self-Expression is Sacred and Fatal Statements," in Christiane Meyer-Thoss, *Louise Bourgeois*, 182.

31. Louise Bourgeois, "Statements 1979," in *Destruction of the Father*, 115.

32. Ibid.

33. Louise Bourgeois in conversation with Jerry Govoroy, 1999. (Louise Bourgeois Archive).

34. Bourgeois witnessed her sister Henriette being fondled by a neighbor, resisting him "for the simple reason that she was menstruating." She sees blood. She thinks that he is killing her. 1997 comment by the artist on a 1973 diary note, *Destruction of the Father*, 71.

35. Louise Bourgeois, quoted in *Louise Bourgeois: Oeuvres récentes/Recent Work* (Bordeaux: capcMusée d'art contemporain de Bordeaux, 1998), 40.

36. "Arena," edited transcript of interview with Bourgeois from the 1994 documentary film directed by Nigel Finch for Arena Films, London, and broadcast by BBC2, in *Destruction of the Father*, 255.

37. "Louise Bourgeois in Conversation with Christiane Meyer-Thoss," in Meyer-Thoss, *Louise Bourgeois*, 132.

38. Ibid., 133.

39. Ibid., 131–132.

40. In the course of an interview Bourgeois is asked "Have you been through analysis yourself?" She replies: "No, but I have spent a life time in self-improvement, self analysis, which is the same thing. My husband said: "We love you when you work." Louise Bourgeois, "Interview with Douglas Maxwell," first published in a longer version in *Modern Painters*, vol. 6, no. 2 (Summer 1993). Reprinted in *Destruction of the Father*, 245.

41. Louise Bourgeois, "On *The Sail*" (17 December 1988), in *Destruction of the Father*, 168–169.

42. Louise Bourgeois, "An Artist's Words," first published in 1954 by the Walker Art Center, Minneapolis, in *Design Quarterly*, no. 30. Reprinted in *Destruction of the Father*, 66.

43. "I keep three kinds of diaries, the written, the spoken (into a tape recorder), and my drawing diary, which is the most important. Having these various diaries means that I like to keep my house in order. They must be up-to-date so that I'm sure life does not pass me by. Most people visit me, and I like to record our conversations or our dialogues." "Tender Compulsions," first published in February 1995 in *World Art*. Reprinted in *Destruction of the Father*, 304–305.

44. Louise Bourgeois, "Interview with Douglas Maxwell," first published in a longer version in *Modern Painters*, vol. 6, no. 2 (Summer 1993). Reprinted in *Destruction of the Father*, 245.

45. "Child Abuse," a project by Louise Bourgeois first published in *Artforum*, vol. 20, no. 4 (December 1982). Reprinted in *Destruction of the Father*, 134.

46. "Louise Bourgeois: Album," first published in 1994 by Peter Blum Edition, New York, and based on the 1983 film *Partial Recall*, Museum of Modern Art, New York. Reprinted in *Destruction of the Father*, 285.

47. "Louise Bourgeois in Conversation with Christiane Meyer-Thoss," in Meyer-Thoss, *Louise Bourgeois*, 137.

48. Louise Bourgeois in "Arena," edited transcript of interview with Bourgeois from the 1994 documentary film directed by Nigel Finch for Arena Films, London, and broadcast by BBC2, in *Destruction of the Father*, 257.

49. Louise Bourgeois, "Self-expression is Sacred and Fatal," in Christiane Meyer-Thoss, *Louise Bourgeois*, 202.

50. Ibid., 197.

51. "Mortal Elements: Pat Steir Talks with Louise Bourgeois," first published in 1993 in *Artforum*, vol. 32, n. 1, p. 86. Reprinted in *Destruction of the Father*, 234.

52. Cited in Louise Neri, "The Personal Effects of a Woman with No Secrets," in *Louise Bourgeois: Homesickness*, Yokohama, 1998, 141.

53. Louise Bourgeois, "Self-Expression is Sacred and Fatal Statements," in Christiane Meyer-Thoss, *Louise Bourgeois*, 184.

54. Louise Bourgeois, "Statements from Conversations with Robert Storr," in *Destruction of the Father*, 217.

55. Louise Bourgeois, "Self-Expression is Sacred and Fatal Statements," in Christiane Meyer-Thoss, *Louise Bourgeois*, 196.

56. "Louise Bourgeois in Conversation with Christiane Meyer-Thoss, in Meyer-Thoss, *Louise Bourgeois*, 127.

57. Louise Bourgeois, "Freud's Toys," artist's review of the exhibition *The Sigmund Freud Antiquities*, first published in *Artforum*, vol. 28, no. 5 (January 1990). Reprinted in *Destruction of the Father*, 190.

58. "In a Strange Way, Things are Getting Better and Better: Interview with Francesco Bonami," first published in *Flash Art*, vol. XXVII, no. 174. Reprinted in *Destruction of the Father*, 265.

59. Louise Bourgeois, "Self-Expression is Sacred and Fatal Statements," in Christiane Meyer-Thoss, *Louise Bourgeois*, 189.

60. Louise Bourgeois, diary entry, January 14, 1994. (Louise Bourgeois Archive).

61. Homesickness becomes housewife blues, a disorder discovered by psychologists during the years Bourgeois was raising her children: "I don't know why the mourning came so frequently in my work, since actually I didn't lose anybody, nobody died. Today this has been recognized as a frequent occurrence—that mothers with young children develop a depression. You were supposed to be overjoyed, but the fact is, that in the afternoon when the children were asleep—the loneliness attacked, and it did it quite often." Louise Bourgeois in interview with Marsha Pels, "Louise Bourgeois: A Search for Gravity," 51.

62. "The Passion for Sculpture: A Conversation with Alain Kirili," first published in *Arts*, vol. 63, no. 7 (March 1989). Reprinted in *Destruction of the Father*, 176.

63. Michael Brenson, "A Sculptor Comes Into Her Own," *The New York Times*, Sunday October 31, 1982, p. H. 29.

64. Louise Bourgeois, "Two Conversations with Deborah Wye," 14 October 1981, published in *Destruction of the Father*, 126–7. The theme of the leg of her sister Henriette reappeared in 1985 in the bronze *Henriette*.

65. Lucy R. Lippard, "Louise Bourgeois: From the Inside Out," *Artforum* (March 1975), 29. And Deborah Wye, *Louise Bourgeois in the 1940s*, unpublished text, 1979 (Louise Bourgeois Archive): "*Portrait of a Brother*, with its hand-shaped indentations serving as handles, become a *portable brother*, ... [that] could be carried around and kept close by."

66. Marsha Pels, "A Search for Gravity," 50.

67. Jeremy Strick, *Louise Bourgeois: The Personages* (Saint Louis: The Saint Louis Art Museum, 1994), 23.

68. "The figures were presences which need the room, the six sides of the cube.... It was a reconstruction of the past." Louise Bourgeois in "Interview with Susi Bloch" first published in *The Art Journal*, vol 35, no. 41 (Summer 1976): 370–3. Reprinted in *Destruction of the Father*, 106.

69. In an interview with Susi Bloch, Bourgeois is asked: "Why did you start thinking in terms of environment?" "The reason was a psychological one. These pieces were presences, missed, badly missed presences. ... It was the reconstruction of the past." *Destruction of the Father*, 105.

70. "There is a great intensity and very great personal emotion. This is apparent in the constant repetition of the word "figure," which expresses the fact that I had left my entire family in Europe... I felt I had abandoned them." "The Passion for Sculpture: A Conversation with Alain Kirili", first published in *Arts*, vol. 63, no. 7 (March 1989). Reprinted in *Destruction of the Father*, 177.

71. Ibid., 179.

72. Louise Bourgeois, "Interview with Douglas Maxwell", in *Destruction of the Father*, 246.

73. Louise Bourgeois quoted in "Daddy Dearest," review of *Destruction of the Father*, in *Artforum* (November 1998), 15.

74. About *Fillette* Bourgeois says: "You can carry it around like a baby, have it as a doll." Quoted in Lucy R. Lippard, "Louise Bourgeois: From the Inside Out," *Artforum* (March 1975), 31.

75. From an interview by Bernard Marcadé for the film *Louise Bourgeois*, by Camille Guichard, Terra Luna Productions, Serie Mémoire, Paris 1993. (Louise Bourgeois Archive).

76. Bourgeois in conversation with Jerry Gorovoy, March 1, 1999. (Louise Bourgeois Archive).

77. August 23, 1980 diary entry. (Louise Bourgeois Archive).

78. Louise Bourgeois with Lawrence Rinder, *Louise Bourgeois, Drawings & Observations*, foreword by Josef Helfenstein. University Art Museum and Pacific Film Archive, University of California, Berkeley. (Boston, New York, Toronto, London: Bulfinch Press, Little, Brown and Company: 1995).

79. Stuyvesant Folly was built in 1869 by Rutherford Stuyvesant, and completed by Richard Morris Hunt. It was inspired by Parisian luxury apartment buildings. It contained sixteen apartments and four artist's studios. Critics skeptical that good families would share a roof dubbed the structure "Stuyvesant's Folly." It was demolished in 1958. (Elizabeth Hawes, *New York, New York. How the Apartment House Transformed The Life of the City 1869–1930*, Henry Holt & Co., New York 1993), 23.

80. "The figures were presences which needed the room, the six sides of the cube.... It was a reconstruction of the past." Louise Bourgeois in "Interview with Susi Bloch" first published in in *The Art Journal*, vol. 35, no. 41 (Summer 1976): 370–3. Reprinted in *Destruction of the Father*, 106.

81. "Interview with Susi Bloch," 1976, reprinted in *Destruction of the Father*, 104.

82. Louise Bourgeois in an interview with Marsha Pels, "Louise Bourgeois: A Search for Gravity," 54.

83. Bourgeois says she "wanted to nail them to the floor," "like a group of people at a party, all in the center." Interview with Michael Auping, 25 October 1996, in *Destruction of the Father*, 353.

84. "The dynamism of the presence in a claustrophobic space such as the top of the stairs under the roof was much more dynamic than the gallery.... But the gallery would not have permitted me to place my personages in a closet which in effect is the way they were conceived." In "Interview with Susi Bloch," *Destruction of the Father*, 106.

85. *Louise Bourgeois, Oeuvres récente/Recent Works*, (Bordeaux: capcMusée d'art contemporain de Bordeaux, 1998), 38.

86. From a taped interview, cited in Deborah Wye, *Louise Bourgeois* (New York: Museum of Modern Art, 1982), 18.

87. Louise Bourgeois in Jerry Gorovoy, Pandora Tabatabai Asbaghi, *Louise Bourgeois: Blue Days and Pink Days* (Milan: Fondazione Prada, 1997), 59.

88. About Adolf Loos' idea of architecture see Beatriz Colomina, *Privacy and Publicity: Modern Architecture as Mass Media* (Cambridge, MA: MIT Press, 1994), 233–281.

89. Adolf Loos, *Das Andere*, no. 1 (1903): 9.

90. Louise Bourgeois, "MacDowell Medal Acceptance Speech," 1990, in *Destruction of the Father*, 198.

91. Louise Bourgeois, cited by Paulo Herkenhoff, "Louise Bourgeois, Femme-Temps," in Jerry Gorovoy, Pandora Tabatabai Asbaghi, *Louise Bourgeois: Blue Days and Pink Days*, (Milan: Fondazione Prada, 1997), 275.

92. Louise Bourgeois, "Rushes: On Robert Mapplethorpe," transcript of a filmed interview, 1993, in *Destruction of the Father*, 202.

93. Louise Bourgeois, "MacDowell Medal Acceptance Speech," 1990, in *Destruction of the Father*, 198.

94. Louise Bourgeois, "Self-expression is Sacred and Fatal," in Christiane Meyer-Thoss, *Louise Bourgeois*, 181.

95. Ibid., 202.

96. Louise Bourgeois, "Arena," edited transcript of interview from the 1993 documentary film directed by Nigel Finch for Arena Films, London, and broadcast by BBC2, in *Destruction of the Father*, 254–255.

97. Louise Bourgeois, "On Janus Fleuri," first published in *Art Now*, vol. 1, no. 7 (September 1969). Reprinted in *Destruction of the Father*, 91.

98. Louise Bourgeois, "On *The Sail*," 1988, in *Destruction of the Father*, 171.

99. "Louise Bourgeois in Conversation with Christiane Meyer-Thoss," in *Louise Bourgeois*, 127.

100. Adolf Loos, "Die moderne Siedlung," in *Sämtliche Schriften, Adolf Loos*, vol. 1 (Vienna and Munich: Verlag Herold, 1962), 402ff.

101. Louise Bougeois in Jerry Gorovoy, Pandora Tabatabai Asbaghi, *Louise Bourgeois: Blue Days and Pink Days*, 21.

102. "Interview with Trevor Rots," 10 May 1990, in *Destruction of the Father*, 194.

103. "A Memoir: Louise Bourgeois and Patricia Beckert," late 1970s, in *Destruction of the Father*, 117.

104. Louise Bourgeois, "The Fabric of Construction," review of the exhibition *Wall Hangings* at the Museum of Modern Art, New York, first published in in *Craft Horizons*, vol. 29, no. 2 (March–April 1969). Reprinted in *Destruction of the Father*, 89.

105. Adolf Loos, "The Principle of Cladding" (1898), in *Spoken into the Void: Collected Essays 1897–1900* (Cambridge, MA: MIT Press, 1982), 66.

106. Louise Bourgeois, "The Fabric of Construction," *Destruction of the Father*, 89.

107. Louise Bourgeois, "Statements from Conversations with Robert Storr," *Destruction of the Father*, 216.

108. "Louise Bourgeois in Conversation with Christiane Meyer-Thoss," in Christiane Meyer-Thoss, *Louise Bourgeois*, 137.

109. Louise Bourgeois, "A Merging of Male and Female," first published on 11 February 1974 in *New York* magazine. Reprinted in *Destruction of the Father*, 101.

110. Louise Bougeois in Jerry Gorovoy, Pandora Tabatabai Asbaghi, *Louise Bourgeois: Blue Days and Pink Days*, 168.

111. Ibid., 160.

Louise Bourgeois:
Woman at Work

CHRISTIANE TERRISSE

FOR PSYCHOANALYSTS, this century began with the Freudian question: "What does a woman want?" and will end with Lacan's response: "Woman does not exist". One by one, women have changed due to the considerable modifications that scientific advances have brought to their lives correlative to a general transformation of behaviour. Louise Bourgeois is one of these women. Her production has stamped this change on the history of art and feminists have been able to see in her work the manifestation of their struggle and follow her footsteps along the path she has forged. But such fertile provocation cannot be reduced to the exaltation of a feminine essence or to an ironical denunciation of the fallacy of the phallus, which are merely conformist supports for the renewal of the never ending war of the sexes.

Louise Bourgeois draws, paints, engraves, sculpts, writes, talks and even sings. The intertwining of these diverse activities is necessary to her creation and her life. For a time, she hoped that psychoanalysis would cure a painfully destructive anxiety –a vain attempt to incorporate into the American way of life precisely what could not be repressed: the vivid remnants of trauma, of the shortcomings of a father unequal to his task of imparting the law. Louise Bourgeois has transmitted the evil encounter with the real of sex, singular in its contingency, universal in its necessity, through constantly insisting on exhibiting what cannot be said, digging what cannot be filled in, telling what cannot be silenced.

From an infancy affected by the First World War (which put an end to 19th century ideals of submission) derive perhaps the accessories of slaughter used to assemble the fragments of bodies on those savage totems she erects to the obscure gods of dismemberment. Out of the context of her industrious childhood,

FIGURE 35. Joséphine and Louis Bourgeois at home, 172 Boulevard Saint–Germain, Paris, ca. 1911

spindles, needles, bobbins, skeins, and threads emerge. Weaving, plaiting and interlacing recall that epoch of diligent darning and mending by hand. Just as time itself does, Louise will not cease to wear out, puncture, bore, wrinkle, empty, and unveil, using both crude and sophisticated materials.

From her youth, she retains the trace of the division between the irrepressible vitality of a plethoric father and the silent grief of a mother mocked in her feminine being (Figure 35). The name "Sadie" inscribes on the feminine the shadow of duplicity and blame, but also poses the revelation of tacit consent and the need for unveiling in future work (Figure 36).

Her training, between classicism and innovation, between utility and *jouissance*, between coding and decoding, traces the encounter between geometrical seriousness and artistic fantasy that was to be inscribed in the reiteration of fruitful ruptures.

Her settlement in the New World –the ferment of the new assurance of a bond and the indefectible suffering

FIGURE 34. *Femme Maison*, 1982

has managed to seize the Organ and carry it under her arm like a soft toy or a handbag. In lending herself to such an illustrated representation of Freudian doctrine, Louise Bourgeois embraces the father of psychoanalysis to the letter, interpreting him just as he himself wished to be, literally. The title raises the girl-phallus equivalence to the level of a *witz* aimed at psychoanalysts, but also refers to the ritual paternal jest associated with peeling oranges, i.e. the mortifying representation of Louise deprived of a phallic attribute (Figure 37). But to make that paradoxical erection the phallic key of the work would mean considering the phallus as a universal master-key and therefore abandoning the search for what cannot be universalized, but which is declined one by one: femininity.

In spite of the fact that "a work of art, as an object, surpasses the intentions that have led to its birth as well as the commentaries, wherever they may come from", we might point to a logic in Louise Bourgeois' path, a logic parallel to the zigzagging trip the subject

FIGURE 36. Louise in Nice with her father, brother and Sadie, ca.1922

of exile– will bring out an enunciation, a distinctive sign of a subject inscribing in the universal the intimate grief of being a woman.

In the Oedipal myth, Freud metaphorizes the drama of the separation of each of us regarding the archaic of an infinite *jouissance* in which the mother figure represents possibility, and the father figure imposes renunciation. The "rock of castration" refers to the rejection of the feminine that Freud was to introduce as a limit to analytical treatment: "For women, penis envy –their desire to possess the masculine genital organ; for men, the rejection of their passive or feminine nature in their relationships with other men"[1]. The portrait of Louise Bourgeois with *Fillette* (1968), photographed by Robert Mapplethorpe in 1982 (Figure 30), is an ironical illustration of the victory of the penis-nied: Bourgeois

FIGURE 37. *Orange Episode*, 1990

goes through in order to "become what he is". The solution of the "runaway girl" to the enigma that she is herself and for herself will be her "invention of signs". Louise Bourgeois, victim of a cruelty that is not shown, that is not expressed, an insecure personage of unsteady balance, a "reed" that never breaks, obstinately continues to investigate, heal, "exorcize" her past through sculpture which, as she said in 1993, is "The only thing that sets me free"[2].

In order to move from grief to interrogation, from interrogation to the real of the answer, Louise Bourgeois chose to privilege art, a way of showing by means of drawing and painting, making present through sculpture, enunciating through titles, commentaries, or poems sometimes accompanied by rap music. This choice has been dictated by the pain of existing as separate, endorsed by the desire "to exorcize" the lingering nostalgia for the homeland, reinforced by the taste for "formal perfection", by the determination to vanquish matter through effort, to transcend that so-called female passiveness through action. But such a choice also owes its existence to the unfathomable decision of being. She can say afterwards without any boasting, "I have disengaged myself", disengaged from beatifying idealism, from "bogus humanitarianism" in whose name so many exactions are made, from frequently conformist sublimations, from the pressures of the *doxa* of art, whose inconsistency was denounced by

FIGURE 39. *Maison Vide* house from ca. 1860 in Staten Island owned by Louise Bourgeois since 1981

Marcel Duchamp, from the demands of the market that reduces an object to merchandise. In fact, for Louise Bourgeois art aims at the real, not to metaphorize in fiction what is intolerable, but to produce a "*fixtion*", an awakening to the real. Psychoanalysis reawakens "*lalangue*" beneath the language, the signifying matter beneath "the babbling" (Louise Bourgeois *dixit*). Louise Bourgeois' work reawakens the *non-sens* from a crowd of subverted meanings, a profusion of disorienting discoveries, a disturbing repetition of dual forms. She alters the frames of reference, displaces the most intimate feeling of the observers leading them beside themselves, towards that "centre of incandescence or absolute zero" a scandalous and unsurpassed "challenge to sensitivity"[3].

Sensitive to the "*pas de sens*" of her work, which is simultaneously the overcoming and denial of all meaning, the Madrid exhibition gives priority to the architectural reference as something which is organized around a void (Figure 39). As "the potter creates the vessel from a hole... so all art is characterized by a particular form of organization around this void"[4] (Figure 38). The artist clears the way, centres on the excluded meaning of Woman. Louise Bourgeois uses forms like a poet uses words, tears them up, displaces them, pushes them off, inventing new associations, repeating them until we are spellbound, creating evidence from vacuity, surprises by accumulation, encounters through divergence.

FIGURE 38. *Twosome*, 1991

The demarcation line of this point of "*ab-sens*" first passes through the erection of effigies symbolizing the absentees –all those people Louise is separated from. These *personnages*, raised on the roof-terrace of her New York home (impregnable, deserted space, protected from time), recall *xoana* –archaic Greek idols capable "of evoking absence in presence, and the elsewhere in what is before our very eyes... establishing real contact with the beyond"[5] (Figure 21). Through this depiction of her private pain, Louise Bourgeois joins the subjectivity of the time which aims at the impossible to bear made real and "creates an object out of a fact". Absence can then be incarnated and that incarnation form "an object that would be an answerer"[6].

Since 1946, the *Femmes Maisons* have brought about the cohabitation of flesh, "*substance jouissante*", hair, a feminine phaner treated as a plant, and the head-house or house-body, source of security and of frustration, indispensable and tyrannical like the woman who inhabits it or that the house inhabits (Figure 40). Representation establishes a link between past and present, between the unflagging attachment to the houses of childhood and the radical difference of the New York skyscrapers, between past and present. It also shows the very excess of femininity, which does not allow itself to remain enclosed within four walls and never stops transgressing the limits of puritanical conformism. What the woman lives through the artist transmits, raising the singular to the level of destiny, transforming her own outcry into a gesture on paper, fabric, plaster, marble or bronze. Whatever the support, the only thing that counts is the insistent display of the intimate grief of a being detached from itself and from others, simultaneously pierced and sealed, exposed and protected, provocative and secret. A captive woman, she captures her own fate and captivates the viewer.

Some twenty years later (1963 and 1965) the *Lairs* are a transformation of the houses into nests or burrows, intermediate forms, human and animal, vegetal and organic. The gesture of the artist gives rise to the polysemy of these "suspended" objects, hanging in the air, awaiting their moment, temporarily deprived of their functions, waivering, undecided, in suspense, divided but neither dissolved nor confused. These forms, rough

FIGURE 40. *Untitled*, 1947. Kröller-Müller Museum, Otterlo, The Netherlands

pottery, with clumsy modelling, arouse as if they were troglodyte caves the wish to penetrate them, "to see"; enigmatic wrappers, undefined habitats, they attract and disconcert. For Louise Bourgeois they recall the industrious *Fée Couturière* (Plate 30), metaphor for the handwork of the mother as well as the act of weaving the family threads almost torn apart. During that period of abundant conflicts these works herald the scandalous series of the hanging penises, relating to the same polysemy, participating in the "suspension" of the all-phallic, which fails to answer the question of the feminine.

On the register of "inner" architecture we should place the presentation of body parts "that only partly represent the function that produces them": mouths, ears, breasts, eyes, depict the course of the passages of *jouissance* not completely associated with the genital. Freud had classified them in phases and they can be

FIGURE 41. Gert Schiff in the performance "A Banquet/A Fashion Show of Body Parts" held at the Hamilton Gallery, New York in 1978

interpreted in terms of partial objects. Lacan related them to sensorial orifices, since in the lack of sex what takes its place is the surplus-enjoyment, "*plus de jouir*" passing through all the holes of the body: "when one advances towards that central void... the body of the other splits up"[7]. Louise Bourgeois cuts out and displays such parts. This fragmentation does not deconstruct the model in the Cubist way or deprive it of realism in the Surrealist manner, without stylization or aestheticism, it reveals the form in all its brutal bareness, its autistic presence, it reproduces the eccentric metonymy of desire and, better than any other discourse, it communicates the fact that possession is reduced to licking the scraps of the body of the other. But the artist does not limit herself to isolating these fragments; with their obsessive proliferation invading the space, they turn into a display of the vacillation of sexual identity, of the continuity of flesh and matter. Plasticity remodels plastic art, the wrapper extends over a body that is treated like a gigantic penis inside a contraceptive sheath burgeoning with bulges. The artist's irony clearly reveals the current invasion of all kinds of prostheses that supposedly stimulate flagging desire, as well as the blurring of singularities for the sake of a conformist model. In *Confrontation* (1978), the ex-girl dressed by Poiret subverts the ritual of the fashion show and clothes the men above all with wild exultation (Figure 41). But she also knows how to lend her body and her image to the deconstruction of appearances, as when she poses

before the flight of steps to her house like Apollinaire's *Tirésias*, with breasts! (Figure 18)

Torso, Self-Portrait (1963-64) (Plate 31) and *The Rabbit* (1970) (Figure 42), in the tearing apart of a nakedness offered up to an inquisitorial *scopy*, evoke not only those indiscreet scale models that reveal the intimate arrangement of places and those roofless ruins within which the traces of destroyed interiors can be perceived, but also the perverse desire to penetrate, beneath the skin, the secret of what is feminine. In *Le regard* (1966) (Plate 33), eyelids, half-closed over a glassy eyeball, suggest half-open labia, the half-drawn curtain of a window, the shutter of a photographic lens, devices of a visual perception that simultaneously reveals and conceals what cannot be seen without blame.

The nipples proliferating on the bust of *She-Fox* (1985) (Figure 43) or on the altar of *Confrontation* (1978) (Figure 17) show the Freudian breast-penis equivalence

FIGURE 42. *Rabbit*, ca. 1970. Solomon R. Guggenheim Museum, New York

of those erectile protuberances whose multiplication stresses and annuls their obscenity just as, on a supermarket shelf, the exhibition of exact copies of merchandise produces an effect that makes us forget their use. Although the plethora of accessories comes near to Baroque profusion, it elides the decorative purpose to

FIGURE 43. *The She-Fox*, 1985. Private Collection

privilege a repetition conceived as a real assault on traditional representation.

The unknotting of the fragment and of the whole is never displayed more daringly than in the hanging works of the *Janus* series and in *Fillette* (1968) (Plate 40), where latex, plaster, bronze, everything, serve to suspend judgement, reverse the point of view, transform established certainty into a hanging pendant, to ill treat a symbol and take it back to its most utterly natural state of appended appendage. It is sufficient for Louise Bourgeois to keep to the real in order for the "primacy of the phallus" to be manifested as "not-all" powerful in the organization of the world in a sub-

version of the male norm more in agreement with Lacan's ideas than Freudian doctrine, close to the psychoanalytical method that attempts to distance the ideal to the advantage of the real. Louise Bourgeois gives a title to most of her works, i.e. she guides the look towards an intention. In this way she curbs the proliferation of meanings and performs the task of interpretation. She teaches the observer to read, just as the analyst teaches the analyzed to read, leading them a side step next to the unknown. The title *Fillette* emphasizes the capricious fragility of the male organ; it stresses the effeminate character of all displays of virility as well as the phallic character of the female being. It is with a *Janus Fleuri* (1968) (Plate 38) causing vertigo that the double face of error finds an ironical representation: the god of two faces, considered the

FIGURE 44. *Sleep II* and *Fillette*, installation view at Musée d'Art Contemporain, Lyon, France, 1990

creator of all things (he gave his name to the arch in the Roman Forum, whose doors, opened or closed, announcing respectively peace or war), embodies the foundational signifying opposition: "there is no one without zero", there is no masculine without its logical supplement, the feminine. For Louise Bourgeois the word cannot be separated from creation, it is an act since its utterance breaks the continuity of perception. Afterwards, one is unable to look at the world as before, one can no longer be unaware.

The work of Louise Bourgeois is logical, arising from the impasse of formalism, attempting, through the working of forms, to depict form as a way of being and a means of expression. It cannot be said that she makes use of forms in the traditional sense, but rather that she elaborates a new artistic ethic that contemporary artists take as a model in installations which sometimes only seem copies of an initial gesture.

Having interpreted and disseminated body and house, in 1991 the artist exhibited a number of almost closed structures, the *Cells* (Plate 66), in which, by way of indication she placed disparate elements united by a complicity that she did not conceal but which, in spite of all explanations, continued to be secretly disturbing. The visitor, restricted by the layout to the role of voyeur, is obliged to slide through the apertures provided by the artist. Believing "that it is discovering the world through the slit of prepuberty", the incited eye attempts to seize some sort of sense to hold on to but loses itself in the details, stumbles around that anomalous arrangement and receives a shock akin to that delivered by Marcel Duchamp with his *Étant donné: 1. La chute d'eau 2. Le gaz d'éclairage* (1946-1966) which Jacques Lacan interpreted as a representation of the building of the pulsion. But the filiation goes no further. For rather than provoking Louise Bourgeois moves, rather than amusing, she disturbs, and rather than attracting, she reprimands. It is a piteous "primitive scene" that leaps to the eye, when it is not the eyes themselves that impose their presence of sheer looking, through an allusive or explicit mirror effect. Whether through the transparency of the glass jars lined up in profusion, the smooth reflection of polished bronze, the unstable reflection of crystal balls or inclined mirrors, everything seems to be there to deceive the eye, to dupe its avidity, to deflect its deadly power, for an instant possessed of an evil ability. The Baroque touch of "exalted obscenity" of the previous works is limited given the spatial location to the erratic inventory of a reverie in which the familiar is transformed and produces that "disturbing strangeness" that Freud associated with the sudden appearance of the "*extime*" for the

FIGURE 45. *Untitled*, 1996. Sammlung Hauser and Wirth, St. Gallen, Switzerland

subject. The *Cells* are not simply a memorial to traumatic childhood scenes but, much more subtly, testimony of those remarkable recollections and their mutation into structural phantasms. Inversely, having deconstructed phallic primacy and *The Destruction of the Father* (1974) (Plate 44) was the crucial moment, the artist was to construct, through indelible images, a surprising world, a world ambiguous and disturbing yet impregnated with a secret and even shameful familiarity. Garments juxtaposed on hangers or layered on a mannequin, isolated fragments, hands sculpted in stone, together on top of a table, a severed ear, a man's decapitated and armless body, in the loneliness of a spasm, rigid, paralyzed, for all to see. Each detail surprises; the whole disturbs like the sudden revelation of a *jouissance* long kept secret, inadvertently exhumed, and which one can no longer elude.

With the *Spiders* (1994-1997) series (Figure 46), a purified form of the *Cells*, we see the emptying of all meaning, the representation of an "empty assemblage" which is only fenced around, cut-out. The central point, now vacant, is found within the unstable circle of the long sci-fi legs, sculpted with intensified realism. The most realistic one of all, twisted through an old injury, no longer seems able to support the tortuously modelled body. They are simultaneously metaphors of the mother's protection and representations of the inconsistency of her response to the issue of the feminine. "My mother: she is the wire framework that keeps me standing up on earth and even the wind that circulates inside"[8]. Contemporary with this fence, the "hangers" (Figure 45), rightly called *Untitled*, scatter and gather together "heterogeneous elements", undergarments and outer clothing, bones literally turned into hangers, heavy trunks, swollen stumps. Wafting in the air in the vicinity is a tomb-like odour, since "the empty structure of the skeleton is the irreducible element around which are arranged other elements, the implements of *jouissance*, necklaces, goblets, weapons: sub-elements more for enumerating the *jouissance* than to make it return to the body"[9].

The continuity of these inverted images allow a reading of the work, of its Möbian knot: both assemblage and elements articulate void and disparity, the absence of "Woman" and the proliferation of her accessories, "the ineffable" of feminine *jouissance* and a multiplicity of commentaries. Better than any authorized annotation on Lacan's famous statement "There is no sexual intercourse", an echo of the lucid Freudian affirmation "There is something in sexuality which is opposed to total satisfaction", the confrontation with the handicapped *Couples* (Plate 71) of the current works reveals both the impossible which must be, unavoidably, endured by every subject for whom undoubtedly 1+1=2 and the acephalia of constant pulsion. The insistence with which Louise Bourgeois retraces her own steps and does not stop "making signs" unites with the endlessness of a real which she is attempting to depict. The manner sometimes allusive, sometimes intrusive of these forms that move from outline to disproportion, from the knot to explosion, relates to the topology that Lacan attempted to establish in psychoanalysis. Louise

FIGURE 46. *Spider*, 1996. Sammlung Hauser and Wirth, St. Gallen, Switzerland

Bourgeois demonstrates through her exposition, the relevancy of that path of investigation.

To produce such creations it is necessary, "beyond dread and pity", to have reached that place where appearances are rejected, that place of utter bareness which characterizes the tragic hero, the saint and the poor in spirit. One must have lost all hope and expect no response from anyone. This step, decisive yet constantly repeated, is produced by the fundamental ignorance as to one's own being and the meaning of one's life. Louise Bourgeois, like so many others, realized this at a very early stage. But she knew how "to make her own way" and thus indicates through her work the arid and fertile road that leads "to the encounter with the real".

Anyone commenting on a work finds himself caught by the trap set by the work, captive of the artist's itinerary, obliged to follow its winding road, and imprisoned by a style that asserts itself beyond the awareness of whoever thought himself free from its glosses. An attraction impossible to resist. The spider has caught in its web the buzzing bla-bla. There resides the strength of a trajectory that commands respect, suspension points and silence.

NOTES

1. Sigmund Freud, *Résultat, Idées, Problèmes* (Paris: Presses Universitaires de France, 1937), 266.

2. Bernard Marcadé and Jerry Gorovoy in an interview for the film, *Louise Bourgeois*, by Camille Guichard, Terra Luna Productions, Série Mémoire/Centre Georges Pompidou, Paris,1993.

3. Jacques Lacan, *Séminaire, livre VII, L'éthique de la psychanalyse* (Paris: Seuil, 1986), 237.

4. Jacques Lacan, ibid, 162.

5. Jean-Pierre Vernant, *De la présentification de l'invisible à l'imitation des apparences, Image et signification* (Documentation Française, 1983) quoted by Gérard Wajcman, 96.

6. Gérard Wajcman, *L'objet du siècle* (Lagrasse: Verdier, Collection Philia), 87.

7. Jacques Lacan, ibid, 237.

8. Christian Prigent, *Une phrase pour ma mère* (Paris: POL, 1996), 58.

9. Jacques Lacan, *Radiophonie, Scilicet 2-3* (Paris: Seuil, 1970), 62.

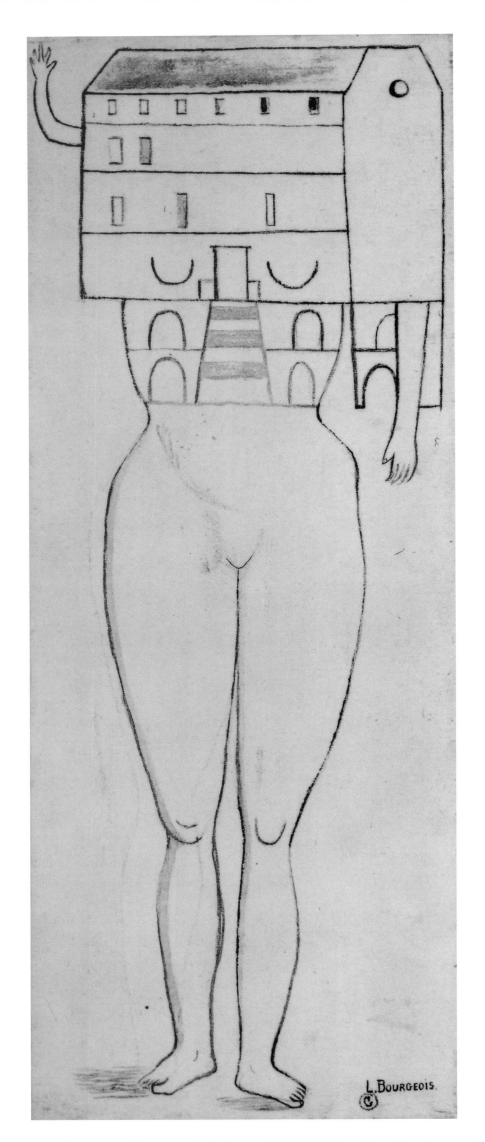

Farewell to the Doll House

LYNNE COOKE

Space does not exist, it is just a metaphor for the structure of our existences.
LOUISE BOURGEOIS

Our house … is our first universe, a real cosmos in every sense of the word
GASTON BACHELARD

THE VOLUPTUOUS FEMALE, her torso encased in a diminutive building, stands enclosed within a narrow stagelike interior, doubly confined. Styled as a substantial bourgeois mansion, the doll house wraps neatly around her figure like a close-fitting garment. But the fit goes beyond a deft exercise in tailoring, since her upper body has miraculously miniaturized and distorted itself in order to conform to the dimensions of the enclosing structure. Her raised arm may be signaling for help, but, equally, it could be a gesture of salutation. In either case the tiny size of this limb attests to the fact that the house infantilizes its occupant. This building both shelters and imprisons: it is at once retreat, fortress, habitat, and gaol. Yet since its dominion does not extend below her waist, her sexuality escapes control and regulation. In *Femme Maison* (1946–47) (Figure 47), Louise Bourgeois reverses standard formulations and traditional paradigms. Female sexuality is no longer privatized, closeted, controlled, and contained within the domestic arena. It is consciousness that is constricted, fettered by the restrictive agencies of domestic, marital, and social mores.

An outline drawing in ink on a linen support, this was the first in a series of four works devoted to the subject of woman and architecture, a trope for Bourgeois' ongoing probing of female experience in its most fundamental terms. Sharing this same title, similar in dimension and format, though now more fully worked in oil, the other three paintings permutate this thematic through a related iconography. One shows a female figure that has been elongated to conform to the profile of an apartment block (Plate 2); another sets the woman within a clapboard building reminiscent of domestic architecture on the northeastern seaboard of the United States (Plate 1), while the fourth depicts a Greek Revival mansion (Plate 3), typical of those found on Southern plantations, clothing its svelte inhabitant. Such reiteration across a gamut of social and cultural contexts reaffirms the ubiquity of the guiding notion as much as its longevity. Of the four versions, the first (Figure 47), with its austere silhouette, is the most compelling. Through the very starkness of its portrayal it becomes a lucid, metaphorical embodiment of what is most essential in this concept. Through its diagrammatic rendering of the nude, stylistically akin to popular graphics and signage, it takes on the manner of the generic. Through its stereotypical formulations of both its principal elements, it seems to situate itself outside time and place.

Concise, iconic, deceptively simple, this painting is closely related to a drawing with the same composition (Figure 48); the drawing's precision and clarity suggests that it may not have served as a preliminary sketch but was designed as a more intimate variant.[1] This version was reproduced on the announcement card for the exhibition in which the suite of paintings was presented: a show at the Norlyst Gallery in New York in 1947. Almost forty years later, in 1984, the same image was reworked

FIGURE 47. *Femme Maison*, 1946–47. Private Collection

into a photogravure that the artist donated to a benefit for the pioneering feminist journal *Heresies*. Six years after, in 1990, it was reissued as a print in a larger format in an edition of sixty. Such literal reiteration is rare in Bourgeois' art, although, typically, she revisits her principal subjects intermittently over the course of many years. Its exceptional recurrence in a career that now spans six

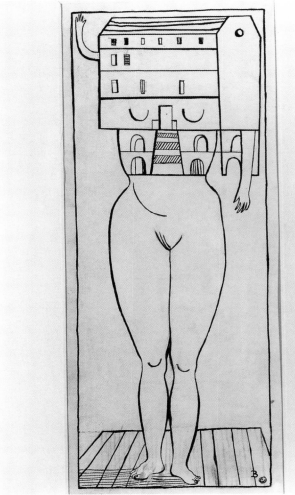

FIGURE 48. *Femme Maison,* 1947. Solomon R. Guggenheim, New York

decades attests at once to the obsessive persistence of the notion of the *femme maison* in her imaginary and, more importantly, to the eloquence and vitality of this particular rendering of the subject.

The potency of this abbreviated, quasi-vernacular version owes almost as much to its humor as to its ambiguity and purported universality. The playfully inverted title is critical to its meaning, and also typical of Bourgeois' quixotic fascination with the allusory character of language. By taking the English construction of "housewife," and reversing and translating it into French, she creates a new entity that fails to conform to the syntactical rules of both languages. Thrust outside the law, the concept is regulated by neither of the cultures to which it is subject.[2] Moreover, switching the normative ordering, so that material property no longer precedes human ownership, effectively shifts focus from the physical to the behavioral, from the passive to the active, thereby stressing that woman may be subject as well as object, agent as well as possession.

Commenting on this schematic image many years later, Bourgeois avoided any acknowledgment of the transgressive ambivalence at its core. "I consider this perfect," she asserted, "it brings the personal together with the environment.... [I]t is a symbiosis of one with the universe...it is a kind of acceptance."[3] Given its uninflected forcefulness, this authoritative declamation, even if heavily freighted with irony, stills critical dispute, cloaking the implicit contradictions between her renderings of the relationship between woman and the world and that deemed normative, and masking the price of any such unity.

The pivotal place of this image in Bourgeois' oeuvre derives not only from its privileged position vis-à-vis the rest of the paintings and drawings exhibited at Norlyst, but also from its prophetic role within her practice at that moment. The works that she created in this crucial period of 1946–47 are generally recognized, by the artist as well as her audience, as her first mature statement. During these seminal years she turned increasingly to three-dimensional forms of expression. The Norlyst exhibition was her last show of paintings. Her debut as a sculptor, some two years later in 1949, was but the first of three exhibitions of the *Personnages* that were held at the Peridot Gallery (Figure 27) (the other two took place in 1950 and 1953). Begun in mid-decade this extensive group of standing totemic figures explore further, if more obliquely, the interrelation between the individual and its environment. In this path-breaking show a number of the hieratic wooden effigies were positioned singly, but many were grouped together. All stood directly on the floor of the gallery, whose space consequently took on an environmental character.

Several possessed pronounced architectonic features, which meant that they had to be presented in close proximity to the walls or corners of a room. Certain titles also alluded to architectural functions, notably *Pillar* (1947–49) (Plate 15), and *the Tomb of a Young Person* (1947–49) (Plate 13), while others referred to emotional and psychic states, for example *Persistent Antagonism* (1947–49) (Plate 14) and *Observer* (1947–49) (Plate 10). Compared with the *Femme Maison* series, these ritualistic figures were more abstract, the architectural references more elliptical. Nonetheless they were invested with a strong animistic presence that enhanced the prevailing mood of somber introspection, isolation, and loneliness.

The sole exception to this was the anomaly within the group, a work that subsequently was exhibited alone, affixed to a wall: *Portrait of Jean-Louis* (1947–49) (Plate 7), an homage to the artist's younger son. Like its pictorial counterparts collectively known as *Femme Maison*, its lower part is human, its upper half architectural. Now, however, the two have harmoniously integrated so that building and child merge into a novel hybrid. The individuation of the figure, by means of the title, is matched by the particularity of the mode of architecture employed: a contemporary skyscraper. Also created during this critical period, *The Blind Leading the Blind* (1947–49) (Plate 8) is a haunting sculpture that fuses the environmental character of the installations at Peridot with a more monumental form, and an even more abstracted language. The culmination of this body of work, it is also the highpoint of that very fertile period. Given its many pairs of long, tapering legs that rest precariously on the ground, it seems to have evolved out of the images of model buildings on stilts, or pylons, found in the concurrent suite of prints *He Disappeared into Complete Silence*. Now, however, with the reduction of the abode to a simple lintel, the whole becomes less overtly figural, more animal-like.

This cryptic series of prints, the other major work in Bourgeois' oeuvre from this crucial formative moment, is, however, ultimately more closely related to the group of paintings clustered under the rubric *Femme Maison*. Initiated in part by the wish to have her art reach a broader audience, as well as in the hope of

augmenting her income, Bourgeois embarked on this suite in 1946.[4] As witnessed in notes written in her daybooks from that and the following year this project proved a major undertaking, requiring a substantial commitment of both time and energy. Yet, in its final stages, the enterprise became somewhat eclipsed: few full sets of the portfolio were ever assembled or distributed, and no definite sequencing of the images was ever concluded.

On each of its nine pages, a text on the left is paired with a drawing on the right (Plates 4 and 5). The relationship between word and image never becomes illustrative, although the brief, autonomous tales are positioned under headings such as "Plate I," "II," etc., as if they were titles or extended captions. Ranging from simple phrases to compressed parables, they inflect the enigmatic images with a mysterious, poetic

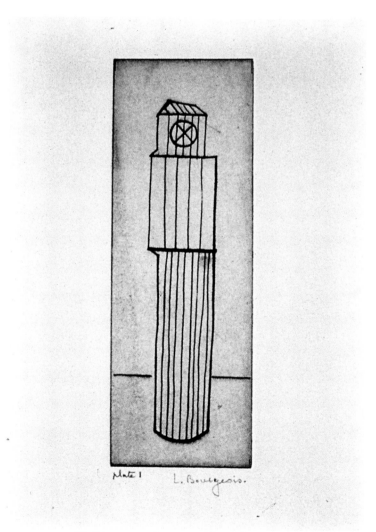

FIGURE 49. *He Disappeared into Complete Silence*, 1947

empty plain, less homely abode than defensive retreat. Silent, closed, impenetrable, walled into themselves, they vividly conjure the hermeticism of the series' title (Figure 49). Only in one instance do they metamorphose into humanoid structures (Figure 50); and it is in this instance alone that a certain anecdotal potential emerges, though it offers little amplification to the schematic plot in general. Elsewhere, the anthropomorphic is sublimated fully into the architectural, creating eloquent metaphors of beleaguered, impotent masculinity. In addition, two provide interior views (Figures 51 and 52). A bare but otherwise ordinary room contains four ladders hanging from its ceiling, suspended above the floor: they offer an image not of escape but its contrary, frustrated egress. Within this homogeneous lexicon of stoic incarceration, the sole transparent dwelling stands out. Where privacy, intimacy, and seclusion would normally prevail, it pro-

FIGURE 50. *He Disappeared into Complete Silence,* 1947

resonance. Most begin in time-honored fashion – "Once...." – thereby projecting the situation back into an undifferentiated past. Equally conventional, all are narrated in relational terms – I/you; mother/son; man/woman – in the standard binary logic of this genre. Although their prototypes are obviously folk and fairy tales, Bourgeois' versions are suffused with a sardonic humor that removes them far from the realm of the child. Terse and elliptical, each ends abruptly, often on a fatalistic note. Bereft of any moral residue, these lapidary accounts offer neither reassurance nor enlightenment: disappointment, if not disaster, is the prevailing legacy.

Engraved with a wiry, taut line and printed darkly onto the paper, the nine pictures in the portfolio are comprised mostly of architectural forms. Strangely isolated, each etiolated cabana is set adrift on an

FIGURE 51. *He Disappeared into Complete Silence,* 1947

Plate 5   L. Bourgeois

FIGURE 52. *He Disappeared into Complete Silence,* 1947

poses an image of shelter now shorn of domesticity and subject to surveillance. Given that this repertoire also includes obelisks and a guillotine, the general impression remains that all these edifices owe more to the typologies of public architecture than to their purely residential counterparts. Once again, as with the cautionary tales, reference may be made to the realm of the juvenile, this time to children's-book illustration. While their graphic style alludes to this genre, which greatly fascinated Bourgeois during this period, the overriding tenor of the portfolio is nonetheless very different. In place of wonder and playfulness something mordant now supervenes.

In the interwar years the burgeoning taste for the naïve, the childlike, the primitive, and the insane was reinforced by polemical claims that such realms were the repositories of not only more archaic, more funda-

mental truths but of primordial modes of expression, languages that stretched across cultures and eras, partaking of the universal and the pre-social. As evidenced in these key early works Bourgeois' subtle engagement with such idioms and beliefs is more tangential than direct. Her debt to contemporary artistic styles is similarly more skewed than straightforward. Influenced by certain of its vocabularies, she nonetheless shied away from Surrealism's delight in assertively provocative formulations, its latent misogyny, and its obsessive fixation on the perverse, the taboo, the transgressive, and the exotic. Thus while her work may at times reveal formal affinities with that of others on its periphery, such as Matta, her existential vision more closely parallels the metaphysics of the Abstract Expressionists, her peers. For example, in *He Disappeared into Complete Silence* she posits an inner solitariness rather than one defined in relation to and conditional upon an urban environment (as found, for example, in De Chirico's haunted cityscapes). Evocative of indeterminate placelessness, the bleak sites limned in this suite memorably encapsulate a signature state of alienation. Ultimately, however, her articulations may owe as much to her formative intellectual milieu, which was shaped by such late-19th-century luminaries as Ibsen, Charcot, and the Symbolists, among others.[5]

While such discourses continue to structure Bourgeois' imaginary, her response to architecture, by contrast, seems to have been somewhat differently determined, inflected as it was by more contemporary debates. A visit to the epochal 1925 Exposition des Arts Décoratifs in Paris resulted in a lasting interest in Art Deco, while simultaneously introducing her to the modernist aesthetic, as manifest in the *Pavillon de l'Esprit Nouveau,* a house that its designer, Le Corbusier, styled "a machine for living." This period of intense theoretical inquiry coincided with Bourgeois' years as a student at the Sorbonne, where, prior to devoting herself to fine art, she studied philosophy, calculus, and solid geometry. The latter proved particularly decisive for her approach to architectural form. Dubbing her vocabulary "symbolic geometry – solid geometry as a symbol of emotional security," Bourgeois conceived of architecture in her early works in terms of simple three dimensional volumes, as witnessed in the following statement: "Euclidean or other kinds of geometry are closed systems where relations can be anticipated and are eternal.... It comes naturally to me to express emotions through

FIGURE 53. *The Quartered One*, ca. 1964–65

relations between geometrical elements." In *He Disappeared into Complete Silence* this "passion for the security geometry affords" was undercut with an ominous tenor as her dual engagement with architecture, as a cultural invention and as the product of an individual act of creation, fully matured.[6]

Bourgeois revitalized this crucial formative encounter during the 1940s in New York when she established connections with a number of architects in exile, Le Corbusier and José Luis Sert among them. At that time Le Corbusier's work was frequently discussed in relation to that of Claude-Nicholas Ledoux, which seemed to presage its elementarism, its concern for the social effects of architecture, and its vision of an ideal city. Ledoux's Neoclassical Platonism, like Le Corbusier's high modernism, shadows Bourgeois' buildings, although her predecessors' idealism has become tinged with a dystopic melancholy. Linking all three is a belief in *architecture parlante*, that is, in an architecture deployed as a symbolic language.[7]

In the mid-1950s, after completing the extended series of the *Personnages*, Bourgeois started to explore alternative methods, modeling rather than carving, and mining biomorphic rather than architectonic idioms, as she concentrated anew on the female form as her preferred subject. From these forays little remains. *Maison*, a small sculpture in plaster of a simple house completed in 1961 but perhaps begun much earlier, seems a diversion (Plate 24). For thereafter she eschewed geometric solids in favor of a more organically defined notion of the architectonic, as manifest in the lairs, caverns, and other womblike configurations that infiltrate her vocabulary over the next two decades. Frequently small, even intimate in scale, and often labyrinthine in structure, the spaces of these sculptures blend interior and exterior, organic and anthropomorphic, part and whole, the microscopic and the monumental, in a radically new conflation of sexuality and habitation. In place of the polarity between human and architecture embodied in those first seminal articulations of a gendered space, notably the *Femme Maison* paintings, works like *Lair* (1962) (Plate 27), *Lair* (1963) (Plate 29), *Double Negative* (1963) (Figure 54), *Fée Couturière* (1963) (Plate 30), and *The Quartered One* (1964–65) (Figure 53) subsume or dissolve this dichotomy into sinuous, formless, amorphous, or unbounded spaces. Articulated very differently from their predecessors, which were structured around a notion of the body based in sexual difference, these sexualized spaces seem either to be grounded in experiences that precede gender distinctions or, alternatively, to be

FIGURE 54. *Double Negative*, 1963. Kröller-Müller Museum, Otterlo, The Netherlands

composite entities comprised of multiple genders. The environments represented in those two complementary bodies of work, *He Disappeared into Complete Silence* and *Femme Maison*, could be described as, respectively, male-identified, and female-identified. As gendered spaces, those realms are constructed in relation to prevailing sexual stereotypes. By contrast, much of Bourgeois' subsequent work from the 1960s and 70s explored space by means of a more abstract, organic vocabulary and by recourse to such subjects as sanctuaries, havens, and cocoonlike sanctums.[8] Places again associated with the contraries of refuge and confinement, such sites no longer belong exclusively to the anthropomorphic world but reference domains utilized by many types of sentient being.[9]

In that key first formulation in 1947 of the *Femme Maison*, four of the five senses were occluded: only touch remained unfettered. That is, engagement with the world was to be mediated tactilely, primarily through the erogenous zones. This signal realignment towards the corporeal and visceral presages the radical reformulation Bourgeois' art would undergo in the early '60s. Such sculptures as *Lair* (1963) and *The Quartered One*, or *Le Regard* (1966) (Plate 33), seem to burgeon forth from their interiors, to become polymorphous, heterogeneous, fragmentary entities, their contours unfixed and fluid. They are best experienced proprioceptively, through the fingers as well as the eyes. Engendered by processes of conflating, splitting, multiplying, magnifying, and proliferating, such spaces often collapse dis-

tinctions between inside and outside, body and environment. In consequence they invite interpretations culled from fantasies of the body riven by drives and undifferentiated by gender, that is, according to a Kleinian model of infantile experience.[10] Complex and interstitial, such structures offer vivid metaphors for the in-betweenness of infantile experience, in which the body is apprehended as decentered, its limits eroded, its psychic life structured by unconscious fantasies generated by innate corporeal drives and unmediated by language.

Inherently disposed to creating spatial interconnections rather than making spatial distinctions, these organic dwellings undermine many of the basic antipodes integral to Bourgeois' previous dwellings, and to the norms of architecture: public/private, male/female, nature/culture. By virtue of complex, seamless, continuously flowing surfaces that appear to twist, bend, warp or stretch through space, they become harbingers of a new architectural language. Derived from topology or based in a branch of mathematics concerned with such geometries as the torus, the Klein bottle, and the projec-

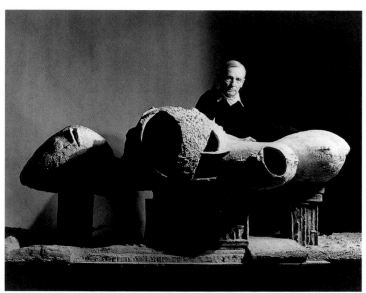

FIGURE 55. Frederick Kiesler photographed by Irving Penn with the maquette of *Endless House*, New York, 1959

tive plane, they evoke "environments of liquid spatiality." In this, they conjure the matrix for a vanguard architecture produced from a structural skin, an architecture of "blobs" as distinct from their more conventional counterparts dubbed, equally derisively, as "boxes."[11] More obvious and less deferred are their affinities with such futuristic postwar experiments as Frederick Kiesler's *Endless House* (Figure 55), which was widely acclaimed at that time on account of its radical exploration of an organic morphology.[12]

In the early 1980s Bourgeois briefly returned to the thematics of the *Femme Maison* (spurred perhaps by a retrospective of the same title held at the Renaissance Society in 1981). In each instance the work she produced was carved, one in black marble, in 1981 (Figure 56), and another in white, in 1983 (Plate 47). In both, a solid, self-contained house is poised atop a base that, in the former, is comprised of tumescent extrusions or anatomical protruberances, in the latter, of mountainous swirling drapery. Divested of overtly figural reference, these composite images juxtapose elements from her vocabulary of the 1960s and 1970s with motifs from her formative years of the 1940s.[13] As witnessed by the release of the editioned print in 1990, the subject of

FIGURE 57. Etienne-Louis Boullée, Monument to Newton, 1784 (Bibliothèque Nationale, Paris)

woman and architecture continued to preoccupy her, its timeliness and topicality undiminished. Viewed through the prism of this resilient revenant *Untitled (with Hand)* (1989) (Plate 55) and *Untitled (with Foot)* (1989) assume a unique identity: performing almost a valedictory homage. From a perfect sphere of rosy pink marble extends, in one case, the tiny arm of an infant, and, in the other, the matching leg. Each sits on a block of roughly carved granite into which the phrase: "I love you" or "Do you love me?" has been carved in a cursive script. Source and sepulcher, womb and tomb, the orb that contains the infant is at once the originary locus and the ideal memorial, an evocative echo of the sublime cenotaph that Etienne-Louis Boullée designed for Isaac Newton (Figure 57). Belated companion to the *Portrait of Jean-Louis*, these tardy progeny of the *Femme Maison* of 1946–47 offer a less problematic synthesis of the individual with its environment. Integrating the man-made and the natural, the geometric and the organic, the rudimentary and the developed, they posit a compelling image of seamless symbiosis.

The initial embodiment of the notion of *Femme Maison* stemmed from fantasies rooted in childhood, fantasies that if maintained in later life prove disabling. After a prolonged gestation of more than fifty years Bourgeois now presented a beguiling heir to that first prophetic statement—an image that may be read as the ideal synthesis of individual with architectural milieu, and as the ultimate gesture of regression.

FIGURE 56. *Femme Maison*, 1981

1. Additional drawings on this theme exist. See, for example, that reproduced in Rosi Huhn, "Louise Bourgeois: Deconstructing the Phallus within the Exile of the Self," *Inside the Visible* (Boston: The Institute of Contemporary Arts, 1996), 141. Here the whole torso is contained within the edifice, and hair, a familiar fetish for the sexual organs, becomes the embodiment of untrammeled expression, unbridled freedom. In addition to other related untitled works from this period, there is a recent reprise, an unexhibited sculpture in which a doll's wig has been assemblaged onto an apartmentlike form that rests on two slender legs (Figure 34). The spider, epitome of yet another telling relationship between the individual and its habitat, also first appears in Bourgeois' work at this time, in a number of drawings.

2. "Womanhouse," the English-language equivalent of this term, was adopted as the title of an influential exhibition, held in Los Angeles in 1972, and organized by the Feminist Art Program at California Institute of the Arts, Valencia, directed by Judy Chicago and Miriam Schapiro. The collective converted a delapidated house into a series of installations, including a *Womb Room* by Faith Wilding and *The Doll House* by Miriam Schapiro and Sherry Brodie.

3. Quoted in *The Prints of Louise Bourgeois* (New York: The Museum of Modern Art, 1994), 148.

4. For a full account see *The Prints of Louise Bourgeois*, op. cit., 72ff.

5. For a more detailed discussion, see Robert Storr, "Arachne on 20th Street," *Louise Bourgeois: Homesickness* (Yokohama: Yokohama Museum of Art, 1997), 131–140. Compare also Bourgeois' first rendering of the *Femme Maison* with the use of the mannequin by the Surrealists, and Masson in particular, in the epochal International Surrealist Exhibition held at the Beaux-Arts gallery in Paris in 1938.

6. Interview with Susi Bloch, *Art Journal*, (Summer 1976), 372, reprinted in *Louise Bourgeois: Destruction of the Father, Reconstruction of the Father* (London: Violette Editions), 102–107.

7. An octroy de Paris, Bourgeois' father's half-brother lived in one of the few extant Ledoux buildings in Paris, an opportunity made possible by his job. Bourgeois' engagement with visionary Neoclassical architecture extended to the work of the other great exponent of that movement, Etienne-Louis Boullée. Burgeoning in the 1930s, this discussion of the work of Le Corbusier in relation to that of Ledoux and Boullée largely grew out of the writings of Emil Kaufmann. Notably, "the City of the Architect Ledoux," "Von Ledoux bis Le Corbusier," (1933), and "Three Revolutionary Architects, Boullée, Ledoux and Lequeux," *Transactions of the American Philosophical Society,* vol. 42, Part 3 (1952). Compare, for example, the drawings of American grain silos in *Vers une architecture,* 1st ed. (Les Editions G. Cres, 1923) with Bourgeois' structures in *He Disappeared…* and with Ledoux's unrealized plans for residences for different professions.

8. Key to this rewriting of the human/architecture dialectic is the critical change in her materials and methods. From the beginning of the 1960s Bourgeois increasingly worked with plaster, and then with latex. The following statement from the end of that decade attests both to the continuity of her abiding concerns and to the significance of this shift in her techniques. "Content is a concern with the human body, its aspect, its changes, transformations, what it needs, wants and feels – its functions./ What it perceives and undergoes passively, what it performs./ What it feels and what protects it – its habitat./ All these states of being, perceiving and doing are expressed by processes that are familiar to us and that have to do with the treatment of materials, pouring, flowing, dripping, oozing out, settling, hardening, coagulating, thawing, expanding, contracting, and the voluntary aspects, such as slipping away, advancing, collecting, letting go." ("Form," late 1960s, reprinted in *Louise Bourgeois: Destruction of the Father, Reconstruction of the Father* [London: Violette Editions, 1998], 76).

9. D'Arcy Wentworth Thompson's influential book *On Growth and Form*, published in 1942, is also important in this regard.

10. In her article "Bad Enough Mother," to which this text is indebted, Mignon Nixon persuasively interprets Bourgeois' installation *The Destruction of the Father* from a Kleinian perspective (*October* 71 [Winter 1995]: 70–92).

11. See Terence Riley, "The Un-Private House," *The Un-Private House* (New York: The Museum of Modern Art, 1999), 29 and passim, for a fuller discussion of these notions.

12. A large-scale model of Kiesler's house was shown several times at The Museum of Modern Art in New York during the 1950s. In 1952 it was exhibited alongside Buckminster Fuller's geodesic dome in "Two Houses: New Ways to Build," and in 1960 it was included in "Visionary Architecture" (The Museum of Modern Art, New York), together with works by Le Corbusier, Bruno Taut, Paul Nelson, Frank Lloyd Wright, and Buckminster Fuller.

13. Several other sculptures that explore the subject of the house should be noted, including *Maison* (1986), a reworking of the image of an open multistoried dwelling first limned in *He Disappeared....* Here it is comprised of seven floors, each containing plaster groupings of polysexual tumescent forms. Yet others, including *Curved House* (1983), are indebted to actual dwellings with autobiographical significance: her childhood home in Choisy and the barn in Easton, Connecticut, which she and her husband purchased in the 1950s, converting it into a country residence. Closer to *The Blind Leading the Blind* and *He Disappeared Into Complete Silence* are two steel sculptures, both titled *Maisons Fragiles*, from 1978.

Beckoning Bernini

MIEKE BAL

. . . the necessity and proper use of anachronism in art history.

HUBERT DAMISCH[1]

ENTRANCE

ARE THEY SCULPTURES? Installations? Buildings? Actually Louise Bourgeois' *Cells* fold such categorical denominations of media and genre one into the other. Triggers of fantasy and strong statements on art, time, and individual and communal life, the question of the architecturality of the *Cells* and, by extension, a great number of Bourgeois' works (including works on paper and in oil) imposes itself. From the series or genre of works called *Femme Maison*, to the overtly built *Cells*, the architectural is present in her art. Present but never straightforward and never alone.

Gigantic and fragmented, enigmatic and suggestive, *Spider* (1997) (Plate 58) belongs to a series of pieces figuring spiders (Figure 59).[2] *Cells* is a series of—to date—thirty large, uniquely significant works, made in the period 1986 to 1999, best characterized as sculptural installations with a sense of habitat that makes them architectural. All different, each work is self-contained, an autonomy to which the concept, form, and title bear witness.

In the following essay, I contend that *Spider*—as a theoretical object—proposes a radical conception of sculpture-as-architecture that is rooted in the Baroque.[3] In particular, it is through a discussion of *Spider* that a case for the passage through both Baroque and modern sculpture to an architectural sculpture whose very terms have been transformed by such a passage may be explored.[4] The "unity of the visual arts" that Irving Lavin[5] saw in Bernini's *The Ecstasy of Saint Teresa* (Figure 61)—but, significantly, analyzed in separate parts—and that characterized Baroque sculpture, was not the ambitious project of Bernini alone. Bourgeois, standing on the other side of modern experimentation, develops, with the *Cells*, another attempt to rethink sculpture as the testing ground of what visual art in general can mean, or rather, in her conception, what it can do.

ARCHITECTURAL SCULPTURE

Like sculpture, architecture is an intervention in space. But architecture is more literal in its intervening. It does not allow for the bracketing off of segments, to constitute a fictional space that suspends the boundaries of real space, in the way that sculpture does. Whether it is seen as occupying, colonizing, or structuring and delimiting space—territorial desire—instead of a fictional free-play of the imagination, is part and parcel of the architectural imaginary. This is why it makes sense that, at the end of the day, Bourgeois refrains from creating architecture in the literal sense. In other words, she does not design buildings; she does not opt for building as her art. Instead, she explores representation and space in terms of arch-shelter and intervention in space, through proposing fictional stories and fantasies. In other words, she deploys architecturality as a language of sculpture.

If, as Rosalind Krauss contends, narratorial omniscience can be said to be a key feature of premodern sculpture, Bourgeois and Bernini stand hand-in-hand on either side of such a threshold. For the Baroque sculptor struggled with precisely the same issues as modern sculptors: to make seeing into one act, not to split it up into the perceptual and the intellectual in order to make comprehending into an act of integration between body and mind, architecture, and sculpture.

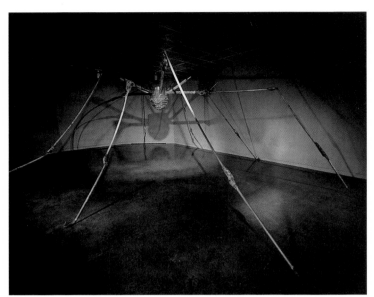

FIGURE 59. *Spider*, 1994. Museo Nacional Centro de Arte Reina Sofía, Madrid

Defying the ambition of omniscience, Bourgeois and Bernini thus pursue similar goals, albeit in different cultural contexts, commenting on the instability of maintaining strict separations between the mediums of sculpture and architecture. Both artists partition off a portion of real space. [6] They therefore overcome one of the central dilemmas of sculpture: Does it occupy space, like a building, or is it a fictitious island? I contend that the answer lies in the notion of sculpture as defined by "architecturality."

Both Bourgeois and Bernini build in limitations that saddle the viewer with the compulsory efforts that counter any "natural" passivity he or she may face when confronted with representation, sculptural or otherwise. The suspended space of their sculpture is not quite fictitious. Although the object that occupies the space commands a "willing suspension of disbelief"–the standard definition of fictionality–it requires a participation in the fiction that, for instance, historical relief does not. For the viewer needs to enter and inhabit the sculpture, so that she can partake of its creation as space. In Bernini's chapel this does not quite lead to the kind of suspension of boundaries that Bourgeois' work commands. For if the chapel requires interiority in its architectural aspect, one still needs exteriority for its transformation into sculpture. The narrativity that inheres in such a transformation must be performed by the

viewer who is invited to inhabit the architecture: an architecture one cannot "penetrate."

In Bernini's *Apollo and Daphne* (1622–25), an adaptation into stone of Ovid's *Metamorphoses*, the story is not only transformed from its literary narrativity into a visual object that retains the original story's movement (Figure 60); it also becomes a story about the tension between movement and stillness. Daphne's existence as a tree fixes her in one place, but allows her to continue to grow. Where her hair sprouts leaves, the sculptor struggles to maintain continuity between the wind-blown hair and the stiff laurel leaves that are beginning to clutter their ends. Roots seem to stream out of her toes like water. Differing registers of the fluidity of live matter are juxtaposed.

But the relevance of Bernini's work to *Spider* becomes most visible at the place where the tree's bark

FIGURE 60. G.L. Bernini, *Apollo and Daphne*, 1622–25. (Galleria Borghese, Rome, Italy)

ture itself transforms marble into representation becoming a representation of transformation.

In midcareer (1647–52), Bernini tried his hand at a religious version of a similar narrative of transformation. Capturing the moment of ecstasy of the 16th-century Spanish mystic Saint Teresa (Figure 61), he again made the transformation itself the subject of his narrative in stone. This time his struggle with layering was more successful. The transformation of Teresa's body happens when it is set on divine fire by the arrow thrust into her breast by an angel (i.e., it is literally embodied). Teresa's body, curved in an obliquely reclining *S*-shape, takes the shape of a flame. But her body's inside cannot be distinguished from its outside. In his 1972–73 seminar, published as *Seminar 20*, Jacques Lacan demonstrates the blindness that comes with obsession when he claims that Teresa's *jouissance* is a matter of her desire to be penetrated again and again (*encore*) by God, the transcendental phallus.[8] However, Bernini's sculpture–and Teresa's writings–suggest that the ecstasy is due to, or rather, consists of, literal ec-stasy (the state of being beside or outside oneself). In other words, the propagation of the fire of love from inside out, so that Teresa's skin, that outer limit of the body, partakes of it; hence, her body's limits are themselves no longer limits. The lusciously folded drapery that iconographically marks the sculpture as Baroque is transformed into flames. Her whole body becomes a flame–each part of it–a surface beneath which nothing else remains. Fire overrules all previous shapes. The transformation, here more aptly called transfiguration, is total.

Transfiguration, including its collusion with death, is not unrelated to what Georges Bataille called "alteration."[9] According to Krauss' account,[10] this concept grasps two totally different logics. The first logic is that of decomposition, the blurring of boundaries through matter's tendency to deteriorate. The second is what we would today call "othering," i.e., the logic of radical distinction. The two meet where death decomposes the body and transforms the former subject into a soul, ghost, or spirit. The two meet, that is, in the transfiguration that both "melts" the body and elevates it to sanctity; which is why flames can so aptly replace decomposition. But flames themselves are in movement, hovering between thing and event. The

begins to cover the woman's soft skin. *Qua* marble as an opaque, solid, hard material, the layering of surfaces rightly earned Bernini admiration. The layer of bark is both thin and coarse, just like bark. It contrasts with the soft skin that covers the flesh that is about to disappear into the wood. But the sculptor can only acknowledge, visually, that body and skin–inner substance and outer layer– must remain separate. The bark, incidentally, covers Daphne's genitals. But it covers them with a detached layer like a fragment of fabric, of clothing, or of decoration.[7]

Apollo and Daphne is a story of transformation in a triple sense. Ovid's narrative, as the title *Metamorphoses* indicates, is devoted to transformation–here, the transformation of Daphne into a laurel tree. Bernini transformed the literary text into a sculpture. And the sculp-

resolution of the hesitation between narrative movement and still visuality could, therefore, not be better shaped than in this all-consuming fire.

The integration of Teresa's inside and outside fires can be seen as programmatic of a sculpture that integrates within itself the architecture that houses it. For the sculpture of Teresa is integrated into a chapel in which the viewer must stand in order to see it. This integration is precisely part of the challenge posed by the *Cells*, where the integration of inside and outside is so dramatically radicalized that the two domains become one. This is due to the architecturality of *Spider*, which offers visual shelter in a cage whose door stands ajar, yet blocks sight through the fragments of tapestry that decorate as well as embody the cage's wall.

But it is in the *Blessed Ludovica Albertoni* (1671–74) (Figure 62), one of Bernini's late sculptures, where the inquiry into narrative sculpture is expanded even further. And it is done through the unification of sculpture and architecture, much as *The Ecstasy of Saint Teresa* did in representing a holy woman in the unified composition of a chapel. In other words, the *Blessed Ludovica Albertoni* represents the moment of death and ascension in the same double movement of body pose and surface shape, representing both lying down and ascending in one form. The body reclines, or rather, just lies down, while the head is bent backward as the holy woman expires. Out of the unity of cloths

FIGURE 62. G. L. Bernini, *Blessed Ludovica Albertoni*, (1671–74). (San Francesco a Ripa, Roma, Italy)

and body, the small but insistent sign of the hand pressing the breast offers a metonymically motivated metaphor. Under her body are the folds of a mattress cover carved in colored marble, to contrast with the white of the figure. As Giovanni Careri has pointed

FIGURE 63. *Homage to Bernini*, 1967

out, these folds indicate a diagonal movement upward. Most strikingly, though, the folds in the garment so completely cover her body that it can be said that the garment and the body are one, indeed, constitute one another, in the same way that the spider constitutes the cage of *Spider*.

As if in reminiscence of Daphne's covered genitals, the drape of the *Blessed Ludovica* extends horizontally between her legs. But that extended fold ends just where it becomes a bit too iconic of the slit it is allegedly covering. This fold is absorbed, elevated, if not *aufgeheben*, in a series of short but firmly erect folds that pull the holy woman up, body and soul. These folds, I cannot help but notice, resonate with the tiny poles inside Bourgeois' *Homage to Bernini*.[11]

These three sculptures–*Apollo and Daphne*, *The Ecstasy of Saint Teresa*, and *Blessed Ludovica Albertini*– stand here for three moments in Bernini's exemplary exploration of sculptural narrative, and the inevitable move toward its integration into architecture. Each sculpture effects this transformation differently. Daphne, taken from a pagan story transformed by a Christian sculptor, was still subject to a division between inner body and outer layer, so that her transformation confined her to the fragmentation to which a subject remains condemned when exteriority and interiority are divided. Teresa's transformation into a voluptuous fire, on the other hand, consumed her entirely. She escaped fragmentation and division, but at the cost of her absorption into the otherness of her desire. Ludovica, whose marble body bending backward resists an easy consummation altogether, insists instead on the body's bodiliness. To the extent that her head resists elevation, it proclaims that her body, *qua* sexed female body, be accepted in the transformation. Like Christ himself, she will ascend whole, in the *aufgeheben* materiality of flesh beyond corruption.

In relation to the issue of Bernini's and Bourgeois' architecturality, these differences are also reflected in the material existence of Bernini's sculptures: their relationship to real space, hence, to architecture. Bernini's two holy women are integrated in a chapel. Daphne, although suffering the excessive bodily proximity of Apollo's desire for her, stands alone when facing the viewer. Like the small vanguard egg in Bourgeois' white marble, very baroque sculpture, *Cumul I* (1969) (Plate 41), which drags heavy folds of fabric below it like a bride carries her veil, Daphne, by means of the front of her body, her most "layered" past, reorients the viewer, who cannot quite live down the illusion that this whirling sculpture is "really" round in the same sense as Bourgeois' *Spider* is. The narrative thus holds the viewer riveted, glued to a linearity that inexorably leads to the front of Daphne's body. Narrative here supersedes sculpturality to the extent that the form remains suspended from real space, encouraging projection rather than absorption. By making her narrativizing *Spider* both outer limit and inner center, Bourgeois provides a radical alternative to Bernini.

As Giovanni Careri pointed out in his discussion of the Ludovica, this sculpture cannot be considered in isolation from the work as a whole. The chapel beckons the viewer, in much the same way as *Spider* does, despite its being situated beyond a threshold over which the

viewer cannot step. The unification of the chapel puts the sculpture of the dying woman inside the space within which the viewer lives out a "fiction of presence" of a reality in which Ludovica and what happens to her could just as well appear and happen to us. Bourgeois' recycling of Bernini, I contend, further elaborates and "invents" this attempt to unify sculpture and architecture into an all-encompassing space of virtuality.

FIGURE 64. *Spider*, 1997 (detail)

In the case of *Spider*, the question is how can this work—with its mutilated putto, its empty chair, and its fragmented fabrics (Figure 64)—relate to a sculpture that has been famously said to embody the "unity of the visual arts"?[12] I contend that it relates to it by way of its own theorizing. Bourgeois does not follow Bernini, despite what her sculpture's title, *Homage to*

Bernini, might suggest; she beckons him. Not satisfied with either influence or opposition, shunning both imitation and mere polemics, "homage" means to take seriously enough to engage with, from the inside. *Homage* is traversal here, as *Lord* (1999) would have it.[13] It is inside her *Homage*, after all, that the tiny poles are polished to the point of receiving a baroque surface.

Take one look at *Homage to Bernini*, from 1967 (Figure 63), which preceded *Spider* by thirty years. Roughly egg-shaped, but with one side caved in, it might be considered a *Spider*'s egg that bred *Spider*. Significantly, the sculptor, who with works such as *Cumul I* has amply demonstrated her interest in producing baroque marble surfaces, has chosen, as her homage to the master of Baroque marble, to cast the work in bronze. No polished surfaces, no white smoothness waiting to be caressed. Instead, this work turns Bernini's painterly surfaces inside-out. Here there is no separate layer of bark; the object *is* bark, just as coarse, but solid and massive. There is no inner wood that it hides. Yet, the object is not entirely solid. It is also hollow. And inside, where you least expect it, is a tiny bit of Berninesque smoothness. Multiple, like the master's folds, but then again, inside-out. There is no suggestion of hollowness in these little protrusions (Figure 65). And in terms of genitals, covered (in *Apollo and Daphne*) or iconically aggrandized (as in *Blessed Ludovica Albertoni*), this sculpture blows such a body part way out of proportion. It is nowhere and everywhere.

If *Homage to Bernini* can be said to have laid an egg for *Spider*, it foreshadows or projects–in a gesture against the anteriority that predominates in art-historical narratives of influence and development–*Spider* as a radically new work which it does not in fact "resemble." Rather, seen from the present, *Homage* becomes a *Spider's*-egg that beckons Bernini from across the thresholds of modern sculpture's passage through time. The time of history, which doesn't only move forward. And the time of narrative, which is constantly interrupted, and remains incomplete. Both temporalities hold up the past like a carrot that can never be reached; neither reconstructed nor eaten and excreted; neither seen nor eliminated. But like such luring carrots, the past is located in front of, *not behind,* the present.

The time that Bourgeois deploys, I contend, is therefore the time of architecture. I don't mean the time it takes to construct a building, or to contemplate one, or the time it takes for the building to become a ruin of fragments that can never become whole again. The architecture of Bourgeois' *Cells*, in a manner comparable to, though more radical than, that of Bernini's women-chapels, requires a temporality of *inhabitation.* As Bourgeois inhabits Bernini by inhabiting the tradition of sculpture in western culture from which she cannot be excluded (yet in which there is no neat niche that can contain her), she inhabits Bernini's work as a parasite. Over time, inhabiting inevitably builds a new logic, invents a host that did not exist before the parasite came to live in and on him.[14] In architect Greg Lynn's words, "A parasite does not attack an already existing host but invents a host by configuring disparate systems into a network within which it becomes an integral part."[15] The shape of *Homage to Bernini*, with its smooth shapes inside and rough ones outside, appears as a model for this theoretical principle.

FIGURE 65. *Homage to Bernini,* 1967 (detail)

In this gesture of beckoning Bernini from over the gap between pre- and postmodern sculpture, the open egg-shaped early work breeds the position of *Spider* at the intersection of Bourgeois' two recent series, themes, or obsessions. *Spider*s and *Cells*, on the one hand, rethink the place of narrative, and on the other, the place of architecture *in,* not *around,* sculpture. This is how *Spider* "thinks" sculpture as inherently architectural, not in the Vitruvian tradition of perfect symmetry, but in the Baroque tradition of wavering scale, coalescing monads or *Cells*, and infinite folds. Indeed, the Baroque's primary figure, its figuration and mathematically precise metaphor, is the *fold*,[16] such as the ones Bernini uses to shift from microscopically small figurations of ecstasy to the macrocosm of the chapel. The coexistence of outside contemplation and inside participation that the Baroque sculptor could only achieve side-by-side, becomes, in the context of Bourgeois' sculpture, a renewed possibility to be explored.

To put it more succinctly: the stories to which the fragments of tapestry allude but which, tantalizingly, we cannot read, inhabit the *Cells*, and are here, in turn, *Spider*'s performances. Inside, on that stage of cellular drama that has no director, only an empty director's chair (Figure 66), the stories constitute the *Cells* that grow and pullulate, producing unpredictable shapes, destroying the unity, and emptying out the center. But the stories can only live inside those spaces, inside *Spider*'s cage, if they are given life, time, subjectivity, body, a viewer – from the outside (Figure 67).

Bourgeois' response to Bernini's search is perhaps most clearly visible in a work from 1983, from yet another series of related works, *Femme Maison* (Plates 1, 2 and 3). Over a number of years, the artist produced, in drawings and sculptures, the semi-transfiguration of a female figure into a house that imprisons and inhabits her body. Many of these houses are square, rectangular, angular, in an almost hostile way. But in the most Berninesque work of this series, the skyscraper voluptuously sinks into a royal robe of folds.[17] (Plate 47)

Unlike Bernini's folds, Bourgeois' refuse all tendency towards regularity. On one side of *Femme Maison*, toward the bottom, where the base becomes sheer matter, the folds confess to the deception of their illusory infinity as surface. Elsewhere, the folds detach themselves from the interior mass, betraying the banal secret of Teresa's transfiguration. Here and there the folds are knotted, turning infinite texture into inextricable confusion, and liberation into imprisonment. The cone-shaped body remains a body, refuses to go up in flames or to be elevated toward transcendence. Firmly fixed on a visible disk-shaped bottom, this body is as heavy as Ludovica's, but does not believe in miracles.

On the top, like a head, stands the angular skyscraper of 20th-century architecture. The gigantic body of folds, and folds of flesh, which surround and incorporate this building, state mutual dependency and threat. Like *Spider*, this sculpture absorbs architecture in a secular, disenchanted, yet merry acceptance of the materiality of the body, house, and sculpture. The house in which women are locked up but also given mastery, a house that confines and protects, weighs the woman's body down.

FIGURE 66. *Spider*, 1997 (detail)

But lest we escape reality by falling for transcendence and tragedy, the folds, knotted around the building as the body's neck, are also just what they appear to be. Between figuration and conceptualism, Bourgeois

FIGURE 67. *Spider*, 1997 (detail)

winks at us when, from one angle, the surface (full of secrets) turns out to be just a garment, warming the lonely house. In this exploration of frightful interventions in space, the architecture, here, encompasses motherly care, humor, and companionship. In opposition to the Vitruvian tradition, this house-woman, while refusing the rigidity of classical symmetry, endorses the caprices of body and matter.

The level at which Bourgeois enfolds and then moves beyond Bernini is, then, one involving the fullest integration of the arts. Architecture comes to stand for this full integration, this embodiment, which the house-enfolding body of *Femme Maison* proposes. Looking forward from this work, we can see how *Spider* is fully architectural: neither as a metaphor nor as a literal building, but

as a most literal acting out of the art of building. *Spider* makes good Bernini's promise to bring unity to the visual arts—except that "unity" is redefined, away from harmony. For the secret of *Spider*'s post-Baroque success is the literalization of the one metaphorical term in Comas' Le Corbusier–inspired modernist definition of architecture, a term that contradicts the pursuit of unity: debate.[18] Bourgeois' work never tires of debating.

JETZ-ZEIT: BOURGEOIS' BECKONING OF BERNINI
Spider, as I have argued here, brings the exteriority of public subjectivity inside. This is why the *Cells* are primarily architectural: they shelter. *Spider*'s exteriority, as a result of the enforced entrance of the viewer within the virtual domain between *Spider* legs and cage, and between body and eye, thus becomes interiority. More effectively because more bodily, the viewer's participation is comparable with Ludovica's levitation of body-and-soul, from between her legs to the folds that will carry her to heaven.

On this level of signification, the shape of the *Spider* becomes particularly relevant. The tall legs are thick, due to their function as columns in the architectural "debate" and achieved through their hyperbolic scale. But they end in fine points that barely touch the ground. This gives the *Spider*, literally, a lightness of being, in spite of its tremendous size. The tall and thick legs are columns, supporting a building they also decorate. But the ballerina-points of the legs, dancing around us, casting operatic moving shadows of great elegance as we walk around the cage, undermine the now striking heaviness of the thick guardians they support. As we recede after the long, sticky time of viewing myopically, peering in to see the perfume bottles and in the process feeling our own body change scale and almost hitting one of those legs, we recede further and the *Spider* remains where it is. This is what makes *Spider* effective, in conveying, persuading, making us experience on all levels of the intellectual and aesthetic, of mind and body, the experience (as experience) of ourselves as individuals and as *Cells*.

Outer layers are not, as Bernini already proclaimed, distinguishable from inner states. The perfectly smooth surface that makes marble look like flesh so that our eye can caress the stone's skin and feel its warmth, is

radically innovative exploration of sculptural narrativity which is in dialogue with both modernism and the Baroque. The tale ends in a building, but one that turns our ideas about building literally inside-out. *Spider* as architectural sculpture does not accept, as Robert Venturi lamented, that "space is what displaced symbolism."[19] To counter such nostalgia for a disembodied symbolism, it is crucial that a form of narrative characterized by the absence of fully comprehensible stories remains a powerful cementing force in Bourgeois' work. By the same token, this revision of the way we look at art rethinks the practice of historicism that is the foundation of art history. This is why it is important, I submit, not only to recognize, but to participate in, the way *Spider* demonstrates how, across a broken and two-way timeline, Bourgeois beckons Bernini.

FIGURE 68. *Spider*, 1997 (detail)

Ludovica's hyperbolic program of sculpture. By making *Spider* more exterior than the outer folds of drapery, yet its egg-laying body (Figure 68) more interior than the viewer's place inside the chapel-as-cage, Bourgeois turns Bernini's sculptural architecture inside out. But even that–this unreliability of our senses to tell us where our body ends and that of others begins–is hyperbolically made to affect us in body, visually, but in a revised visuality that operates by way of a theoretical object that speaks through the senses.

It speaks, that is, in a *Jetz-zeit*–my word here to summarize, through Walter Benjamin, the primary effectivity of this work in engaging the viewer in the act of viewing. In other words, the sculpture as forbidden home tells itself through me. This is how *Spider* offers a

1. In Careri, *Bernini: Flights of Love, The Art of Devotion*: viii. Damisch is referring to Careri's invocation of Soviet filmmaker Sergei Eisenstein to understand Bernini.

2. Most of the works have been superbly published and thoroughly discussed and analyzed as a series in a recent book, which ought to be considered as background for the present essay (Rainer Crone and Petrus Graf Schaesberg, 1998). I will try to avoid overlap with this in-depth study, an attempt that entails sacrificing aspects of the 1997 *Spider* that would otherwise require commentary.

3. This formulation refers to Rosalind Krauss' title. Hereafter I take Krauss' study as the paradigm of modern sculpture, to which Bourgeois responds but to which she does not in any simple sense belong (1977).

4. See Lavin, *Bernini and the Unity of the Visual Arts*.

5. Krauss, *Passages in Modern Sculpture*, 114; *Bachelors*, 65.

6. Where Bernini covered the woman's genitals, Bourgeois– or her mother–so the famous anecdote tells us, cut out the genitals of that quintessentially Baroque male figure of the putto. Iconographic reversal seems, here, ludicrously incidental, unless it is a caricature, part of Bourgeois' mildly mocking smile. But as *Homage to Bernini* indicates, Bourgeois has other ways of addressing Bernini. Inside the coarse hollow shape, a few tiny, shiny poles prop up, like miniature male genitals, fingers or pods or plants–or, again, mocking all of the above –inside a gigantic hollow space that could be a house, or a gigantic womb.

7. See, for the relevant fragments, Mitchell and Rose, eds., *Feminine Sexuality*, 137–61.

8. Rosalind Krauss uses Bataille's term to elaborate a concept for the analysis of Sur-realism beyond the formalist argument that considered Surrealism not formally innovative. See Krauss, *Bachelors*, 7–8.

9. Krauss, *Bachelors*, 8.

10. On Bernini's work in general, see Wittkower (1955); Scribner (1991). On *Apollo and Daphne*, Herrmann Fiore (1997); on *The Ecstasy of Saint Teresa*, Lavin (1980), who made the point about the folds looking like flames. On the *Blessed Ludovica*, Perlove (1990) and, most relevantly, Careri's brilliant study of the integration of sculpture within architecture, which he discusses in terms of montage (1995).

11. See Lavin, *Bernini and the Unity of the Visual Arts*.

12. Traversing, here, also alludes to the psychoanalytical concept of traversal. Catherine Lord (*The Intimacy of Influence*) discusses and deploys this concept in an analysis of literary interactions among George Eliot, Virginia Woolf, and Jeanette Winterson. This study of relations of intimacy among artists across history is highly relevant here.

13. Michel Serres made the parasite an emblem of innovation from within (*The Parasite*, 35).

14. Lynn, "Body Matters," 62.

15. See Deleuze, *The Fold: Leibniz and the Baroque*, and, for an account of the fold in contemporary art, Bal, *Quoting Caravaggio: Contemporary Art, Preposterous History*.

16. *Femme Maison* (1983), marble, 25 x 19½ x 23 in.

17. See Comas, "Modern Architecture, Brazilian Art Corrolary."

18. Venturi et al. (*Learning from Las Vegas*, p. 99), quoted by Wagner ("Bourgeois Prehistory," p. 39) in the framework of a discussion of postmodernism in architecture.

REFERENCES

Bal, Mieke, *Quoting Caravaggio: Contemporary Art, Preposterous History* (Chicago: University of Chicago Press, 1999).

Benjamin, Walter, *Illuminations*. Edited and with an introduction by Hannah Arendt. Trans. Harry Zohn. (New York: Schocken Books, 1969).

Careri, Giovanni, *Bernini: Flights of Love, the Art of Devotion*. Trans. Linda Lappin. (Chicago: University of Chicago Press, 1995).

Comas, Carlos Eduardo, "Modern Architecture, Brazilian Corrolary." *AA Files* 36 (1988): 3–13.

Crone, Rainer and Petrus Graf Schaesberg, *Louise Bourgeois: The Secret of the Cells.* (Munich/London/New York: Prestel-Verlag, 1988).

Deleuze, Gilles, *The Fold: Leibniz and the Baroque*. Foreword and translation by Tom Conley. (Minneapolis: University of Minnesota Press, 1993).

Herrmann Fiore, Kristina ed., *Apollo e Dafne del Bernini nella Galleria Borghese* (Milan: Silvana Editoriale, 1997).

Krauss, Rosalind E., *Passages in Modern Sculpture* (Cambridge, MA: MIT Press, 1977).

Krauss, Rosalind E., *Bachelors* (Cambridge, MA: MIT Press, 1999).

Lavin, Irving, *Bernini and the Unity of the Visual Arts* (New York: [for] Pierpont Morgan Library [by] Oxford University Press, 1980).

Lord, Catherine, *The Intimacy of Influence* (Amsterdam: ASCA Press, 1999).

Lynn, Greg, "Body Matters," *Journal of Philosophy and the Visual Arts. Special Issue: The Body*, ed. Andrew Benjamin (no vol. or issue no.) (1993), 60–69.

Mitchell, Juliet, and Jacqueline Rose, eds., *Feminine Sexuality: Jacques Lacan and the Ecole Freudienne*. Trans. Jacqueline Rose (London: Macmillan, 1982).

Perlove, Shelley Karen, *Bernini and the Idealization of Death: The Blessed Ludovica Albertoni and the Altieri Chapel* (University Park, PA: Pennsylvania State University, 1990).

Scribner, Charles III, *Gianlorenzo Bernini* (New York: Harry N. Abrams, 1991).

Serres, Michel, *The Parasite*. Trans. Lawrence R. Schehr (Baltimore, MD: Johns Hopkins University Press, 1982).

Venturi, Robert, Denise Scott Brown, and Steven Izenour, *Learning from Las Vegas* (Cambridge, MA: MIT Press, 1972).

Wagner, Anne, "Bourgeois Prehistory, or the Ransom of Fantasies," *Oxford Art Journal* (in press).

Wittkower, Rudolf, *Gian Lorenzo Bernini: The Sculptor of the Roman Baroque* (London and New York: Phaidon, 1955).

Passages Impliqués [1]

JENNIFER BLOOMER

HERE IS A BIG CAGE made of chain-link fence and welded steel, housing a collection of objects that seem much like a cast-aside, ragtag accumulation one might find in a musty attic. It is a large cage, perhaps 9 meters long, 3 meters wide and 2½ meters high, and comprises a long corridor with small cagelike rooms off to either side. The envelope of chain link is a great tapestry of intersections of innumerable xs: symbols of loving embrace, symbols of the forbidden. *Passage Dangereux* is an ethereal house-passage, a section from the passing of a life. It is not a glass house, although it is completely pellucid. It is a house built of hundreds of links: transparent, weblike, and unyielding.

If we take an imaginary guillotine and slice the *Passage* across the middle, the resulting transverse section resembles that of a basilica or a cathedral: high central corridor, lower side rooms, more or less axially symmetrical.

Here is the hint of a door, an entrance, but it is locked. Just inside, on either side of the jambs are a plaster breast-pear and an ancient key about five inches long. The key dangles out of reach behind the membrane [2] As we track down the corridor and into each room by circumnavigating the exterior, we see displayed a collection of allegorical artifacts, both found and made, objects that form the nodes where our desires and those of Louise Bourgeois meet.

What do we see? A long empty bottle of Shalimar; a pink marble megalith sprouting translucent, pink, perfectly formed bunny ears; glass globes holding bones and nothing; a delicate ferrous spider; bits of faded, ragged tapestry; a troupe of signifying chairs on floor and ceiling; a bed with copulating, cast-metal feet attached to mechanical rods, the bigger pair on top with toes pointed down; tiny broken glass and metal animals.

And mirrors, lots of mirrors: moments of passage into virtual spaces: links to somewhere else, nowhere else, but also links to the viewer. The space that each mirror offers is completely dependent upon the position of the viewer. I can only begin to pass through the world of Louise [3] when I bend down a bit, transforming my point of view towards what I imagine to be hers. The mirrors are adjustable and adjusted, on sticks like the crooked lollipop mirrors at the dentist's. Mirrors for looking into obscure spaces, these rings of reflection are icons that transport us somewhere we could not otherwise be.

The *Passage* is a transparent architecture of slippery scales: a large dollhouse, a small house, a miniature basilica, a good-sized conservatory.

As we approach, the *Passage Dangereux* calls to mind the London Crystal Palace, the glass-and-steel Leviathan that dominated Hyde Park in The Great Exhibition of 1851 (Figures 70 and 71). A technological wonder filled with objects from all over the world and a generous smattering of undulating Victoriana, the Crystal Palace was a great, glass house, an enormous jewel box inspired by the hothouses of its designer, the English landscape gardener Sir Joseph Paxton. *Une serre*, a hothouse or conservatory, is a place where precious and vulnerable collections of plants are preserved, protected from the surrounding elements. In the conservatory, the glass wall is a transparent membrane that allows the passage of sunlight and the human gaze, but forbids wind, rain, snow, and unwelcome animals.

Passage Dangereux is a conservatory of memory. But that is not quite right.

Let us allow the object of our attention to slip to another scale, one between the palace and the house. For this cage of old, broken junk is also another building type: a *passage*, the glass-covered arcade of 19th-century Paris. The *passage* is a notable building type in that it is accurately described more as absence than presence, and as interior space more than exterior form. It is a corridor of space that runs from street to street at midblock, through the mass of the building it occupies. The *passage* is an interior architectural space whose only exterior manifestations are its two portals and the iron-and-glass roof that allows natural light to enter and protects the space from the elements (Figure 72). As the public space of the *passage* is traversed, the eye is drawn by the visual spectacle of hundreds of objects displayed for sale in the small spaces of display off the primary corridor (Figure 73).

Architecturally, the *passage* is the scion of the conservatories of Joseph Paxton, the department store, the enclosed shopping mall, and the World Wide Web: all spaces constructed for the display of objects that summon desire and consumption.

Walter Benjamin, in his essay, "Paris, Capital of the Nineteenth Century," points out that the *passage* was Charles Fourier's inspiration for the architectural form of the phalanstery. Fourier (who as a boy had filled his bedroom with several inches of soil for growing plants, making of his living space a kind of greenhouse), transformed the commercial display space of the passage to the dwelling spaces of his new, utopic visions. (This is a remarkable inverse prefiguration of the *Passage Dangereux*, in which the dwelling space of a middle-class family has become the space of display of old, private desires.) The public circulation space of Fourier's vision of public housing took its form from the arcades, a form that would have lasting significance in the history of architecture and urbanism. And as the glass-

covered street is the dwelling place of the collective for Benjamin, Fourier, Le Corbusier, *et al.*, in Louise Bourgeois' *Passage Dangereux*, the transparent central corridor into which no one can actually pass is the dwelling place of individual memory which reaches out to a collective desire. We look into this space and although we cannot inhabit it, through it we literally and figuratively can connect to each other—and, most importantly, we might believe, to Louise.

In the opening passage of his novel *Thérèse Raquin* (1867), Émile Zola described the *passages de Paris* from the point of view of the late 19th century—in ruin:

[L]orsqu'on vient des quais, on trouve...une sorte de corridor étroit et sombre qui va de la rue Mazarine à la rue de Seine.[5] Ce passage a trente pas de long et deux de large, au plus; il est pavé de dalles jaunâtres, usées, descellées, suant toujours une humidité âcre; le vitrage qui le couvre, coupé à angle droit, est noir de crasse.

A gauche, se creusent des boutiques obscures, basses, écrasées, laissant échapper des souffles froids de caveau. Il y a là des bouquinistes, des marchands de jouets d'enfant, des cartonniers, dont les étalages gris de poussière dorment vaguement dans l'ombre; les vitrines, faites de petits carreaux, moirent étrangement les

FIGURE 72. Passage des Panoramas, Boulevard Montmartre, Paris, ca. 1864

marchandises de reflets verdâtres; au-delà, derrière les étalages, les boutiques pleines de ténèbres sont autant de trous lugubres dans lesquels s'agitent des formes bizarres.

A droite, sur toute la longueur du passage, s'étend une muraille contre laquelle les boutiquiers d'en face ont plaqué d'étroites armoires; des objets sans nom, des marchandises oubliées là depuis vingt ans s'y étalent le long de minces planches peintes d'une horrible couleur brune. Une marchande de bijoux faux s'est établie dans une des armoires; elle y vend des bagues de quinze sous, délicatement posées sur un lit de velours bleu, au fond d'une boîte en acajou.

Au-dessus du vitrage, la muraille monte, noire, grossièrement crépie, comme couverte d'une lèpre et toute couturée de cicatrices.

Note the dreadful, haunting beauty of this passage, delicately and horrifyingly attending all the possibilities of signification of the word "*passage*."

Read Zola's passage aloud in its original language – the text itself delineates the age and fullness of the architecture, its musty odors, its dampness, the powerful seduction of the relic. The effect of this text – its approach to something ineffable and powerful – is precisely the effect of Louise Bourgeois' *Passage Dangereux*, and its siblings, the *Cells*. For they are constructions formed *couturées de cicatrices*, slashed with scars.

Zola's *passage* seems far removed from those described by Walter Benjamin a half-century later:

> These arcades, a recent invention of industrial luxury, are glass-roofed, marble-walled passages cut through whole blocks of houses, whose owners have combined in this speculation. On either side of the passages, which draw their light from above, run the most elegant shops, so that an arcade of this kind is a city, indeed, a world in miniature.[5]

Benjamin cites a *passage* from a past that was distant to him in the 1920s, when he was constructing the first segment of his *Passagenwerk*, or Arcades Project, the essay reworked in the '30s and known as "Paris, Capital of the Nineteenth Century." Like his study of the Baroque German Tragic Drama and its subject of the 17th century, the *Passagenwerk* was to have been an immense montage of citations and allegorical fragments that encompassed the 19th century and the effects of burgeoning capitalism upon social processes. And like *Die Trauerspiel*, the *Passagenwerk* loops repeatedly around three main themes and their interrelations: myth, nature, and history.

The project was never completed, indeed hardly begun, but it was intimately related to Benjamin's contemporaneous oeuvre over twenty years, and therefore it both does and does not exist. What explicitly does exist is an amazing "filing system" of Benjamin's notes, in which masses of historical documentation were organized under a series of words or phrases. Each word or phrase served as a key or icon locating a body of information, which was then intricately subdivided by a code of numbers, each accompanied by a letter representing the key word(s). Susan Buck-Morss gives us the list of keys:[6]

A   Arcades, Novelty Shops, Salesmen
B   Fashion
C   Ancient Paris, Catacombs, Demolitions, Ruin of Paris
D   Boredom, Eternal Recurrence
E   Haussmannization, Barricade Fighting
F   Iron Construction
G   Methods of Display, Advertising, Grandville
H   The Collector
I   The Interior, Trace
J   Baudelaire
K   Dream City and Dream House, Dreams of the Future, Anthropological Nihilism, Jung
L   Dream House, Museum, Fountain Hall
M   The Flâneur
N   Epistemology, Theory of Progress
O   Prostitution, Gambling
P   The Streets of Paris
Q   Panorama
R   Mirror
S   Painting, Jugendstil, Newness
T   Forms of Lighting
U   Saint-Simon, Railroads
V   Conspiracies, Compagnonnage [trade guilds]
W   Fourier
X   Marx
Y   Photography
Z   Doll, Automaton

FIGURE 73. Passage de l'Opéra, Paris, ca. 1922–23

And the list goes on into a series of lower-case letters.

Thus, Benjamin presented history as a great construction of artifice that he likened to the 19th-century urban building type after which the work is named: the *passages* or arcades. History not as a line, but as what he would call petrified nature, and also what we might call an architectonic construction. For the *Passagenwerk* represents a virtual architecture: an architecture of knowledge and an architecture of thinking. This is an architecture of multiply linked points of intersection, systems of interlacing systems that rely on logics both rational and not.

As Benjamin points out, two conditions intersected in the building of the Paris arcades from 1822 to 1840: a great supply of and demand for textiles, and the development of iron as a building material.[7] Reminiscent of the Arab souk, the market in a narrow street defined by fabric canopies and abundance of textiles and other material objects for sale, the *passage* also looks forward typologically through the department store (often with glass dome over a central space) to the American shopping mall. An enclosed space through which the individual walks and sees a vast proliferation of objects of desire that are for sale, the *passage* is the reification of desire and consumption. Benjamin correctly identified commodity fetishism with this artifact, and tied it to the great world exhibitions of the 19th century. Louise Bourgeois knows something deep and true about Walter Benjamin's strange equation of myth, nature, and history. Only for her, history is intensely and explicitly personal.

The *Passage Dangereux* is a passage through time and space: a difficult voyage, a dark arcade, a poignant passage of text of personal history. Like the *passages de Paris*, it is both a transparent, skeletal architecture and a gloomy, obscure space oozing with unrecognizable liquids and odors, strewn with unascertainable detritus: what Jonah saw. All envisioned through the nearly nine-decades-old eyes of a child who, like Walter Benjamin, has been working on a very present but intangible project most of her adult life: the project of coming to terms with childhood injury and pain. And like his, her work is not as much lament as it is a melancholic form of research. Louise Bourgeois' entire oeuvre is her *Passagenwerk*, an interlinked constellation of objects that call to us as if from dreams. And the *Passage Dangereux* is her architecture of keys, a filing system for her memory documents. Buck-Morss notes that the Paris arcades were for Benjamin a "precise material replica of the collective unconscious and collective dream desires."[8] This is why the arcades were the model for his *Passagenwerk*.

And, while Louise Bourgeois traverses the *passage* at the scale of the individual unconscious and individual dream desires, her obsession with the past, the nature of history and memory, and time and space locks into Benjamin's. This is why the arcade is a model for her *Passage Dangereux*.

What is this *Passage Dangereux* and how can we be swallowed into it by these words that are being imagined in one language, played upon in a second, and translated into yet another? In English, the word "passage" has both temporal and spatial connotations. We refer to the passage of time and to passage through a space, a building, a city. We represent them both in passages of text and of pigment on canvas. We have missed the boat in not referring to the theater and the cinema as passage. But, with this construction, Louise Bourgeois has her tiny feet firmly planted on this boat. For what we see before us is a cinematic *nature morte*, a stage set, *un tableau mort*, an allegorical architecture where, in the words of the late Italian architect Aldo Rossi, "something is about to happen," and what is about to happen is completely woven around something that has already happened, has happened long ago. A musty shop of strange, figurative Proustian madeleines, moldy cakes that have not made a proper passage, that have stuck in the craw. *Un Passage Dangereux*. Nonetheless, like Proust's more aromatic and palatable bits, they are souvenirs of memory.

What we have here is a dead body. A house skeleton filled with a collection of invented souvenirs, of objects to stir the memory. But what is a house, what is anybody's house in a certain sense, but a carapace of objects of personal memory, a collection of niches and surfaces on which are placed a collective petrified projection of the local narcissist? For Benjamin, objects were transformed from merchandise on display and for sale in the arcades to projections of the self. In the *Passage Dangereux*, Louise displays herself as a hothouse narcissus, a rare cultivar, but significantly related to the other members of the species. She has constructed a self-projection booth that is simultaneously house, conservatory, self-portrait, collection, catharsis, aversion therapy, art, homeopathic pharmacy, and theater of memory.

The subjects of architecture and memory are inextricably intertwined. What is it that a great public building or monument represents? What does it call forth? Memory: of nation, of culture, of event, of agent. It is a commonplace that a house is a container of objects that evoke memories. The house (the home) is literally the object of nostalgia (Greek, *nostos*, the longing for home, and *algia*, pain). A house of childhood revisited can be an overpowering catalyst for memories long forgotten or repressed. In our dreams, it is said, the house represents the self.

There is another way in which architecture and memory are linked: through the ancient *ars memoria* itself. In the classical art of memory, an imaginary building served as an artificial memory apparatus for oratory. Quintilian described it this way:

> In order to form a series of places in memory, he says, a building is to be remembered, as spacious and varied a one as possible, the forecourt, the living room, bedrooms, and parlours, not omitting statues and other ornaments with which the rooms are decorated. The images by which the speech is to be remembered ... are then placed in imagination on the places which have been memoried in the building. This done, as soon as the memory of the facts requires to be revived, all these places are visited in turn and the various deposits demanded of their custodians.[9]

By means of such an architectural apparatus, a collection of disjointed ideas might be ordered into an unbroken narrative or logical argument.

In the 16th century, the architect Giulio Camillo constructed what he called a *Theater of Memory*, a small, occupiable wood construction of prototypic artificial intelligence. Vigilius Zuichemus, writing in 1532 to Erasmus of his trip to Venice, where he met Camillo and entered the device with him, said that the theater allowed anyone who entered to "to discourse on any subject no less fluently than Cicero."[10] Vigilius wrote:

> The work is of wood, marked with many images, and full of little boxes.... He calls this theatre of his by many names, saying now that it is a built or constructed mind and soul. And now that it is a windowed one. He pretends that all things that the human mind can conceive and which we cannot see with the corporeal eye, after being collected together by diligent meditation may be expressed by certain corporeal signs in such a way that the beholder may at once perceive with his eyes everything that is otherwise hidden in the depths of the human mind. And it is because of this corporeal looking that he calls it a theatre.[11]

The theater consisted of seven gangways arranged as a Roman theatre. Off each of the gangways, or passages, were seven doors, each embellished with images. These doors, with their images, were the prompters of memory. In Camillo's theater, there was no audience, and there was only one player, the spectator, who played to himself.

According to Frances Yates, the sevenfold structure of the theatre referred to the seven pillars of Solomon's House of Wisdom,[12] as well as to the seven then-known planets, and other cosmological symbols. Giulio Camillo's *Theater of Memory* and Louise Bourgeois' *Passage Dangereux* are thus structurally resonant, and exist at the extremes of a continuum: from the universal and divine to the personal and profane. And, as in the nature of extremes, they are easily seen to correspond.

Passage Dangereux is a palace of disjointed memories placed in ordered niches, a collection of souvenirs of the deeply nonrational, rationalized. This passage is a crystal palace, a glass house of painful memories. *Dans serre ou*... And, in appropriate *mise en abîme*, it is one of a grander collection of itself: the entire *Cells* series, and all of the *Femmes Maisons*. These represent the house of

a dream. This is Louise's house and Louise's house is Louise. *Femme Maison*.

But the *Femmes Maisons* that appear as forms throughout Louise's oeuvre and which have been interpreted as feminist critique are more importantly clues or markers of something much more profound. In the later works it is the interior architectural spaces, NOT the monstrous architectural woman forms, that capture us. This is where the relation of architecture and memory becomes serious indeed.

FIGURE 74. *Cell (Eyes and Mirrors)*, 1989–93. Tate Gallery, London

> When history is what it should be, it is an elaboration of cinema.... The true historical reality is not the datum, the fact, the thing, but the evolution formed when these materials melt and fluidify. History moves; the still waters are made swift.[13]

Let us pass through the membrane of the *Passage* and look down the line of the corridor. The French call the corridor *le couloir*, which also denotes a tracking shot–

a continuous uninterrupted segment of filming. The geometry of the *couloir*, whether corridor or cinematic tracking shot, is the geometry of the line.

The line is an omnipresent tool of the architect, who uses it for all manner of things: to mark the centers of buildings, spaces, or elements; to delineate boundary conditions of walls, rooms, buildings, and sites; to mark imaginary cuts through projected buildings; to mark out territory on which buildings will be built; to establish cardinal points and relations between horizontal and vertical. This list could continue, but here is the point: the architect throws lines, and with those lines, establishes multiple relations among various materials, ideas, and codes which altogether constitute a construction that is about to happen. The line, the protagonist of geometry, is the architect's tool for orienting herself in relation to her projected construction. The line is the tool for establishing the architect's points of view.

Geometry is Louise Bourgeois' tool for orienting herself, for calming her terror of being lost. She has said:

Once I was beset by anxiety. I couldn't tell right from left or orient myself. I could have cried out with terror at being lost. But I pushed the fear away by studying the sky, determining where the moon would come out, where the sun would appear in the morning. I saw myself in relation to the stars. I began weeping and knew I was alright [sic]. That is the way I make use of geometry. The miracle is that I am able to do it by geometry.[14]

Louise here describes herself as a voyager on the sea, navigating safe passage by a web of lines drawn among points.

If we were to imagine the diagram of a passage, whether a passage of time, space, or text, that diagram would always be a line, a line projected from one point, the here-and-now, to another, the possible, the there-and-then. And if we were to cut a center line through *Passage Dangereux*, this line from front to back down the middle of the empty corridor would resemble a line cut down the center of a century, a line of narration of a tale, a line of the tapestry shuttle moving across the lines of warp, or that of a threaded needle dipping in and out of its punctured surface, the line of the mapping of an ocean voyage, the line of a scar on a sea captain's face gashed by an aggressive white whale, or a line projected in space by a threaded harpoon headed towards its quarry. But not a single one of these lines would be anything more than an abstraction of something unfathomably more complex, rich, and meaningful.

When José Ortega y Gasset fashioned the history of painting about a line, this line traced the conventional art-historical line of serial chronology, but its force derived from Ortega's seeing the line as simultaneously spatial. In his essay "On the Point of View in the Arts," Ortega imagined a line of movement from the Renaissance to Surrealism, which simultaneously spanned the distance between the surface of a canvas and the inner space of the artist's mind. Ortega saw the history of art as one great, sweeping movement along this line. And what was it that was moving down this line, this passage? The artist's point of view, which changed over time (Ortega) from a proximate vision focused on particular things to a distant vision taking in increasingly wider whole pictures until in the art contemporaneous with Ortega – Surrealism – the picture included its own reflexive, critical, and psychoanalytic dimensions.

The work of Louise Bourgeois represents a strange, but logical, extension of the line of Ortega: her work takes the line of the movement of the point of view into a topological involution into itself, both beyond Surrealism and tracking back into the inner realms of proximate apprehension. Against the authoritative diagnoses of her critics, Louise declares herself not a surrealist, but an existentialist.

The difference between Louise Bourgeois and the Surrealists is that while the Surrealists worked around a general theory of desire and the unconscious, Louise makes it particular and local. She is up-front, forthright. What is so discomfiting about this work is that she is eighty-seven years old and insists on revealing the dreadful secret that an adult skin can be an envelope of childhood pain and rage. This is far more embarrassing than nudity. Get over it, we might say. Why are we indignant and want so badly for her to get over it? Because we know what she is doing. She is not controlling herself; she is not keeping her distance. She lets herself go. She is out of line.

The work of the Surrealists optimistically continued the direction of Ortega's line. This is a line that moves in a continuous direction, a line headed towards a goal, a way out. Jean-Paul Sartre described genius as "the brilliant invention of someone who is looking for a way out."[15] The genius of Louise Bourgeois lies in the fact that she recognizes that the only way out is to keep going back in, causing the line to loop around on itself, shuttling between extremes.

Let us now look to our left, into the first "room" of the *Passage* (Figure 75).

On center at the rear of this little space is a small shelf with six levels. On each sits a gentleman's detachable starched white cuff laundry-marked "Bourgeois": the name-of-the-father. Each cuff is set up as a tiny theater set, open to the door of the niche, six little stages prefiguring the six little rooms off the central corridor of the *Passage*. Within the lowest, the last, an empty bottle of Shalimar occupies center stage. Held in the powerful embrace of a band that once encircled the wrist of Louis Bourgeois, the beautiful, empty vessel displays its metonymic contents.

A translucent blue, shell-like stopper crowns the bottle, the cast glass folds of which echo the characteristic folds of a baleine surface. Lower down the folds are cinched by a circlet of glass, and continue down to form a balanced base, the whole reflective of a triumphal trophy or a cinerary urn. The bottle possibly contains a potent molecule or two of Shalimar, an elixir made from the oils of flowers and whale detritus. Its name recalls the exotic and romantic garden of India, constructed to celebrate the love of a king for his queen, a love which further engendered the construction of the Shish Mahal, the Palace of Mirrors. Shalimar, the scent of grown-up ladies dressed to go out.

On the floor below the shelf, floating on a soft-cornered slab of marble that rests on two horizontal, hollow steel legs, is a slab of beguiling pink marble formed like nothing so much as a guillotined whale, rear end missing; or is it the living-room coffee table? Perched on a corner surface sit two sweet pink bunny ears, translucent and delicate stone-flesh, enveloping and casting shadows an architect would die for. It is a vulnerable and easily terrified creature. And weighty—this creature cannot move no matter how threatened it is; it remains, listening, held captive by its own inert nature.

It is a soft pink creature with a substance of hard stone. It has more resistance than its soft pink color and delicate ears would suggest. The Shalimar bottle would shatter into pieces were it to come into serious contact with this creature. Soft leviathan, sweet bunny tucked into its bed of stone.

FIGURE 75. *Passage Dangereux* (detail), 1997

There are three round mirrors in this room, two small and one a bit bigger. And, as we pass through the corridor again and encounter the next room (Figure 76), a tableau of small chairs and transparent globes enclosing piles of white bones (Figure 77) and strange not-quite-natural objects, we note more mirrors. What does it mean when a mirror is held up before you? It means, "Hey, LOOK." For Louise, it often means, "You want to look at me? Well, here, have a look at yourself, because that is all you want to see, and therefore all you are going to see, when you look at me." But here, in this little room and others, the relation of the mirror and the viewer is more complicated: because one does not see oneself in the mirror; one sees specific details of the installation itself. "See here, see this, see Louise, see you. See what you want. See what you see. What you see is what you get." The mirrors serve as *puncta*[16] – little holes in the space of the passage that throw lines to the unconscious, that catch its attention, that say, "Look and see much more than what appears to be here."

This collection of small reflecting holes is our connection to an underground passage, a secret passage, already tunneling through this essay. In his influential long essay on the 17th-century inventor/philosopher Gottfried Wilhelm Leibniz and the Baroque, *Le Pli*, Gilles Deleuze, in a passage devoted to color and Baroque painting in which he refers to Leibniz's concept of the monad, writes of an allegorical bifurcated space of light and darkness. This space, to be thought

FIGURE 77. *Passage Dangereux* (detail), 1997

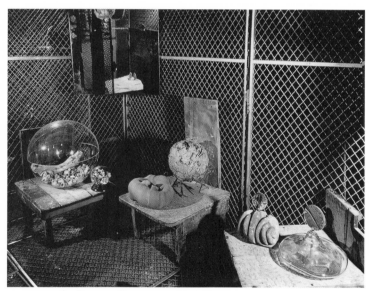

FIGURE 76. *Passage Dangereux* (detail), 1997

of as "two levels of the world separated by a *thin line of waters* [emphasis mine]" is a contained space of one level folding into the other rather than a divided space of opposition. The upper level is an obscure room that is completely interior, without windows or doors. And yet there are light and color. How? Leibniz, in *Profession de foi du philosophe*, described the light as sliding in "through a slit in the middle of shadows."[17] Deleuze carries our imaginations further into the nature of this

space by suggesting that the light coming through the narrow slit is multiplied or folded by "a great number of small reflecting mirrors," and that a certain "whiteness" appears or is "produced through all the tiny inner mirrors."[18] (Figure 74)

Do you see the whiteness that is produced through all the tiny reflecting mirrors of the obscure interior space that is *Passage Dangereux*? What is it that appears in this constellation of mirrors? It is spectral, white, haunting, there and not there, punctuated by these *puncta*, these puncture wounds, these slits. As through the surface of dark water, we perceive a shadowy image: a great, white whale, riddled with marks of harpoons, *couturée de cicatrices*.

And his name is Moby Dick.

Moby Dick, long considered one of a few truly great American works of literature, was written by Herman Melville and released to the public in 1851. (That same summer, the doors of the monstrous steel-and-glass Crystal Palace, its surfaces reflecting sunlight as a great whiteness like many thousand mirrors, were opened to the public attending the Great Exhibition.)[19]

The American poet Charles Olson opens his remarkable study of *Moby Dick*, *Call Me Ishmael*, with a rumination on Melville's treatment of space. Melville's protagonist of space was Captain Ahab, a sea captain obsessed with finding and destroying a white whale that, many years ago, had taken off his leg and left a long scar-line down the side of his face:

> This Ahab had gone wild. The object of his attention
> was something unconscionably big and white. He had
> become a specialist: he had all space concentrated
> into the form of a whale called Moby Dick.

Olson wrote,

> Melville had a way of reaching back through time
> until he got history pushed back so far he turned
> time into space. He was like a migrant backtrailing
> to Asia, some Inca trying to find a lost home.[20]

Olson's Melville goes back in time in order to go forward in space. Olson again:

> Ortega y Gasset puts it that the man of antiquity,
> before he did anything, took a step like a bullfighter
> who leaps back in order to deliver the mortal thrust.[21]

With *Passage Dangereux*, Louise Bourgeois presents a key to her oeuvre, a key that involves a certain wildness, a turning of time into space, a leaping back in order to deliver a mortal thrust. The object of her attention is something unconsciously big and white: white-faced adults in white flannel pajamas, white frocks, and white cuffs, by whom she was maimed no less than Ahab was maimed by the great white whale.

> In this photograph, it is about one o'clock in the
> afternoon and it is Sunday brunch (Figure 78). You
> see him here. He just got up so he is in one of his
> negligés, of flannel, white flannel, there on the
> left. . . . [T]he mother is not there. Sure enough, I
> guess she's seeing that the food is being prepared.
> But Sadie is there, in white. You see that pussycat
> face on the right? And I am right next to her. But
> you see how everybody is proper and well dressed –
> except him. So if you say, why I object to my father's
> behavior, it's that he broke the rules all the time.[22]

On the left, the woman in white is The Mistress.[23]

This is the mistress, showing off all in white.[24]

Louise's memories of her father and his mistress are tinted white: the hubris of the white pajamas, the white stones Louis Bourgeois collected as markers of good memories, the blondeness of Sadie's hair, the paleness

FIGURE 78. The Bourgeois family gathered at home for target-shooting party, Antony, France, 1925

of her blancmange face, her clothing. Whiteness in Louise's memories of them is a cloak for what frightens and betrays her. White, the color worn by "good guys," the innocent, and neoclassical (including modern) buildings, is always ambiguous in its significance. Whiteness is the emblem of what is not to be trusted, what is therefore to be feared. Louise's father and the great white whale are both objects of longing, both elusive, both benign creatures of nature, innocently dangerous and damaging; both also figures of cultures that establish and maintain certain conditions of damage and danger. And both are accommodated in gentle, domestic ferocity by *la mère*.

> Of all the elements, water fascinates me the most.
> Everything is always connected with water. . . . All
> architecture depends on the flow of water.[25]

Louise's quarry (her quest) is the quarry (the mine) of her work. And Louise has piled her rage onto her object no less than Ahab "piled upon the whale's white hump the sum of all the general rage and hate felt by his whole race from Adam down."[26]

If we hack off the tail of *Passage*, what remains is *Pass*, the haunting white creature that Louise carved out of a cube of Carrara marble in 1988–89 (Figure 79). Severely implicated, benign and threatening, nature and myth, this creature looks at you as if it could swallow you whole down the long passage that surely lies beyond its comely slit-beak: a deeply ambiguous voyage with the unquestionable destination of a belly. Louise herself described the work of producing *Pass* as a voyage, a voyage "inside the cube."[27] *Pass* was for her the elusive quarry of a voyage, just as was *Moby Dick* for Ahab. Memory, fear, and pain drive the voyages of Louise and Ahab; and both voyages are fueled by passions that consume themselves and others. The force of this consumption is nowhere better inscribed than in Louise's 1974 work, *The Destruction of the Father*, the residual of an exorcising fantasy of her family at the dinner table turning on and eating the pompous and tyrannical father. *The Destruction of the Father* (Plate 44) an interior biomorphic space, the unrecognizably dismembered body of the father and the cavernous belly of the whale. It has been said[28] that *Pass* represents a threshold in Louise Bourgeois' work. (Let us not forget that a possible meaning of the French verb *passer* is to vent one's anger.) What might we call the architecture — the obscure, articulated construction of Louise's voyage beyond this threshold? We might call it a dangerous passage.

In the corridor, just outside the next room, is a dark, heavy rubber bat hanging from the ceiling. It is pricked with needles, a baleine St. Sebastian, a figure of Ahab's dream: the whale subdued by the lines of harpoons. From one of the needles flies a line of thread.

Inside the room, we see a small legless chair of wood slats suspended with S-hooks by chains from the ceiling: a small child's swing (Figure 80). On the seat is a cushion covered in burlap, in the center of which is placed an old piece of tapestry on which there seems to be a grimacing face. Behind the swing and covering nearly the entire back wall is an ancient, worn tapestry with three foreground figures: a woman, a man, and a young girl holding flowers. The faces of the adults have been completely worn away: they are literally defaced. They wear blue robes, the folds of which are Byzantine in their vivid wildness. The girl, who is held in front of the man by his imprisoning arms, looks beseechingly to the woman, whose body is turned away from the child, while her featureless face looks back to the girl. In front of the ensemble, leaning against the right wall is a long slat of mirror.

FIGURE 79. *Pass*, 1988–89. The Ginny Williams Family Foundation

When I was growing up, all the women in my house used needles. I've always had a fascination with the needle, the magic power of the needle. The needle is used to repair the damage. It's a claim to forgiveness. It is never aggressive, it's not a pin.[29] (Figure 81)

Louise's mother restored tapestries. She repaired images, bridging the gap between what is and what was by bridging the gaps of tears, her needle dipping in and out of the tapestry surface, its line of wool following behind, like a harpoon's shaft with its line of rope projecting ever forward to suture the gap between man and beast. In French, *faire une tapisserie* means to make a tapestry, and in its idiom, to be a "wallflower," a fearful one who hides against the wall (as if a tapestry). Like a spider, the epitome of the architect who works with thread. The Arachnid: industrious, silent, delicate, potentially deadly.

My mother was a restorer, she repaired broken things. I don't do that. I destroy things. I cannot go the straight line. I must destroy, rebuild, destroy again.

FIGURE 80. *Passage Dangereux* (detail), 1997

My rhythm is not the same. My mother moved in a straight line; I go from one extreme to the other.[30]

Need we point out that going from one extreme to the other is precisely the movement of the weaver and tapestry maker? Let us simply say that, regardless of our wishes, daughters are more like their mothers than we like to think. And this is more of a good thing than we think. *Nota bene* the small, pale, seemingly gossamer-wrapped object in the little bed at the top of the spiral stair in *Cell VII*. Pricked by needles, with threads flying, it is Sebastienne, yes, but also Sebastien, another harpooned whale (Figure 82).

The needle is not a pin; nevertheless it creates punctures as it mends. There is a constellation of tiny holes in the weave of the tapestry through which we perceive another image: spectral, there and not there. Beneath the undulations of the fabric as beneath the undulations of the sea—as Ahab glimpsed the whale beneath the surface of the sea—we can glimpse the

subliminal image of Louise's quarry through this surface of holes.

Let us turn back to look at the room across the passage and its neighbor, into which we have peeked before (Figure 76). The dominant presence in both rooms is a grouping of chairs upon which sit various objects, mostly orbs and biomorphs. In the previously visited room, the three chairs are crudely "homemade." On one sits a large plastic globe with what seems to be vertebrae and a stocky mammalian femur lying desolately inside, and a smaller, empty glass snow globe, also displaying dry bones, on a painted wood stand. The middle chair sports a great sphere of hornets' nest on a thin, pale gray marble slab in a glass box. The third offers a closed glass bell-jar with three depressions in the bottom that serve as feet; a stuffed stocking doughnut with three protuberances and a strange joint; and a familiarly Louise biomorph of masonry coils punctuated with small wounds of metal. The first and last are surmounted by small round lollipop mirrors. In one corner, hung at an angle, is the

FIGURE 81. *Needle (Fuseau)*, 1992

grandest mirror of the entire ensemble. When we stand where we can see in the mirror, our vision is split down the middle by the corner of the cage in the foreground. We see a double image–both the object and its reflection–a blonde-hair-and-steel basket suspended before the mirror and superimposed upon our own image. If we scrunch down to what we imagine as the artist's height, we now see ourselves only from the waist down, the hair basket hanging between our legs.

The second space is a schoolroom of four chairs (Figure 83). One is a large steel chair with tapestry cushion, its burlap-bag back worked in what looks like giant trapunto, and a large green glass globe perched on it. And there are three small school chairs, two identical and graced with smaller green glass globes, the third smaller and less sturdily constructed, with tiny blue glass globe. The small chairs are clustered attentively around the large one. High in one corner is mounted a small steel and stone platform that displays two figurines: a glass horse that once held liqueur, its tail a spout stoppered with cork and its head largely missing,[31] standing over a stout, bronze bull (Figure 84). The fragile, injured horse seems protective of its sturdier companion. Or is it

FIGURE 83. *Passage Dangereux* (detail), 1997

standing over the smaller beast in triumphant control? Look closely, and you will see that inside the horse there is the body of a fly, an innocent creative seduced by sweetness, and trapped. This tableau is reflected in a pair of lollipops mounted on the platform. The nose of each animal points to its own respective mirror, each of which becomes yet another round glass world.

> Transparency interests me. I want to be transparent. If people could see through me, they could not help loving me, forgive me. What is the difference between the two? None.[32]

All of these small glass worlds invoke the melancholy of containment, of being closed off to the outside. Their similarity to their gargantuan cousins–the Crystal Palace, the arcades and department stores of the 19th century–halts at the threshold of material description. Here, we are in the realm of the glass menagerie, a fragile and isolated world of memory, longing, and pain. In her book *Women and Madness*,

FIGURE 82. *Cell VII*, 1998 (detail)

FIGURE 84. *Passage Dangereux* (detail), 1997

Phyllis Chesler quotes the writer Ellen West, who describes this world:

> I feel myself excluded from all real life. I am quite isolated. I sit in a glass ball. I see people through a glass wall, their voices come to me muffled . . . I stretch out my arms toward them; but my hands merely beat against the walls of my glass ball.[33]

In the BBC film produced by Nigel Finch, Louise herself describes the glass globes as individuals, so near and yet so far from each other, each "in a world of their own," passing each other "like ships in the night." Herman Melville notes such invisible prison cells: "Though in many of its aspects the visible world seems formed in love, the invisible spheres were formed in fright."[34]

The *Passage Dangereux* and the *Cells* defy the common wisdom that people who live in glass houses shouldn't throw stones. Louise throws hard, she intends to shatter, and she shows that we all live in

glass houses: fragile, brittle houses of fear. We are all made of cells and we live in cells. Cells are environments for retreat or incarceration for the safety of others. Safe passages. And each of us, she and he, *celle* and *celui*, is a living, transparent glass globe. Each of Louise's *Cells*, including the agglomerate *Passage Dangereux*, is a *celle*, the "she" who is an interior, *une femme maison*; but let us not forget the fact that each is also, significantly, a *Cell-Louis*.

A stone's throw across the corridor, we encounter a room dominated by a vivid representation of authority, power, punishment, and constraint. There are only two objects in this room: a chair and a six-inch lollipop mirror to its right at the head height of a seated person (Figure 85). In this room alone of all the furnished rooms of the passage, the chair does not bear its customary benign connection to domesticity. This chair is crudely built, with only the slightest embellishment of the back. It has arms and the chair's structure suggests that it is meant to be borne on something else: to be put on a pedestal as spectacle, perhaps, or to be carried as a

FIGURE 85. *Passage Dangereux* (detail), 1997

FIGURE 86. *Passage Dangereux* (detail), 1997

son. Imprisoned in this cell, in this chair, and, as always with the *Femmes Maisons*, with arms restrained and legs planted on the ground. But it is only an image. Who is the intended occupant of the chair? *Celle, ou celui?*

Let us, at last, return to the corridor and face what is ahead of us: the end of the *couloir*, the end of the line, the apse, the final room, the way out.

But is there in fact a way out? Or is this a passage with No Exit? (Recall that Sartre's title *A Huis Clos*, translated into English as *No Exit*, suggests something else in French: an environment of privacy.) This is a private space, a bedroom, on display for all to see and full of chairs for the witnessing of the spectacle that is occurring in the room (Figure 86). On a bare steel bed frame rests a rectangular section of steel pipe of torso proportions. From within the pipe, attached to separate struts by rings that seem to allow rotation, emerge two pairs of steel poles; one pair a bit longer than the other, one pair pristinely treated against rust, and the other grizzled with ferrous oxide; the rusty pair parallel and poised above and between the slightly spread, unsullied pair. At the ends of each pair are a pair of cast metal feet, anatomically appropriate to what, we have no doubt, is going on.

The present condition of this room is LEGS: the two pairs of copulating legs on the bed; the supporting legs of the surrounding school chair with desk and dining chair binding them to the floor; the dangling legs of the multitude of chairs hanging from the ceiling (In storage? Theoric witnesses?); the eight delicately poised legs of the spider in the corner; the crippled leg of Louise's sister Henriette implied by the brace that floats flaccidly near the also absent, but implicated, legs of the large, ratty, professional chair posed on axis with the bed. (The point of view of an occupant of this chair would be directly in line with doors to implied body passages, into the belly of the whale at hand.) The legs, the doors, of Louise Bourgeois' life and work are all here.

We enter any room through the parted legs (*jambes*) of a door, as we enter the world, slimy and trusting, through parted legs. In *Passage Dangereux*, these jambs, these customary sites of support and enclosure, implicate the site of betrayal of a child's trust and safety.

Ahab's prosthetic whalebone leg, which he plants in a hole on the deck of his ship to maintain balance at sea, is

sedan. This is a chair of power and authority. This is a chair that threatens punishment, constraint, even, perhaps, death. There are two leather straps near the ends of the chair's arms. One is dark brown and smooth, not adjustable; the other is a dark honey color and has five pairs of holes for adjustment of its circumference.

A chair always speaks of the body; it has arms, legs, a back, and a seat. In accommodating the bend at the hips of a seated human being, the chair mimics it. Unlike the bed and the door, which are ambivalent toward the body, the chair is precise in its universalizing abstraction of the body: back against back, seat on seat, feet on floor. And look here, wrists inserted in leather bands.

Who is in the chair, who is being restrained and punished? The chair is empty, but look closely at a certain published image of it: there is a ghostly image of lines projected onto the two planes of the chair's back and seat. It is a woman; it is a building. It is *une Femme Mai-*

ing gossamer architecture of her own? In the BBC film, we learn that when Louise feels threatened, she holds up mirrors, literal or figurative, to deflect the dangerous question. But she also hides, seeks shelter, slides into slots in the walls of her studio and simply disappears (Figure 87). When she looks into her mirrors herself, looking for her ghostly quarry, I wonder, can she see in the intricate construction of small points of glassy reflectivity, in the crystal passages of memory, can she see the exquisite spider that is there?

FIGURE 87. Louise Bourgeois on the staircase of her house on West 20th Street, New York, 1992

the souvenir of the leg of flesh and bone that the white whale "reaped away . . . 'as a mower a blade of grass in the field.'"[35] So these parted metal legs mark, not the nostalgic site of Louise's original home, but the place where her at-homeness in the world was mown down.

The *jambage*, the jambs of the door at the end of the passage, that might exit this room, are *faux*. Fake legs, they allow No Exit. What is there to do at this end of the line, this passage with No Exit? Look to the spider in the corner. What is she doing? Where is she going? Is she leaving, or is she preparing to climb up into the farthest corner to watch, joining the passive chair spectators above; is she, in fear and rage, about to inject venom, or is she, involuting, preparing to spin and weave a glisten-

1. With many thanks to Danielle Tilkin for her substantial support, to Jerry Gorovoy for insightful comments at beginning and end, to Karen Bermann for critical reading, and to Louise Bourgeois for magnificence and ice cream.

2. Although the artist intended the *Passage* to be an architectural space open to visitors, when installed in museums it remains closed to protect its fragile contents.

3. How ludicrous it seems to refer to this person who has boldly removed so many trappings of propriety and polite posturing from her work and life as "Ms. Bourgeois" or "Bourgeois." I implore the reader not to interpret my calling the artist "Louise" as a conventional sign of American disrespect for the female and aged. Because the generatrix of *Passage Dangereux* and other work is the occupation of her child-self through memory, I refer to the artist as Louise in order to honor that child, as well as a sign of (maternal? filial?) affection for her.

4. The rue de Seine is a tiny street, hardly longer than *Passage Dangereux*, just on the left bank of the Seine. Is it meaningful that, in the long passage of Louise Bourgeois' life, the first place she headed when she left her father's house in Choisy-le-Roi was an apartment in the very same rue de Seine? Of course it is.

Translation of the Zola Passage (by Jennifer Bloomer):

"As one comes up from the river, one finds … a sort of cramped and dark corridor that connects the rue Mazarine and the rue de Seine. This passage is thirty paces long and at most two paces wide; it is paved with yellowish tiles, worn down and loose, which always reek of an acrid dampness; the steep pitched glass roof which covers it is black with grime.

On the left, are sunken dark, mean, and ruinous shops from which cold, cellar-like air whispers. Here, there are booksellers, dealers in children's toys, and cardboard merchants, whose shop windows are gray with dust and lie dimly idle in the shadows; the showcases, made of small panes of glass, eerily cast watery, greenish reflections on the merchandise. Beyond, behind the displays, the shadow-filled shops are all the more dismal holes in which strange patterns fidget about.

On the right, along the entire length of the passage, runs a wall against which the shopkeepers opposite have put up narrow cupboards; where along slender shelves painted an appalling brown color are displayed some nameless objects, merchandise lying forgotten for twenty years. A woman selling costume jewelry is set up in one of these cupboards; here she sells fifteen-sous rings, each daintily set on a bed of blue velvet in the bottom of a mahogany box.

Above the glass roof rises the thick black wall, crudely rough-cast, as if covered with leprosy and slashed with scars."

5. Walter Benjamin, "Paris, Capital of the Nineteenth Century," in *Reflections: Essays, Aphorisms, Autobiographical Writings*, ed. Peter Demetz (New York: Harcourt Brace Jovanovich, 1978), 146–147.

6. From Susan Buck-Morss, *The Dialectics of Seeing: Walter Benjamin and the Arcades Project* (Cambridge, MA: MIT Press, 1989), 50–52.

7. Benjamin, 146–147.

8. Buck-Morss, 39.

9. Frances A. Yates, *The Art of Memory* (London: Routledge and Kegan Paul, 1966), 18.

10. Vigilius quoted in Yates, 135.

11. Ibid., 136–137.

12. Ibid., 142.

13. José Ortega y Gasset, "On the Point of View in the Arts," in *The Dehumanization of Art and Other Essays* (Princeton: Princeton University Press, 1968), 107.

14. Marie Darrieussecq, *Dans la maison de Louise* (1988), 1.

15. Quoted in Sylvia Nasar, *A Beautiful Mind* (New York: Simon & Schuster, 1998), 15.

16. See Roland Barthes' beautiful essay, *Camera Lucida: Reflections on Photography*, transl. Richard Howard (New York: Hill and Wang, 1981). The essay was originally published as *La Chambre Claire* and was dedicated in homage to Jean-Paul Sartre's *L'Imaginaire*.

17. Gilles Deleuze, *The Fold: Leibniz and the Baroque* [*Le Pli: Leibniz et le baroque*, Minuit, 1988], transl. Tom Conley (Minneapolis: University of Minnesota Press, 1993), 32.

18. Ibid.

19. Thus, 1851 is a significant node in our implicated passage. There is another: precisely a century later, in 1951, when Louise's father Louis Bourgeois left this world, and I entered it.

20. Charles Olson, *Call Me Ishmael* (San Francisco: City Lights Books, 1947), 14.

21. Ibid.

22. Louise Bourgeois, *Destruction of the Father, Reconstruction of the Father: Writings and Interviews 1923–1997*, Eds. Marie-Laure Bernadac and Hans-Ulrich Obrist (London: Violette Editions, 1998), 284.

23. Ibid., 133.

24. Ibid., 283.

25. Ibid., 291.

26. Olson, 183.

27. Rainer Crone and Petrus Graf Schaesberg, *Louise Bourgeois: The Secret of the Cells* (Munich, London, New York: Prestel, 1998), 54.

28. Ibid.

29. Christiane Meyer-Thoss, *Louise Bourgeois: Designing For Free Fall* (Zurich: Ammann Verlag, 1992).

30. Jerry Gorovoy and Pandora Tabatai Asbaghi, *Louise Bourgeois: Blue Days and Pink Days* (Milan: Fondazione Prada, 1997), 21.

31. Jerry Gorovoy tells me that the glass horse was a gift to Louise from the Swiss architect Le Corbusier, whose formal quotations of the *Passages de Paris* are well-known, and whose penchant for controlling women has been documented by Beatriz Colomina. See, for example, her "Battle Lines: E.1027," in Francesca Hughes, ed., *The Architect: Reconstructing Her Practice*, (Cambridge, MA: MIT Press, 1996).

32. 3 October, 1987 diary entry. From *Destruction of the Father, Reconstruction of the Father*, 132.

33. Phyllis Chesler, *Women and Madness* (New York: Harcourt Brace Jovanovich, 1972), 15.

34. Quoted in Olson, 43.

35. Olson, 83.

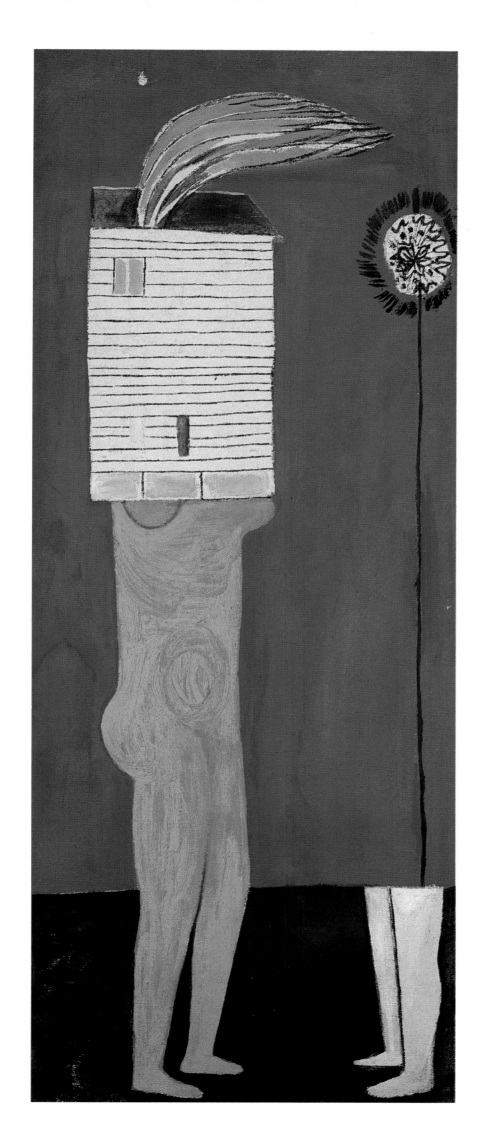

2.
FEMME MAISON
Oil and ink on linen
36 x 14 inches
ca. 1946–47
Private collection

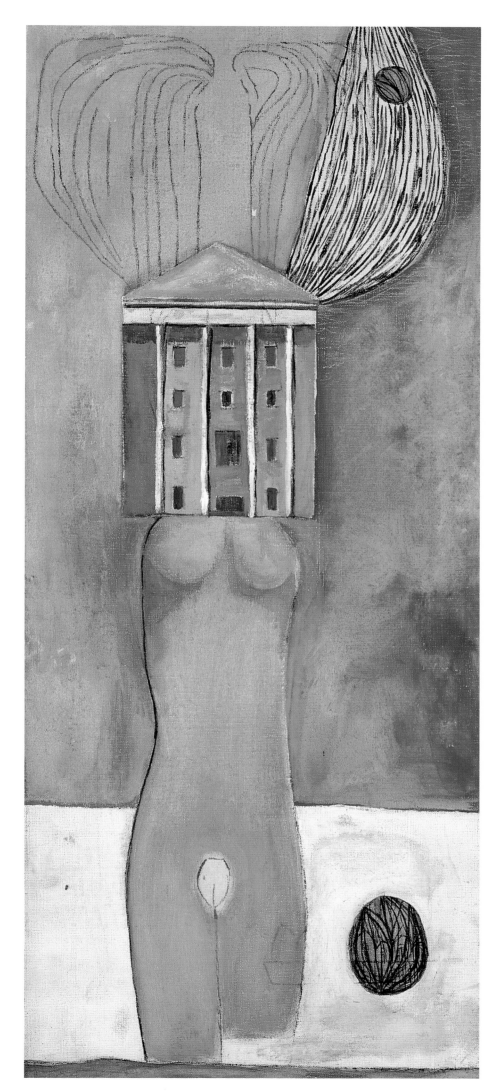

3.
FEMME MAISON
Oil and ink on linen
36 x 14 inches
ca. 1946–47
Private collection

Plate 2

The solitary death of the Wool-
worth building.

4.
HE DISAPPEARED INTO
COMPLETE SILENCE
Set of nine engravings and text
10 x 14 inches
1947

Plate 5

Once a man was waving to his friend from the elevator.

He was laughing so much that he stuck his head out and the ceiling cut it off.

5.
*HE DISAPPEARED
INTO COMPLETE
SILENCE*
Set of nine engravings
and text
10 x 14 inches
1947

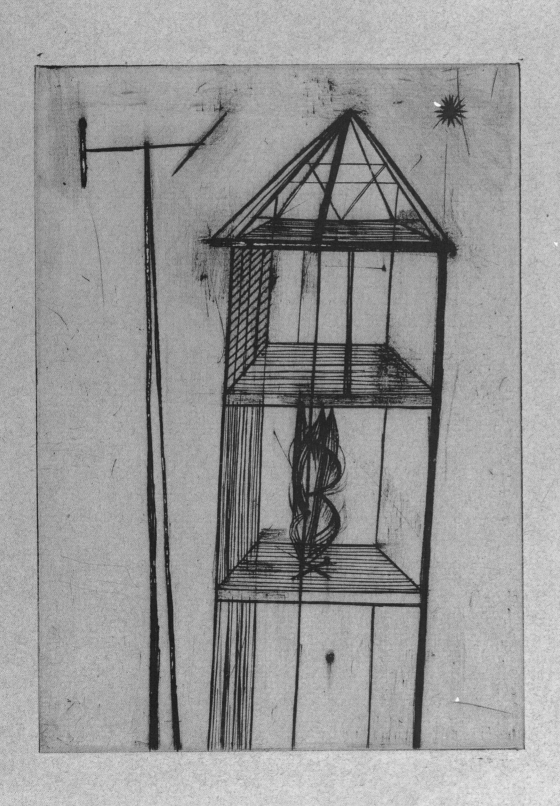

IV

6.
UNTITLED
Painted wood
59 x 12 x 12 inches
1947–49

7.
PORTRAIT OF JEAN-LOUIS
Bronze
35 x 5 x 4 inches
1947–49

9.
PORTRAIT OF C. Y.
Bronze and nails
66½ x 12 x 12 inches
1947–49

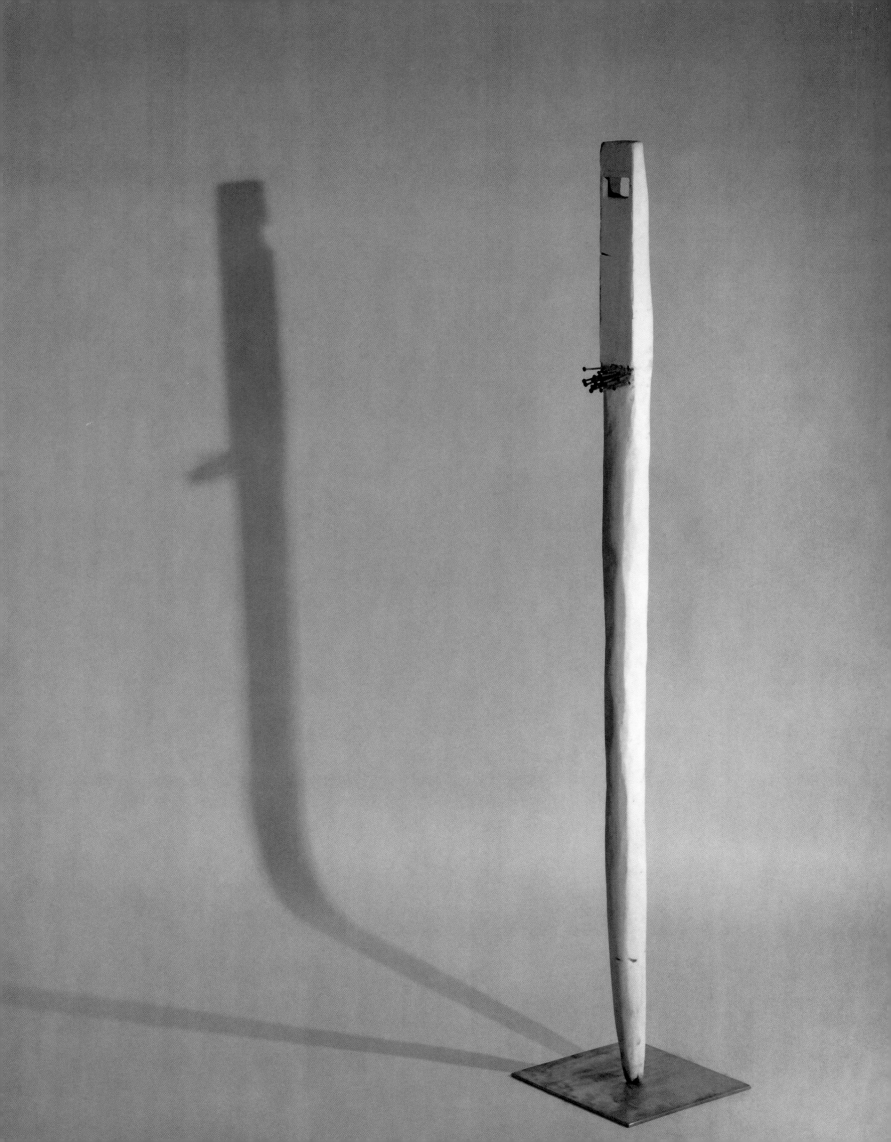

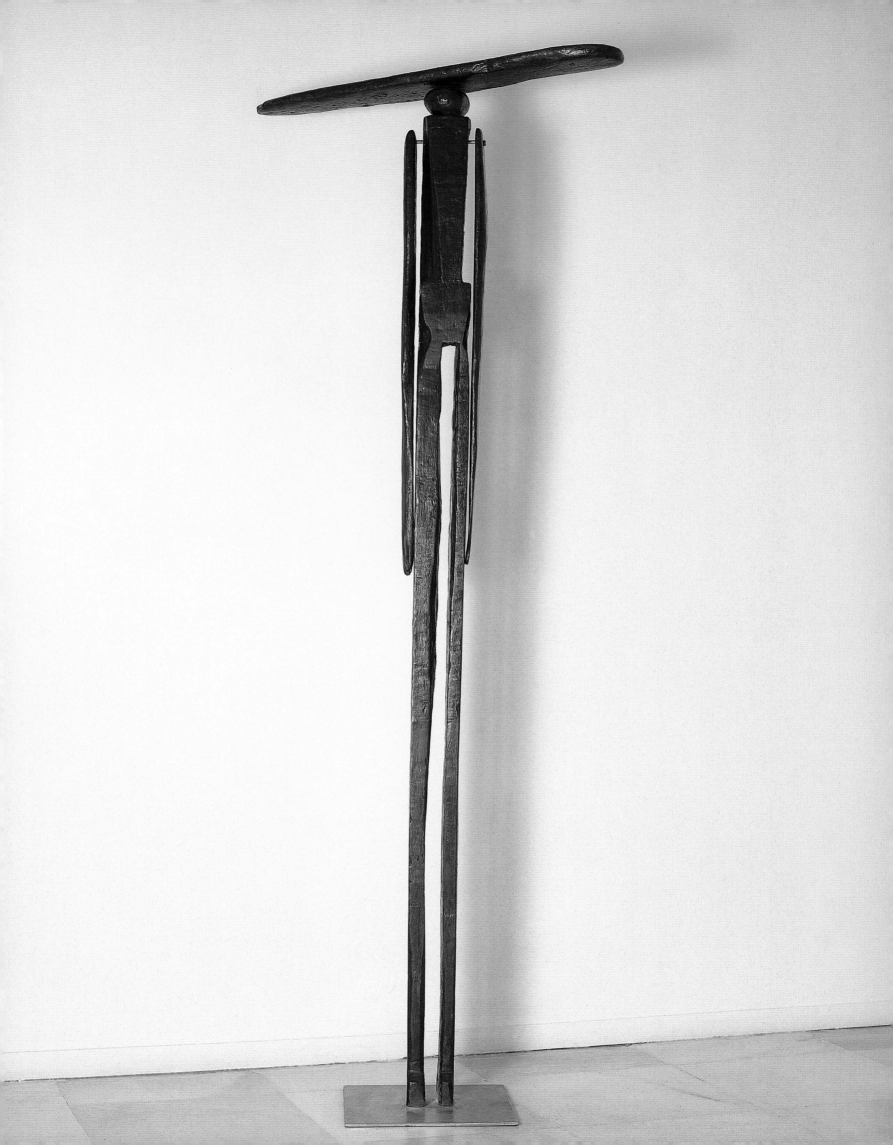

CORNER PIECE
Bronze
84 x 12 x 12 inches
1947–49

PERSISTENT ANTAGONISM
Bronze
66 x 12 x 12 inches
1947–1949

PILLAR
Painted wood and stainless steel
61½ x 12 x 12 inches
1947–49

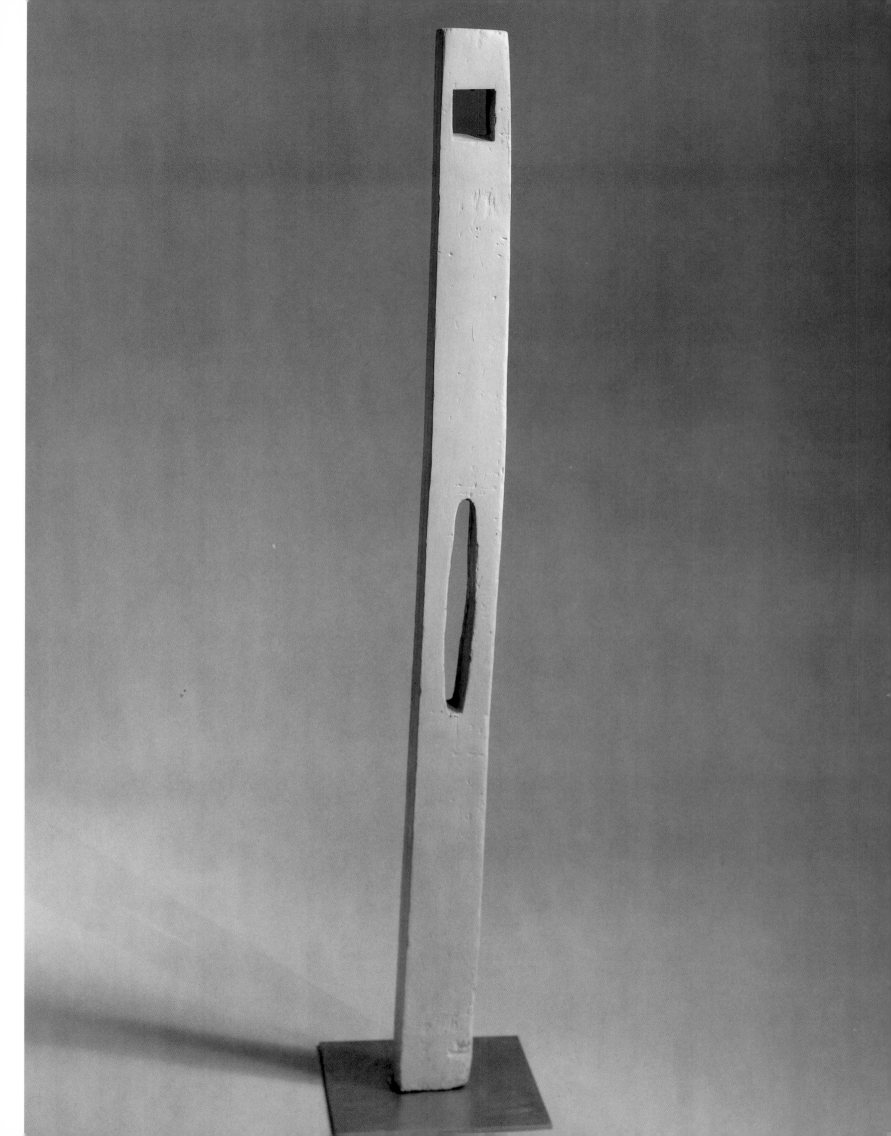

16.
WOMAN WITH PACKAGES
Bronze, white patina
65 x 18 x 12 inches
1949

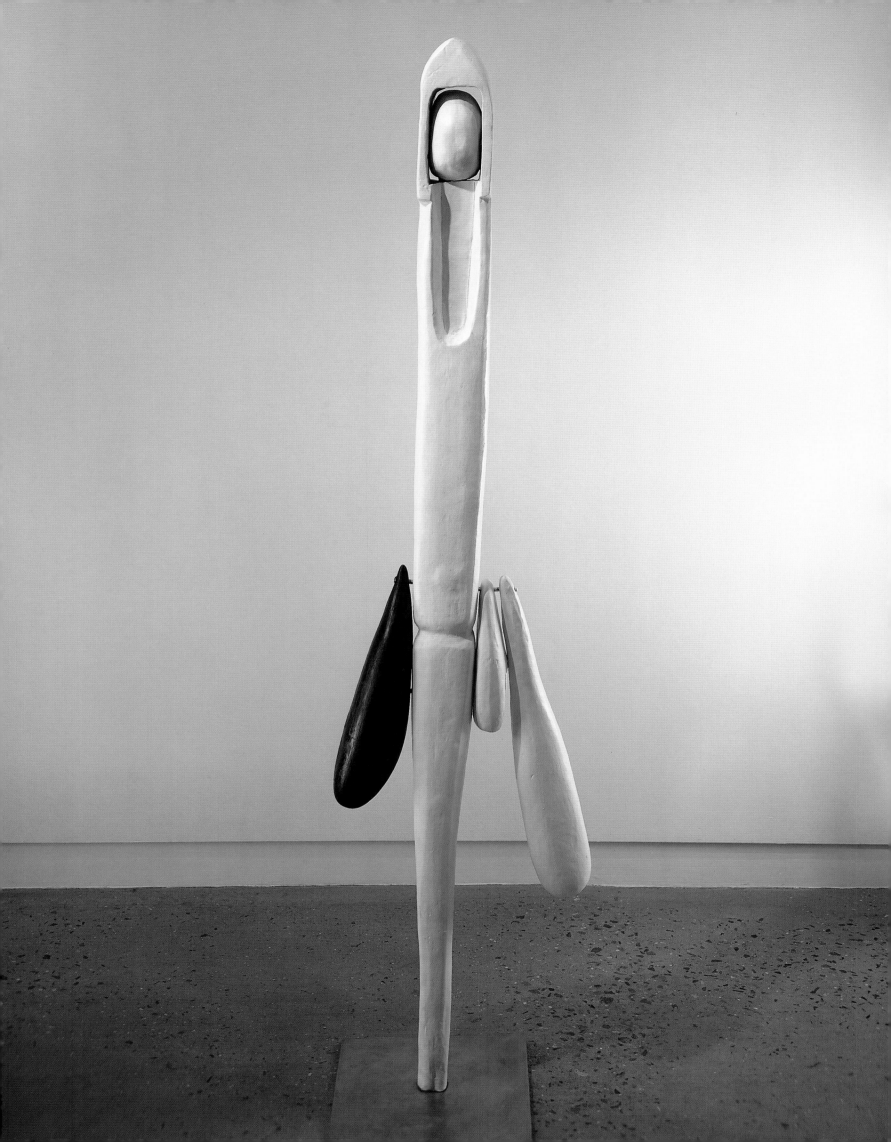

17.
KNIFE COUPLE
Painted wood
68½ x 12 x 12 inches
1949

18.
PILLAR
Bronze
63½ x 12 x 12 inches
1949–5o

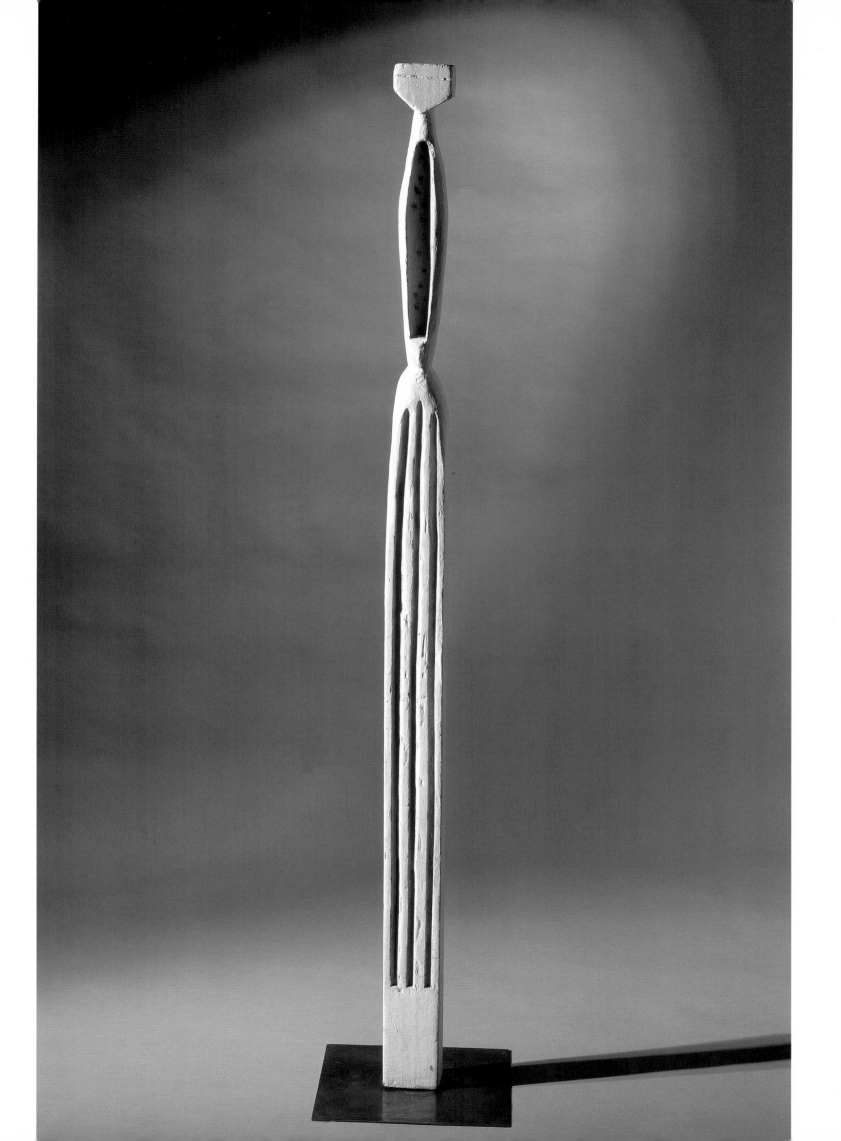

20.
UNTITLED
Painted wood
63 x 12 x 12 inches
1950
The Ginny Williams Collection

23.
UNTITLED
Painted wood
59¼ x 8½ x 7½ inches
1953

25.
CLUTCHING
Plaster
12 x 13 x 12 inches
1962

27.
LAIR
Plaster
22 x 22 x 22 inches
1962

28.
LAIR
Plaster
18½ x 29⅛ x 21⅜ inches
1962–63

LAIR
Latex
9½ x 16¾ x 14⅜ inches
1963

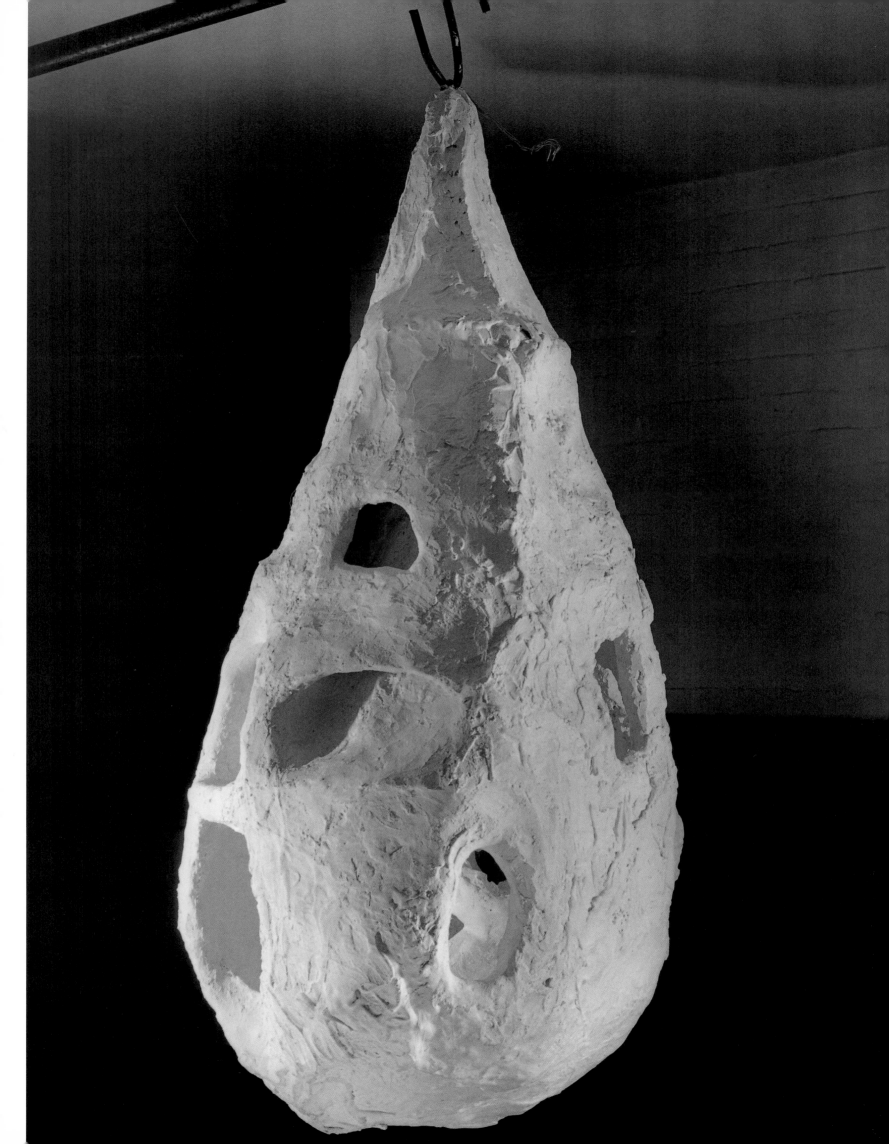

31.
TORSO, SELF PORTRAIT
Bronze, white patina
24¾ x 16 x 7⅞ inches
1963–64

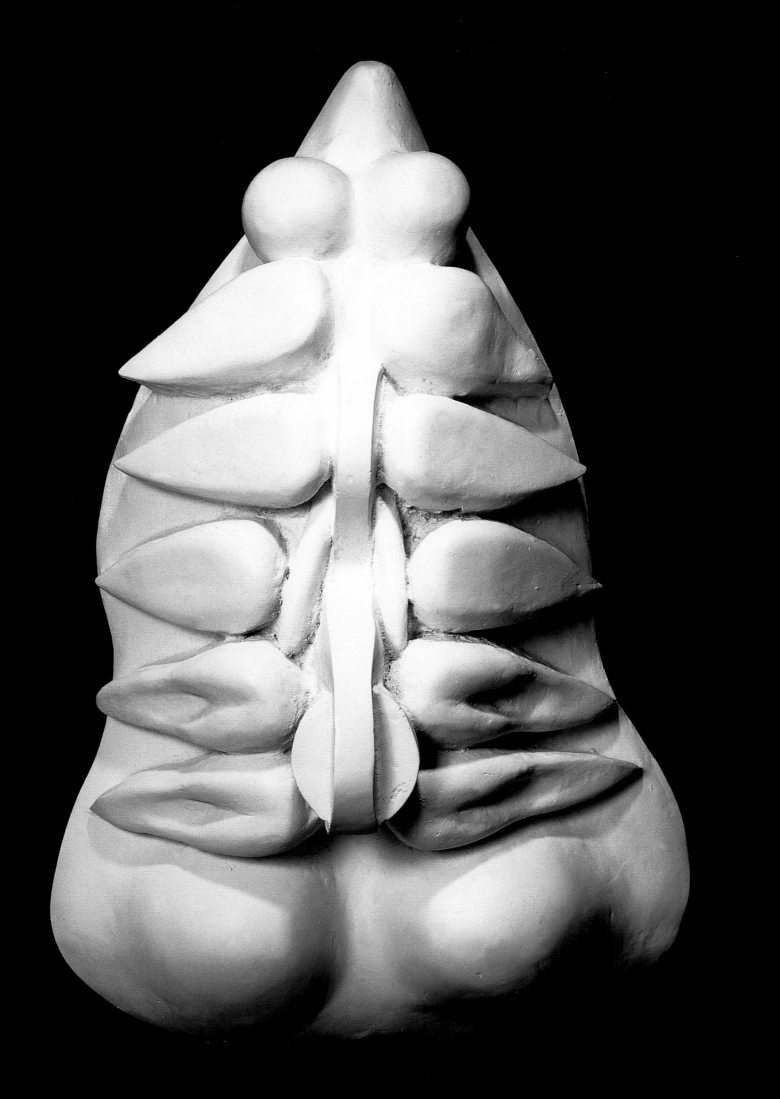

32.
AMOEBA
Plaster
37½ x 28½ x 13¼ inches
1963–65

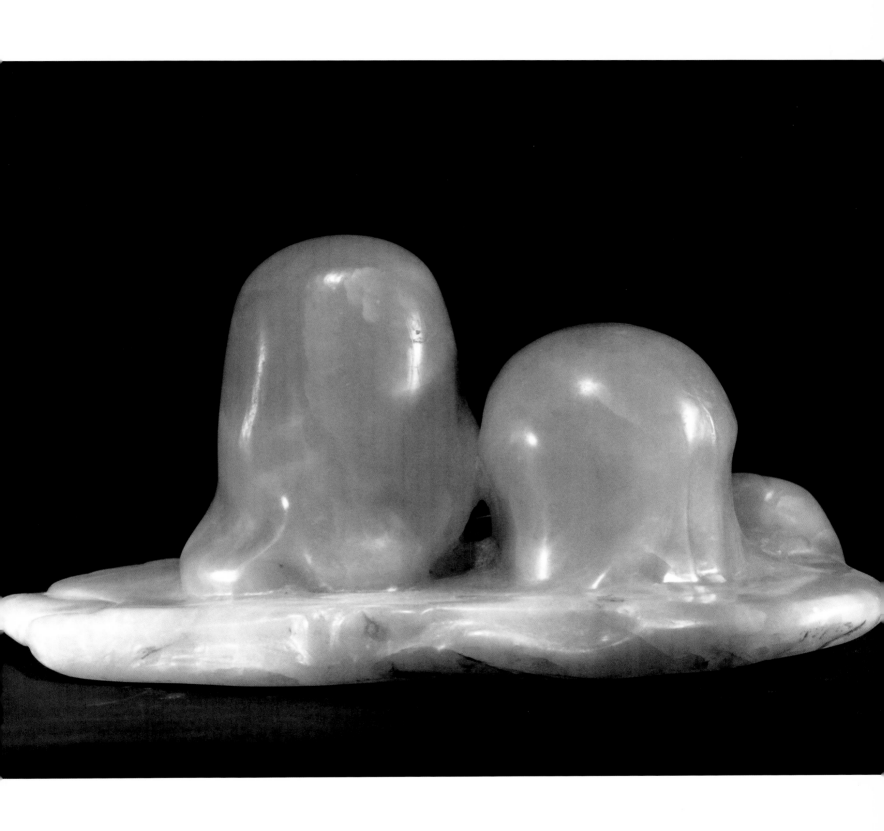

35.
UNCONSCIOUS LANDSCAPE
Bronze
12 x 22 x 24 inches
1967–68

37.
JANUS IN LEATHER JACKET
Bronze
12 x 22 x 6½ inches
1968

39.
AVENZA
Latex
21 x 30 x 46 inches
1968–69

40.
FILLETTE (SWEETER VERSION)
Latex over plaster
23½ x 10½ x 7¾ inches
1968 cast 1999

41.
CUMUL I
White marble
22⅜ x 50 x 48 inches
1969
Centre Georges Pompidou, Paris
Musée National d'Art Moderne/Centre de Création Industrielle

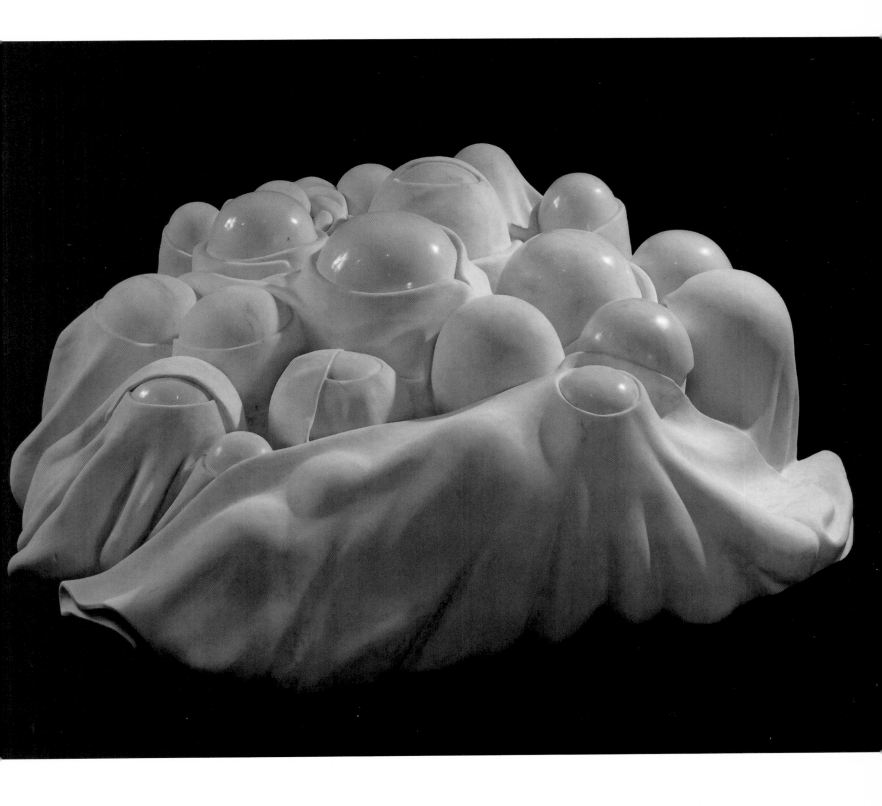

42.
FEMME PIEU
Wax and metal needles
3½ x 2½ x 6 inches
ca. 1970
Collection of the Museum of New Mexico
Museum of Fine Arts, Lucy Lippard Collection

FRAGILE GODDESS
Bronze, gold patina
10¼ x 5⅝ x 5⅜ inches
1970

46.
FEMME COUTEAU
Pink marble
2¾ x 15¼ x 4 inches
1982
Collection Ellen Kern

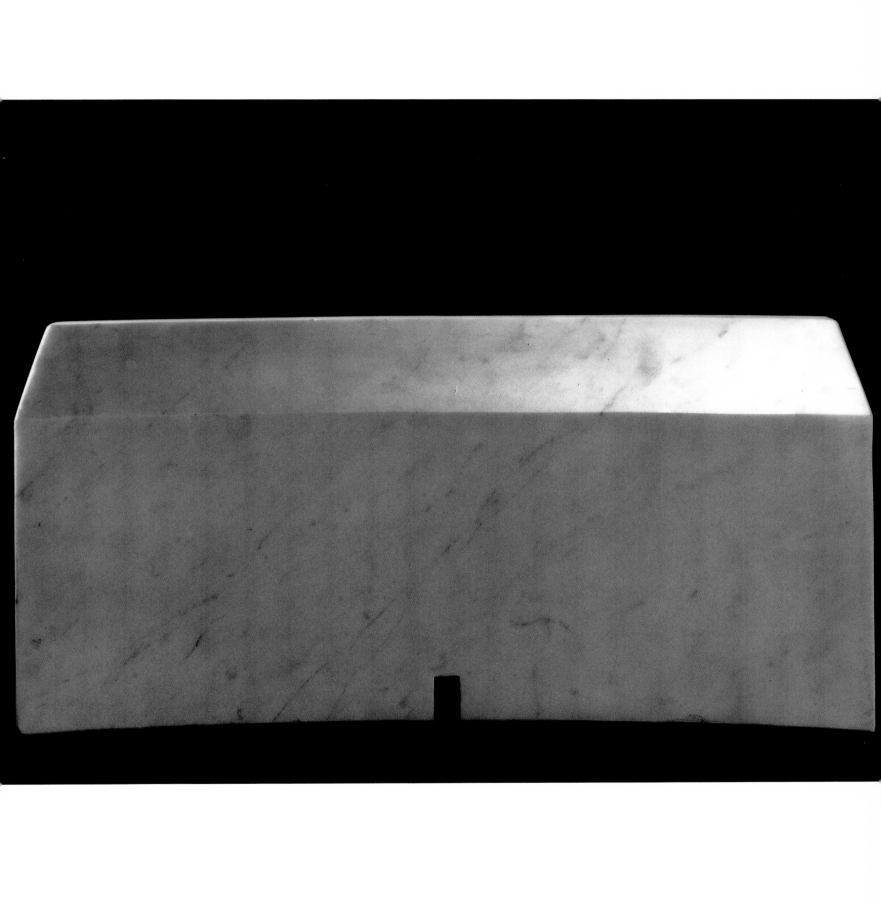

49.
BELLY
Bronze
4¼ x 11 x 5¼ inches
1984

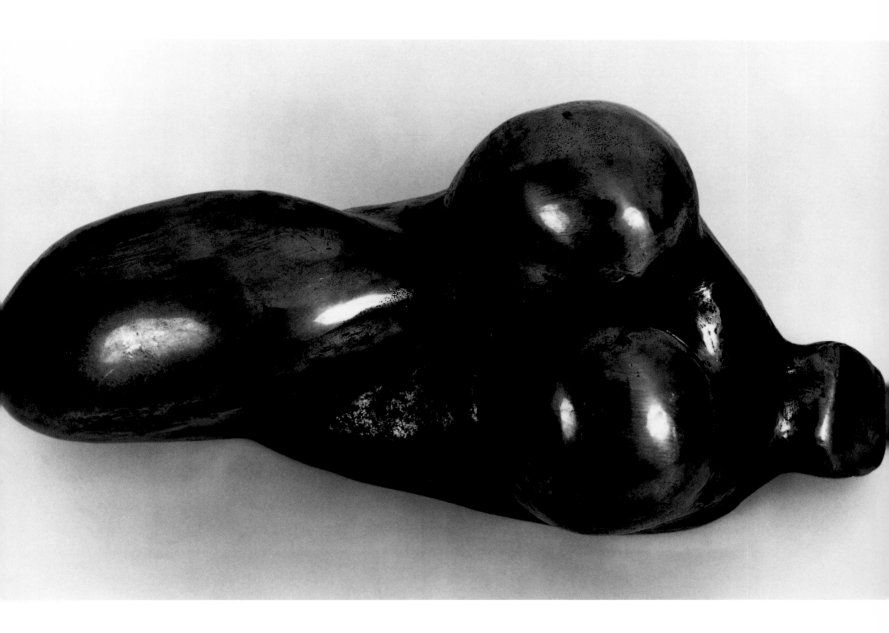

51.
LAIR
Rubber
43 x 21 x 21 inches
1986

52 and 53.
ARTICULATED LAIR
Painted steel, rubber and stool (metal)
111 x 258 x 193 inches
1986
The Museum of Modern Art, New
York, Gift of Lily Auchincloss and the
artist in honour of Deborah Wye
(by exchange), 1993

54.
LEGS
Rubber
123 x 2 x 2 inches
1986

55.
UNTITLED (WITH HAND)
Pink marble
31 x 30½ x 21 inches
1989
Private collection

57.
THE PURITAN
Suite of 8 hand colored engravings and text
26 x 39½ inches
1990 (text 1947)

Do you know the New York sky? You should, it is supposed to be known. It is outstanding. It is a serious thing. Can you remember the Paris sky? How unreliable, most of the time grey, often warm and damp, never quite perfect, indulging in clouds and shades; rain, breeze and sun sometimes managing to appear together. But the New York sky is blue, utterly blue. The light is white, a glorying white and the air is strong and it is healthy too. There is no foolishness about that sky. It is a beautiful thing. It is pure.

There was a street in New York and it was full of the New York sky. It spread over it like a blue aluminum sheet. At that particular place I know why that sky was so blue, so completely himself. Because right under him the most formidable building in the world was standing up. In that street, close to that sky and close to that building, there was a house. The sky, the building, and the house, knew each other and approved of each other.

58.
THE PURITAN
Suite of 8 hand colored engravings and text
26 x 39½ inches
1990 (text 1947)

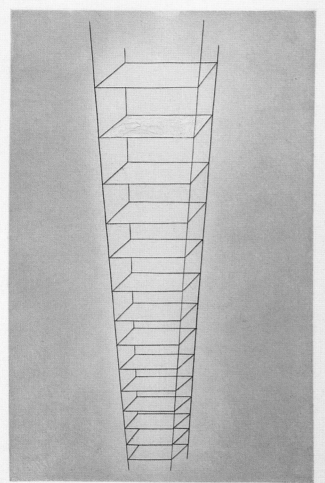

Louise Bourgeois.

59.
VENTOUSE
Marble, glass and electrical light
34 x 78 x 32 inches
1990

60.
MAMELLES
Rubber wall relief
19 x 120 x 19 inches
1991

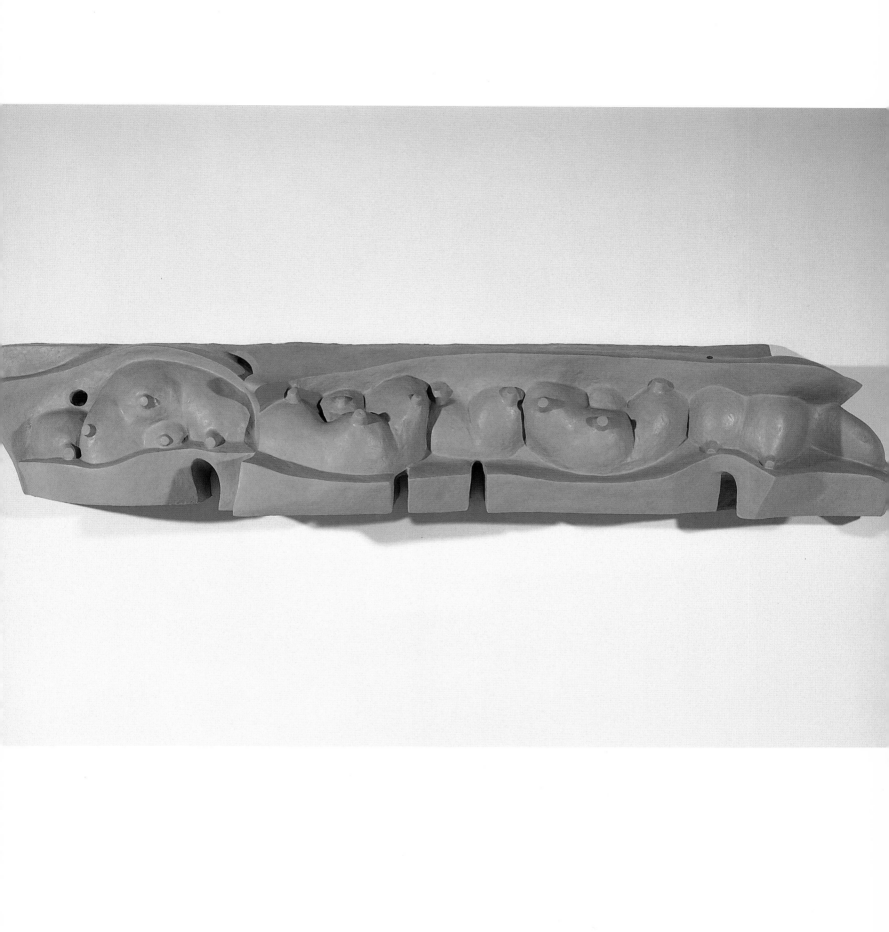

61.
CELL II
(Detail)
Mixed media
83 x 60 x 60 inches
1991
Carnegie Museum of Art, Pittsburgh; Heinz Family Fund, 1991

62.
PRECIOUS LIQUIDS
Wood, metal, glass, alabaster, cloth, water
168 x 174 inches
1992
Centre Georges Pompidou, Paris. Musée National d'Art
Moderne/Centre de Création Industrielle.

63.
PRECIOUS LIQUIDS
Wood, metal, glass, alabaster, cloth, water
168 x 174 inches
1992
Centre Georges Pompidou, Paris. Musée National d'Art
Moderne/Centre de Création Industrielle.

POIDS
Steel, glass and metal
177 x 147 x 24¼ inches
1992

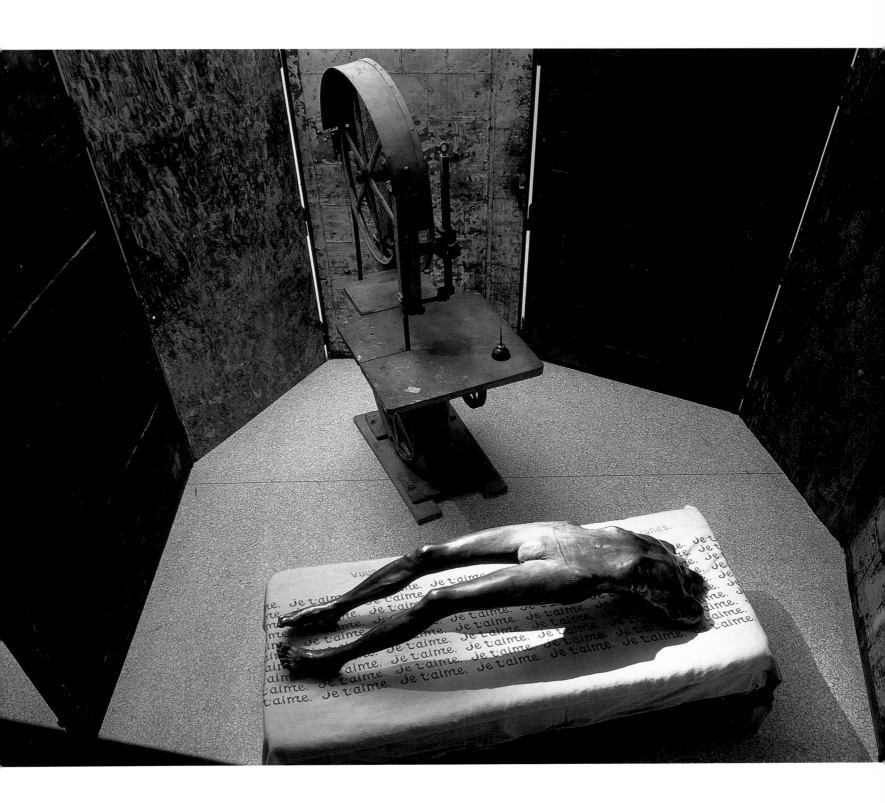

67.
RED ROOM (CHILD)
Mixed media
83 x 139 x 108 inches
1994
Collection Musée d'Art Contemporain de Montréal/The
Musée d'Art Contemporain de Montréal Collection

71.
COUPLE III
Fabric, leather and steel arm brace
28 x 39 x 71 inches
1997
Private collection

72.
SPIDER
Steel and mixed media
175 x 262 x 204 inches
1997

73.
PASSAGE DANGEREUX
Mixed media
104 x 140 x 345 inches
1997
Sammlung Hauser & Wirth, St. Gallen, Switzerland

75.
PASSAGE DANGEREUX
Mixed media
104 x 140 x 345 inches
1997
Sammlung Hauser & Wirth, St. Gallen, Switzerland

76.
PASSAGE DANGEREUX
(Detail)
Mixed media
104 x 140 x 345 inches
1997
Sammlung Hauser & Wirth, St. Gallen, Switzerland

78.
CELL VII
Mixed media
81½ x 87 x 83 inches
1998

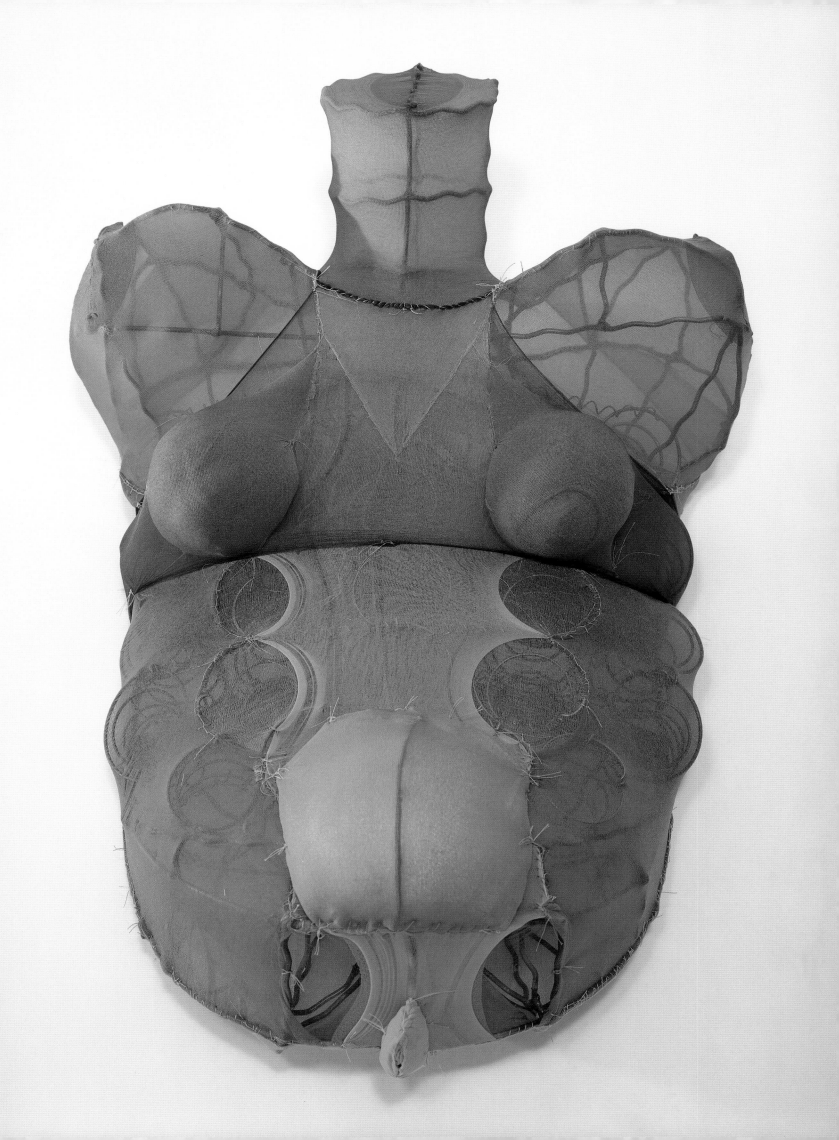

81.

UNTITLED (CHAIR AND THREE MIRRORS)
Steel and mirrors
9 x 13 x 10½ inches
1998
Private collection

83.
CELL (TWELVE OVAL MIRRORS)
Steel, wood and 12 oval pivoting mirrors
90 x 96 x 132 inches
1998

84.
THE MIRROR
Cast and polished aluminum
94 x 34½ x 44 inches
1998

85.
UNTITLED
8 holograms
11 x 14 inches
1998

Works in the Exhibition

*works not reproduced in the catalogue

*EASTON HOUSE, 1946
Ink on graph paper
8½ x 11 inches; 21.5 x 27.9 cm
Courtesy Cheim & Read, New York

1. FEMME MAISON, 1946–47
Oil and ink on linen
36 x 14 inches; 91.4 x 35.5 cm
Collection of Agnes Gund, New York

2. FEMME MAISON, ca. 1946–47
Oil and ink on linen
36 x 14 inches; 91.4 x 35.5 cm
Private collection

3. FEMME MAISON, ca. 1946–47
Oil and ink on linen
36 x 14 inches; 91.4 x 35.5 cm
Private collection

*UNTITLED, 1947
Ink on graph paper
8½ x 11 inches; 21.6 x 27.9 cm
Galerie Lelong, Zurich

*UNTITLED, 1947
Ink and charcoal on paper
11⅛ x 8½ inches; 28.3 x 21.6 cm
Courtesy Cheim & Read, New York

4 and 5. HE DISAPPEARED INTO
COMPLETE SILENCE, 1947
Set of nine engravings and text
10 x 14 inches; 25.3 x 35.5 cm
Courtesy Cheim & Read, New York

6. UNTITLED, 1947–49
Painted wood
59 x 12 x 12 inches; 149.8 x 30.4 x 30.4 cm
Courtesy Cheim & Read, New York

7. PORTRAIT OF JEAN-LOUIS, 1947–49
Bronze
35 x 5 x 4 inches; 88.9 x 12.7 x 10.2 cm
Courtesy Cheim & Read, New York

8. THE BLIND LEADING THE BLIND,
1947–1949
Painted Wood
67⅛ x 64⅜ x 16¼ inches; 170.4 x 163.5 x 41.2 cm
The Ginny Williams Family Foundation, Collection of
Ginny Williams

9. PORTRAIT OF C. Y., 1947–49
Bronze and nails
66½ x 12 x 12 inches; 168.9 x 30.4 x 30.4 cm
Courtesy Cheim & Read, New York

10. OBSERVER, 1947–1949
Bronze, dark patina
76 x 28 x 12 inches; 193 x 71.1 x 30.4 cm
Courtesy Cheim & Read, New York

11. CORNER PIECE, 1947–49
Bronze
84 x 12 x 12 inches; 213.3 x 30.4 x 30.4 cm
Courtesy Cheim & Read, New York

12. DAGGER CHILD, 1947–49
Bronze
75⅝ x 12 x 12 inches; 192 x 30.4 x 30.4 cm
Courtesy Cheim & Read, New York

13. *THE TOMB OF A YOUNG PERSON*, 1947–49
Painted wood
46 x 12 x 12 inches; 116.8 x 30.4 x 30.4 cm
Courtesy Cheim & Read, New York

14. *PERSISTENT ANTAGONISM*, 1947–1949
Bronze
66 x 12 x 12 inches; 167.6 x 30.4 x 30.4 cm
Courtesy Cheim & Read, New York

15. *PILLAR*, 1947–49
Painted wood and stainless steel
61½ x 12 x 12 inches; 156.2 x 30.4 x 30.4 cm
Courtesy Cheim & Read, New York

16. *WOMAN WITH PACKAGES*, 1949
Bronze, white patina
65 x 18 x 12 inches; 165 x 45.7 x 30.4 cm
Courtesy Cheim & Read, New York

17. *KNIFE COUPLE*, 1949
Painted wood
68½ x 12 x 12 inches; 173.9 x 30.4 x 30.4 cm
Courtesy Cheim & Read, New York

18. *PILLAR*, 1949–50
Bronze
63½ x 12 x 12 inches; 161.2 x 30.4 x 30.4 cm
Courtesy Cheim & Read, New York

19. *MORTISE*, 1950
Bronze, painted red and black
55¾ x 18 x 18 inches; 141.6 x 45.7 x 45.7 cm
Courtesy Cheim & Read, New York

20. *UNTITLED*, 1950
Painted wood
63 x 12 x 12 inches; 160 x 30.4 x 30.4 cm
The Ginny Williams Collection

21. *MEMLING DAWN*, 1951
Painted wood
67¼ x 12 x 12 inches; 170.8 x 30.4 x 30.4 cm
Collection Frances Dittmer

22. *SPIRAL WOMAN*, 1951–52
Wood and steel
50 x 12 x 12 inches; 127 x 30.4 x 30.4 cm
Courtesy Cheim & Read, New York

23. *UNTITLED*, 1953
Painted wood
59¼ x 8½ x 7½ inches; 150.4 x 21.5 x 19 cm
Courtesy Cheim & Read, New York

24. *MAISON*, 1961
Plaster
16 x 14 x 9¼ inches; 40.6 x 35.5 x 23.4 cm
Courtesy Cheim & Read, New York

25. *CLUTCHING*, 1962
Plaster
12 x 13 x 12 inches; 30.4 x 33 x 30.4 cm
Courtesy Cheim & Read, New York

26. *LABYRINTHINE TOWER*, 1962
Plaster
18 x 12 x 10½ inches; 45.7 x 30.5 x 26.7 cm
Galerie Karsten Greve Köln Paris Milano

27. *LAIR*, 1962
Plaster
22 x 22 x 22 inches; 55.8 x 55.8 x 55.8 cm
Courtesy Cheim & Read, New York

28. *LAIR*, 1962–63
Plaster
18½ x 29⅛ x 21⅜ inches; 46.9 x 73.9 x 54.2 cm
Courtesy Cheim & Read, New York

29. *LAIR*, 1963
Latex
9½ x 16¾ x 14⅜ inches; 24.1 x 42.5 x 36.5 cm
Courtesy Galerie Karsten Greve Köln Paris Milano

30. *FEE COUTURIERE*, 1963
Plaster
39½ x 22½ x 22½ inches; 100.3 x 57.1 x 57.1 cm
Courtesy Cheim & Read, New York

31. *TORSO, SELF PORTRAIT*, 1963–64
[*Torso, auto-retrato*]
Bronce, pátina blanca
62,8 x 40,6 x 20 cm
Cortesía Cheim & Read, Nueva York

32. *AMOEBA*, 1963–65
[*Ameba*]
Escayola
95,2 x 72,3 x 33,6 cm
Cortesía Cheim & Read, Nueva York

33. *LE REGARD*, 1966
[*La mirada*]
Látex y tela
12,6 x 39,3 x 36,8 cm
Cortesía Cheim & Read, Nueva York

34. *SOFT LANDSCAPE II*, 1967
[*Paisaje blando*]
Alabastro tallado
16,5 x 36 x 25 cm
Kunstmuseum Berna

35. *UNCONSCIOUS LANDSCAPE*, 1967–68
[*Paisaje inconsciente*]
Bronce
30,4 x 55,8 x 60,9 cm
Cortesía Cheim & Read, Nueva York

36. *GERMINAL*, 1967
[*Germinal*]
Mármol
13,9 x 18,7 x 15,8 cm
Colección privada

37. *JANUS IN LEATHER JACKET*, 1968
[*Jano con chaqueta de cuero*]
Bronce
30,4 x 55,8 x 16,5 cm
Cortesía Cheim & Read, Nueva York

38. *JANUS FLEURI*, 1968
[*Jano en flor*]
Bronce, pátina dorada
25,7 x 31,7 x 21,2 cm
Cortesía Cheim & Read, Nueva York

39. *AVENZA*, 1968–69
[*Avenza*]
Látex
53,3 x 76,2 x 116,8 cm
Cortesía Cheim & Read, Nueva York

40. *FILLETTE (SWEETER VERSION)*, 1968/99
[*Niña (versión más dulce)*]
Látex sobre escayola
59,7 x 26,7 x 19,7 cm
Cortesía Cheim & Read, Nueva York

41. *CUMUL I*, 1969
[*Cúmulo I*]
Mármol blanco
56,8 x 127 x 121,9 cm
Centre Georges Pompidou, París. Musée National
d'Art Moderne/Centre de Création Industrielle

42. *FEMME PIEU*, ca. 1970
[*Mujer estaca*]
Cera y agujas de metal
8,8 x 6,3 x 15,2 cm
Colección del Museum of New Mexico
Museum of Fine Arts, Colección Lucy Lippard

UNTITLED, ca. 1970
[*Sin título*]
Pintura sobre tabla
119,4 x 149,9 cm
Colección privada

43. *FRAGILE GODDESS*, 1970
[*Diosa frágil*]
Bronce, pátina de oro
26 x 14,2 x 13,6 cm
Cortesía Cheim & Read, Nueva York

44. *THE DESTRUCTION OF THE FATHER*, 1974
[*La destrucción del padre*]
Escayola, látex, madera y tela
237,8 x 362,2 x 248,6 cm
Cortesía Cheim & Read, Nueva York

45. *MAISONS FRAGILES*, 1978
[*Casas frágiles*]
Acero, dos elementos
213,3 x 68,5 x 35,5 cm
Cortesía Cheim & Read, Nueva York

46. *FEMME COUTEAU*, 1982
[*Mujer cuchillo*]
Mármol rosa
6,9 x 38,7 x 10,1 cm
Colección Ellen Kern

47. *FEMME MAISON*, 1983
Marble
25 x 19½ x 23 inches; 63.5 x 49.5 x 58.4 cm
Courtesy Cheim & Read, New York

48. *THE CURVED HOUSE*, 1983
Marble
11⅛ x 23⅝ x 4¼ inches; 28,4 x 60 x 10,8 cm
Kunstmuseum Bern

49. *BELLY*, 1984
Bronze
4¼ x 11 x 5¼ inches; 10.7 x 27.9 x 13.3 cm
Courtesy Cheim & Read, New York

50. *SPIRAL WOMAN*, 1984
Bronze with slate disc
19 x 4 x 5½ inches; 48.3 x 10.2 x 14 cm
Courtesy Cheim & Read, New York

51. *LAIR*, 1986
Rubber
43 x 21 x 21 inches; 109.2 x 53.3 x 53.3 cm
Courtesy Cheim & Read, New York

52 and 53. *ARTICULATED LAIR*, 1986
Painted steel, rubber and stool (metal)
111 x 258 x 193 inches; 281.7 x 655.7 x 555.6 cm
The Museum of Modern Art, New York,
Gift of Lily Auchincloss and the artist in honour of
Deborah Wye (by exchange), 1993

54. *LEGS*, 1986
Rubber
123 x 2 x 2 inches; 312.4 x 5 x 5 cm
Courtesy Cheim & Read, New York

55. *UNTITLED (WITH HAND)*, 1989
Pink marble
31 x 30½ x 21 inches; 78.7 x 77.4 x 53.3 cm
Private collection

56. *NO EXIT*, 1989
Wood, painted metal and rubber
82½ x 84 x 96 inches; 209.5 x 213.3 x 243.8 cm
The Ginny Williams Family Foundation;
Collection of Ginny Williams

57 and 58. *THE PURITAN*, 1990 (Text 1947)
Suite of 8 hand colored engravings and text
26 x 39½ inches; 66 x 100.3 cm
Courtesy Cheim & Read, New York

59. *VENTOUSE*, 1990
Marble, glass and electrical light
34 x 78 x 32 inches; 86.3 x 198.1 x 81.2 cm
Courtesy Cheim & Read, New York

60. *MAMELLES*, 1991
Rubber wall relief
19 x 120 x 19 inches; 48.2 x 304.8 x 48.2 cm
Courtesy Cheim & Read, New York

61. *CELL II*, 1991
Mixed media
83 x 60 x 60 inches; 210.8 x 152.4 x 152.4 cm
Carnegie Museum of Art, Pittsburgh;
Heinz Family Fund, 1991

62 and 63. *PRECIOUS LIQUIDS*, 1992
Wood, metal, glass, alabaster, cloth, water
168 x 174 inches; 427 x 442 cm diameter
Centre Georges Pompidou, Paris. Musée National
d'Art Moderne/Centre de Création Industrielle.

64. *POIDS*, 1992
Steel, glass and metal
177 x 147 x 24¼ inches; 449.5 x 373.3 x 61.5 cm
Courtesy Galerie Karsten Greve Köln Paris Milano

65. *CELL (ARCH OF HYSTERIA)*, 1992–93
Steel, bronze, cast iron and fabric
119 x 145 x 120 inches; 302.2 x 368.3 x 304.8 cm
Centro Andaluz de Arte Contemporaneo. Junta de
Andalucia

*SPIDER, 1994
Watercolor, pencil and gouache on paper
10 x 8 inches; 25.3 x 20.3 cm
Collection John Cheim

66. Installation view, RED ROOMS, 1994

67. RED ROOM (CHILD), 1994
Mixed media
83 x 139 x 108 inches; 210.8 x 353 x 274.3 cm
Collection Musée d'Art Contemporain de
Montréal/The Musée d'Art Contemporain de Montréal
Collection

68 and 69. RED ROOM (PARENTS), 1994
Mixed media
97½ x 168 x 167 inches; 247.6 x 426.7 x 424.1 cm
Sammlung Hauser & Wirth, St. Gallen, Switzerland

70. LE DEFI IV, 1994
Painted wood, glass, mirror and mixed media
73½ x 65 x 24 inches; 186.6 x 165 x 60.9 cm
Courtesy Cheim & Read, New York

*ODE A MA MÈRE, 1995
Suite of 9 drypoint etchings
12 x 12 x 2 inches; 30.5 x 30.5 x 5.1 cm
Courtesy Cheim & Read, New York

71. COUPLE III, 1997
Fabric, leather and steel arm brace
28 x 39 x 71 inches; 71.1 x 99 x 180.3 cm
Private collection

72. SPIDER, 1997
Steel and mixed media
175 x 262 x 204 inches; 444.5 x 665.4 x 518.1 cm
Courtesy Cheim & Read, New York

73–77. PASSAGE DANGEREUX, 1997
Mixed media
104 x 140 x 345 inches; 264.1 x 355.6 x 876.3 cm
Sammlung Hauser & Wirth, St. Gallen, Switzerland

78. CELL VII, 1998
Mixed media
81½ x 87 x 83 inches; 207 x 220.9 x 210.8 cm
Courtesy Cheim & Read, New York

79 and 80. UNTITLED, 1998
Fabric and steel
10 x 25½ x 18 inches; 25.3 x 64.7 x 45.7 cm
Daros Collection, Switzerland

81. UNTITLED (CHAIR AND THREE
MIRRORS), 1998
Steel and mirrors
9 x 13 x 10½ inches; 22.8 x 33 x 26.6 cm
Private collection. Courtesy Galerie Karsten Greve
Köln Paris Milano

82. UNTITLED (CHAIR), 1998
Steel and glass
7½ x 8 x 10 inches; 19 x 20.3 x 25.3 cm
Private collection. Courtesy Galerie Karsten Greve
Köln Paris Milano)

83. CELL (TWELVE OVAL MIRRORS), 1998
Steel, wood and 12 oval pivoting mirrors
90 x 96 x 132 inches; 228.5 x 243.8 x 335.2 cm
Courtesy Cheim & Read, New York

84. THE MIRROR, 1998
Cast and polished aluminum
94 x 34½ x 44 inches; 238.7 x 87.6 x 111.7 cm
Courtesy Cheim & Read, New York

85. UNTITLED, 1998
8 holograms
11 x 14 inches; 27.9 x 35.5 cm
Collection of the artist. Courtesy C Project, Miami
Beach, Florida. (Exhibition set underwritten by Guy
and Nora Lee Barton)

86. TOPIARY III, 1999
Steel, fabric, wood and beads
27 x 20 x 21 inches; 68.6 x 50.8 x 53.3 cm
Private collection. Courtesy Galerie Karsten Greve
Köln Paris Milano

Chronology

I need my memories. They are my documents. I keep watch over them. They are my privacy...
If you are going to them [your memories], you are wasting time. Nostalgia is not productive.
If they come to you, they are the seeds for sculpture.

LOUISE BOURGEOIS

ca. 1902
Emile Fauriaux introduces his sister Joséphine to landscape architect Louis Bourgeois. Emile Fauriaux and Bourgeois have become friends through their interest in aviation and gliding.

1904
Henriette Marie Louise Bourgeois is born to Joséphine Fauriaux and Louis Bourgeois on March 4.

1905
Joséphine Valerie Fauriaux marries Louis Isadore Bourgeois in Paris. They live at 206 Boulevard Saint-Germain in Paris. At 212 Boulevard Saint-Germain, Joséphine's mother runs a tapestry gallery called *Maison Fauriaux* that deals in repairing and selling Medieval and Renaissance tapestries (Beauvais, Gobelins, Aubusson) and antiques. Louis Bourgeois begins to work with Joséphine and her mother at the *Maison Fauriaux*.

1910
Louis Bourgeois takes over the Fauriaux business and moves the tapestry gallery from 212 Boulevard Saint-Germain to 174 Boulevard Saint-Germain, as *Maison Louis Bourgeois*. In the 1990s, Louise Bourgeois will incorporate the metal sign that hung outside of the gallery, *Aux Vieilles Tapisseries*, into the sculpture *Cell (Choisy)* (1990–93). Fragments of tapestry similar to those used in her parents' atelier will also be incorporated into *Spider* (1997), *Passage Dangereux* (1997) and *Cell VIII* (1998).

1911
Louise Joséphine Bourgeois is born in Paris on December 25. She resembles her father and will become his favorite offspring. The family rents an apartment at 172 Boulevard Saint-Germain on the fourth floor, above the Café de Flore.

1912
The Bourgeois family rents a house in Choisy-le-Roi outside of Paris at 4 Avenue de Villeneuve-St.-Georges. Until 1917 they will live there in a large house built in the mid-19th century. Behind the house is a two-story atelier for the tapestry workers.

The Bourgeois family will leave the Choisy house in 1917 because the Seine River, which is behind the house, is not accessible enough for the tapestry workers, nor does it have the proper amount of tannin required for dyeing of tapestries. Bourgeois will incorporate a marble replica of the Choisy home in *Cell (Choisy)* (1990–1993) and in *Cell (Choisy Two)* (1995). A bronze version of the house will also appear in *Cell VII* (1998).

1913
Pierre Joseph Alexandre, Bourgeois' brother, is born on January 24.

1915–1918
Louis Bourgeois and his brother Desiré are mobilized to fight in World War I. As a result of the war, the Bourgeois family moves to Aubusson. Desiré's wife Madeleine, and her children Jacques and Maurice, accompany them. Desiré is killed during the first week of the war.

FIGURE 88. The Bourgeois family in Choisy-le-Roi, France, ca. 1915

1919

In May, the Bourgeois family acquires a property in Antony at 11 Avenue de la Division Leclerc. The property includes a house, a rear atelier, a hothouse and gardens that are separated by the banks of the Bièvre River, whose tannin is needed for the dyeing of the tapestries.

1920

Louise, Pierre, and Henriette attend school in Antony.

1921–1927

Bourgeois attends the Collège Sévigné and the Lycée Fénelon in Paris. Her brother Pierre goes to the Lycée Lakanal in Sceaux. It is en route to the Lycée Lakanal that Bourgeois discovers the house built by the engineer François Hennebique (1842–1921) for his family. The eccentric structure, with its turret, utilizes the possibilities of reinforced concrete that Hennebique was known for.

At the age of twelve, Bourgeois is asked to use her drawing skills to help out in the tapestry workshop when Monsieur Gounod, from the Gobelins, does not show up for work. She helps out by drawing in the sections of the missing parts that are to be restored. Since it was often the bottoms of the tapestries that were in the worst state of disrepair, Bourgeois became an expert at drawing legs and feet. This imagery would reoccur throughout her entire body of work.

1921

Just after World War I, Bourgeois' mother contracts the Spanish flu. Bourgeois' education is subsequently interrupted so that she can take care of her mother, whom she accompanies to the Hotel des Anges in Le Cannet.

1922

Sadie Gordon Richmond is hired by Louis Bourgeois to teach English to the Bourgeois children. She starts on November 16, 1922 at the Villa Marcel, Le Cannet. Sadie will then live with the Bourgeois family periodically until 1932. During this time she becomes Louis Bourgeois' mistress.

1923–1928

The Bourgeois family rents the Villa Marcel in Le Cannet. They spend the winters at Le Cannet and summers at Antony. Bourgeois attends the Lycée International in Cannes. Louise and her mother become friendly with Pierre Bonnard.

1925

Bourgeois visits the celebrated *Le Salon des Arts Décoratifs et Industriels Modernes* exposition where she sees the Pavillon de la Maitrise, the Tour des Renseignements et du Tourisme by Mallet Stevens, the Pavillon de L'Afrique Française and Le Corbusier's Pavillon de L'Esprit Nouveau. She encounters the Art Deco style for the first time, as well as the works of Frederick Kiesler and Vladimir Tatlin.

1929

Bourgeois travels to England.

From 1929 to 1932 the Bourgeois family winters in Cimiez-Nice at the Villa Pompeiana.

1930

Bourgeois continues to study English at the Berlitz School in Nice and continues her education by correspondence at the École Universelle in math, physics, and chemistry.

1931

Bourgeois visits the *Exposition Coloniale* in Paris.

1932

Bourgeois enters the Sorbonne briefly to study calculus and geometry, receiving the Baccaluréate in Philosophy from the University of Paris. Her dissertation is on Blaise Pascal and Emmanuel Kant.

Through family friends Bourgeois travels along with a medical group to the Baltic countries and Russia.

Louise's mother Joséphine dies on September 14 in Antony.

1933–1938

Bourgeois is disillusioned by the turn in mathematics towards abstraction and so begins to

FIGURE 89. Louise in Paris, ca. 1932

pursue art. Over the next several years, she studies in various artists' ateliers in Montparnasse and Montmartre. In 1934, at the suggestions of her teacher Paul Colin, she makes a second trip to Russia, this time to see the Moscow Theater and the work of the Russian Constructivists.

During this period she studies at the Académie d'Espagnat (1936–1937); the atelier of Roger Bissière at the Académie Ranson (1936–1937); at the Ecole des Beaux-Arts (1936–1938) with Devambez and Colarossi; at the Grande-Chaumière (1937–1938) with Othon Friesz in painting and Wlérick in sculpture; as well as at the Académie Julian (1938) and the Académie Scandinavie (1938) with Charles Despiau, who was Auguste Rodin's assistant.

In the years 1936–1938, Bourgeois is an assistant, or *massière*, at the Académie de la Grande-Chaumière in the studio of Yves Brayer. Her role is to hire the models, who are mostly prostitutes. She also studies under Marcel Gromaire, André Lhote, and Fernand Léger (1938). It is during this time that Léger suggests that Bourgeois' sensibility leans more toward the three-dimensional.

Bourgeois exhibits a painting at the Salon des Indépendants and the Salon des Artistes Français.

1936
Bourgeois rents her first apartment at 31 rue de Seine. From May 1937 through February 1938, André Breton will open and direct the gallery Gradiva in the same building. He will exhibit the works of the Surrealists such as Hans Arp, Hans Bellmer, Giorgio de Chirico, Salvador Dalí, Marcel Duchamp, Alberto Giacometti, Stanley William Hayter, Joan Miró, Pablo Picasso, Man Ray, and Yves Tanguy, among others. The building also houses the Théatre de l'Académie Raymond Duncan as well as a prosthesis maker named M. Perrot. Later in her career, Bourgeois will incorporate the prostheses of M. Perrot in pieces such as *Henriette* (1985), *Couple II* (1996), *Couple III* (1997), and *Passage Dangereux* (1997).

Bourgeois exhibits at the Galerie de Paris in the *Exposition de L'Atelier de la Grande Chaumière* (June 23 to June 30).

1937–1938
Bourgeois moves to a first-floor apartment at 18 Rue Mazarine. She studies art history at L'Ecole du Louvre in order to become a fully certified docent at the Louvre. She exhibits with the Ranson group at Galerie Jean Dufresse in an exhibition called *Le Groupe 1938–1939*.

1938
Bourgeois partitions off part of her father's space at 174 Boulevard Saint-Germain to open up her own art gallery dealing in prints and paintings by Delacroix, Matisse, Redon, Valadon, and Bonnard. There she meets Robert Goldwater, an American art historian who is in Paris doing further research on his doctoral thesis "Primitivism in Modern Painting."

Robert Goldwater proposes to Bourgeois, and they marry on September 12 in Paris at the Église Saint-Sulpice.

1938–1939
Bourgeois moves to New York City with Robert Goldwater. They live at 63 Park Avenue. Goldwater has been an instructor in art history at New York University since 1924. He also teaches at Queens College from 1938 until 1957. In 1957 he is hired as a Professor of Art History at the Institute of Fine Arts, New York University. He is the editor of the *Magazine of Art* from 1947–1953, and from 1957–1963 is the Director of the Museum of Primitive Art in New York City.

1939–1945
Bourgeois enrolls at the Art Students League in New York City, studying with Vaclav Vytlacil. She begins making prints.

Throughout the 1940s and 1950s, because of Robert Goldwater's position as a professor of art history and editor, Bourgeois circulates within a world of art historians that includes such figures as Alfred Barr, René D'Harnoncourt, Walter Friedlander, Lloyd Goodrich, Clement Greenberg, Belle Krasne, Dwight McDonald, Erwin Panofsky, Philip Rahv, John Rewald, Michel Seuphor, Meyer Shapiro, James Johnson Sweeney, David Sylvester, and Lionel Trilling.

Bourgeois and Goldwater also socialize with gallery owners Leo Castelli, Charles Egan, Peggy Guggenheim,

FIGURE 90. Portrait of Louise by Brassaï at the Académie de la Grande-Chaumière, Paris, 1934

Sidney Janis, Pierre Matisse, Betty Parsons, Ellie Poindexter, Lou Pollack, and Curt Valentine, as well as American artists John Cage, Ralston Crawford, Stuart Davis, Willem de Kooning, Franz Kline, Loren McIver, Louise Nevelson, Maurice Prendergast, Hans Richter, and Mark Rothko. European artists such as André Breton, Marcel Duchamp, Max Ernst, Fernand Léger, André Masson, Piet Mondrian, and Yves Tanguy are also in New York City after World War II. Along with these artists, art historians, and gallery owners, Louise and Robert socialize with architects such as Le Corbusier, Edgar Kaufman, Philip Johnson, José Luis Sert, and Paul Nelson. Through Le Corbusier Louise becomes friends with Matta and Nemecio Antunez, both of whom worked for Le Corbusier.

1939
Louise and Robert move to 333 East 41st Street, where they will live for two years. They return to France to arrange for the adoption of Michel Olivier, an orphan, who was born in Margaux near Bordeaux in 1936.

Bourgeois exhibits in the United States for the first time in a print exhibition at the Brooklyn Museum.

1940
Jean-Louis Bourgeois is born to Louise Bourgeois and Robert Goldwater on July 4.

1941
On July 30, the Bourgeois family puts a deposit down to rent 142 East 18th Street. The building is called "Stuyvesant Folly" and is the oldest apartment house in New York City. The family also acquires a house in Easton, Connecticut.

Alain Matthew Clement, Louise and Robert's second son, is born on November 12.

1943
Louise Bourgeois participates by contributing prints to an exhibition under the auspices of Artists for Victory at the Metropolitan Museum of Art.

Bourgeois receives an honorary award for her participation in the exhibition *The Arts in Therapy* at the Museum of Modern Art in New York. She exhibits a tapestry based on the work of Torres Garcia.

1945
Bourgeois has her first solo show, *Paintings by Louise Bourgeois*. The exhibition opens on June 4 at the Bertha Schaefer Gallery, New York City. Included in the group of twelve canvases are *Peaceable Kingdom, Connecticutiana, Natural History,* and *Mr. Follet.*

She curates *Documents, France 1940–1944: Art-Literature-Press of the French Underground* at the Norlyst Gallery (June 4 to 19) with the help of Marcel Duchamp. The exhibition includes underground anti-Nazi press by *Défense de la France, Résistance* and *Le Populaire;* art by Bonnard, Picasso, and Dubuffet; poetry by Louis Aragon, and Jean Cassou; and prose by Jean-Paul Sartre, André Gide, and Gertrude Stein.

Bourgeois is included in a group show of work by women artists called *The Women* (June 12 to July 7) at Peggy Guggenheim's Art of This Century Gallery in New York. Also included in the show are Leonora Carrington, Fanny Hillsmith, Lee Krasner, Loren MacIver, Alice Paalen, Irene Rice Pereria, Kay Sage, Hedda Stern, Pegeen Vail, and Catherine Yarrow.

Guggenheim's gallery opened in 1942 and was designed by architect and set designer Frederick Kiesler. Bourgeois spends time with Kiesler and Duchamp during this period.

Bourgeois exhibits for the first time at the Whitney Museum of American Art in the *Annual of Painting*. The work shown is *Painting on Red and White* which depicts a self-portrait hidden within a bouquet of flowers. She will also be included in the Annuals of 1946, 1947, 1948, 1951, and 1952.

1946
Bourgeois begins to learn about printmaking at Stanley William Hayter's Atelier 17. Other members of the workshop are Nemecio Antunez, Joan Miró, Yves Tanguy, Ruthven Todd, and Le Corbusier. Le Corbusier is in New York because his schema has been accepted as the working model for what will become the United Nations building. Le Corbusier stays at the Grosvenor Hotel on Fifth Avenue, and comes to dinner at Louise and Robert's home on November 12. He opens dozens of oysters in the sink and talks about Claude-Nicholas Ledoux. Bourgeois' diary entry dated December 3, 1946,

FIGURE 91. Louise Bourgeois and Joan Miró in New York in 1947

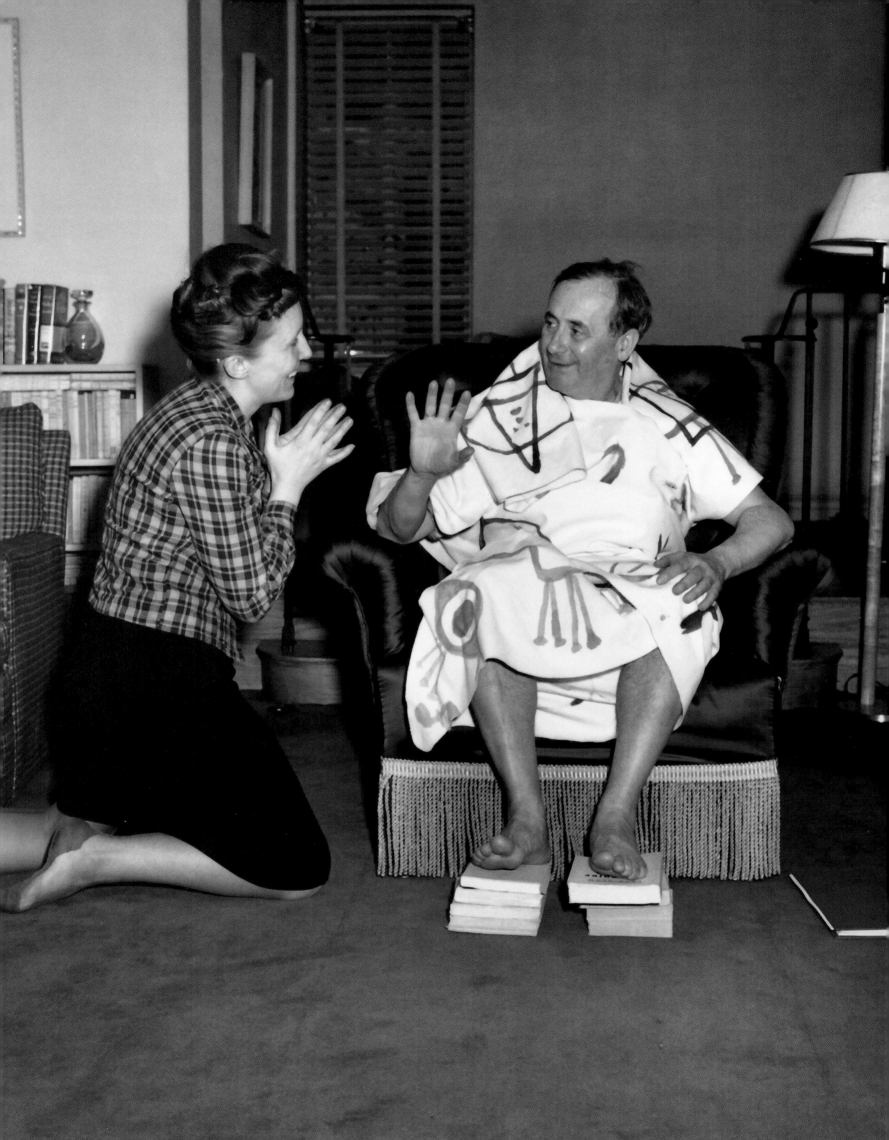

contains drawings of Le Corbusier prints. Bourgeois helps to arrange the printing of Le Corbusier's drypoints and takes them to the Buchholz Gallery. She studies his writings: "City of Tomorrow," "Urbanism," "Vers une Architecture," and "La Ville Radieuse 1933." Le Corbusier gives Bourgeois an original drawing for her own collection. Le Corbusier and Alexander Calder introduce her to José Luis Sert.

1947

Bourgeois completes the suite of nine engravings accompanied by parables, *He Disappeared Into Complete Silence,* that she began at Atelier 17. She finishes the project on a press installed in her home at 142 East 18th Street with the help of Kenneth Kilstrom. Marius Bewley, who worked at Peggy Guggenheim's gallery, writes the introduction for the portfolio.

Bourgeois exhibits seventeen paintings at Norlyst Gallery at 59 West 56th Street in New York from October 28 to November 8, 1947. The paintings shown are *Ceremony; Red Night; Portrait; Game of Bilboquet; Conversation Piece; Jeffersonian Courthouse; Regrettable Incident in the Louvre Palace; Processed Flowers; Southern Scene; Two Figures from a Cotton Mill District; One Way Traffic; It is Six Fifteen, Trilogue; Pole of Joy; Attentive Figures; Roof Song; Child Asleep in a Skein of Wool.* The announcement for the exhibition depicts a woman's body whose head and torso are replaced by a house. This suite of images is later called *Femme Maison.*

1949

Bourgeois' sculptural debut, *Louise Bourgeois, Recent Work 1947–1949: Seventeen Standing Figures in Wood,* takes place at the Peridot Gallery in New York City (October 3 to October 29). Exhibited are *The Tomb of a Young Person; Persistent Antagonism; Portrait of C.Y.; Friendly Evidence; Woman in the Shape of a Shuttle; Ship Figure; New York City Doorway With Pillars; Attentive Figures; Pillars; Rear Façade; Lettre à un frère; Woman Carrying Packages; Wedges Forms; Captains' Walk on Irving Place Building; Weedy Shore; Coordinates; The Blind Vigils.* This show takes place at the invitation of gallery director Louis Pollack and his friend Arthur Drexler, who would later become the Director of the Department of Architecture and Design at the Museum of Modern Art.

Bourgeois is included in *13th Annual Exhibition of the American Abstract Artists* at the Riverside Museum in New York City. Her work will also be shown there in 1954 and 1956.

1950

Bourgeois has a second exhibition, *Louise Bourgeois: Sculptures,* at the Peridot Gallery (October 2 to 28). The fifteen sculptures shown are titled on the announcement: *Figure qui apporte du pain; Figure regardant une maison; Figures qui supportent un linteau; Figure qui s'appuie contre une porte; Figure qui entre dans une pièce; Statue pour une maison vide; Deux figures qui portent un objet; Une femme gravit les marches d'un jardin; Figures qui attendent; Figures qui se parlent sans se voir; Figure endormie; Figure pour une niche; Figure quittant sa Maison; Figure de plein vent; Figure emportant sa maison.*

1950–51

Robert Goldwater receives a Fulbright Scholarship (to conduct research in France) in 1950. The Bourgeois family returns briefly to France in 1951 and lives in Antony. They travel to London, where Bourgeois meets Francis Bacon. They eventually rent a house at 77 Rue Daguerre in Paris, where Bourgeois will have a studio until 1955.

1951

Louis Bourgeois passes away on April 9. Bourgeois is devastated by her father's death as well as with having to deal with the closing of the family business.

Alfred Barr acquires *Sleeping Figure* (1950) from the Peridot Gallery for the Museum of Modern Art in New York City.

1952

Bourgeois designs the sets for *The Bridegroom of the Moon,* a dance performance by Erick Hawkins–the husband of Martha Graham–which takes place at Hunter Playhouse in New York on January 19.

FIGURE 92. Louise Bourgeois in the studio of her apartment at 142 East 18 Street, New York, in 1946

1953

Bourgeois has her third solo show at the Peridot Gallery. It is called *Louise Bourgeois: Drawings for Sculpture and Sculpture* (March 30 to April 25) and includes the work *Forêt (Night Garden)*. Bourgeois also participates in group shows at Stable Gallery and Poindexter Gallery and exhibits in the Annuals of the Whitney Museum of American Art from 1953 to 1957.

On June 17, Louise, Robert, and the children depart for Europe. They visit Bourges, Aubusson, Aix, Magagnose, and the caves at Lascaux. Bourgeois' cavelike *Lairs* of the 1960s are inspired by Lascaux. The family also goes to Italy and visits Peggy Guggenheim and Philip Johnson.

During the summers of 1955, 1957, and 1959 the family returns to Paris.

1955

On October 4, Louise Bourgeois becomes an American citizen.

1956

The Whitney Museum of American Art acquires the sculpture *One and Others* (1955).

1958

The building Robert and Louise have lived in since 1941, Stuyvesant Folly, is sold and designated to be demolished. The family moves to 435 West 22nd Street.

Bourgeois opens Erasmus Books and Prints in an effort to bring money to the family. The first location is on 10th Street but it is moved later to 922 Madison Avenue at 73rd Street.

1959

Bourgeois exhibits eleven wood personages in the Festival of Contemporary Arts at The Andrew Dickson White Art Museum of Cornell University, Ithaca, New York (April 5 to 25).

1960

Bourgeois teaches in the public school system in Great Neck, New York.

Her work is included in the Annuals of 1960 and 1962 at the Whitney Museum of American Art in New York.

Galerie Claude Bernard in Paris organizes *Aspects de la sculpture Américaine* (September 30 to October 31). The artists included are Harry Bertoia, Louise Bourgeois, John Chamberlain, Herbert Ferber, Naum Gabo, Sidney Geist, David Hare, Frederick Kiesler, Gabriel Kohn, Ibram Lassaw, Jacques Lipschitz, Seymour Lipton, Louise Nevelson, Isamu Noguchi, José de Rivera, James Rivera, James Rosati, Theodore Rozack, David Smith, Georges Spaventa, and Richard Stankiewitz.

Bourgeois' brother Pierre dies.

1961

Bourgeois is accepted into the graduate School of Arts and Sciences at New York University. She enrolls in "The Evolution of French Theater from Renaissance to Symbolism" and "Main Currents of 15th Century French Painting" among other courses.

1962

The Bourgeois family moves to 347 West 20th Street, where Louise Bourgeois still lives today.

1963

Bourgeois teaches at Brooklyn College.

1964

After eleven years without a solo show, Bourgeois exhibits a new body of work at the Stable Gallery (January 7 to 30), installed by Arthur Drexler. Bourgeois exhibits *Labyrinthine Tower, Double Negative, Fée Couturière, Inner Ear, Lair,* and *Clutching*. This show coincides with *Recent Drawings by Louise Bourgeois* at the Rose Fried Gallery in New York City (January 14 to 29).

1965

Bourgeois exhibits the bronze *Spring* at the Musée Rodin's and the Museum of Modern Art's exhibition *Les Etats-Unis: Sculpture du XX Siècle,* which is part of the series *American sculpture in Paris* held at the Musée Rodin and at the chapel which once served as Rodin's studio. The show is curated by René D'Harnoncourt (Director of the Museum of Modern Art) and Frank O'Hara (Associate Curator of Painting and Sculpture). The exhibition includes works by William Zorach, Elie

FIGURE 93. Louise and Robert at the opening of the Franz Kline exhibition at the Sidney Janis Gallery, New York, March 7, 1960

Nadelman, Gaston Lachaise, and other contemporary artists.

1966
Bourgeois spends the summer in Europe travelling to Spain and Greece. In Barcelona she visits the Gaudí buildings. In September she is included in the exhibition *Eccentric Abstraction* organized by Lucy Lippard at the Fischbach Gallery in New York. Her work is shown with a younger generation of artists, such as Eva Hesse and Bruce Nauman.

1967–1968
Bourgeois makes her first trip to Pietrasanta, Italy, to work in marble and bronze. She will continue to return regularly to Pietrasanta through 1972.

Bourgeois' *Sleep II* (1967) is shown at the Whitney Museum of American Art's *Annual Exhibition: Sculpture.*

Louise and Robert travel to Nigeria with Robert Farris Thompson and Roy Seiber to an international symposium on African Art.

1970
Bourgeois begins her involvement with the feminist movement, taking part in demonstrations, benefits, panels, and exhibitions.

Her work is shown at the Whitney Museum of American Art's Annuals of 1970 and 1973.

Bourgeois is included in the exhibition *L'Art vivant aux Etats-Unis* at the Fondation Maeght in St. Paul de Vence (July 16 to September 30).

1973
The marble floor piece *Number Seventy-Two (The No March)* is exhibited in the 1973 Whitney Museum of American Art's Biennial. It is subsequently acquired by Storm King Art Center in Mountainville, New York.

The Musée National d'Art Moderne in Paris acquires *Cumul I* (1969). The sculpture is transferred to the Centre Georges Pompidou in 1976.

Bourgeois designs the sets, costumes, and poster for the Women's Inter Art Center's production of Tennessee Williams' *This Property is Condemned* and

August Strindberg's *The Stronger.* Both are produced and directed by Alice Rubinstein.

She receives an artist's grant from the National Endowment for the Arts.

Her husband Robert Goldwater dies on March 26th.

1974
Bourgeois has a solo show at 112 Greene Street (December 14 to December 26). It includes *Eye to Eye, Colonnata, Baroque,* hanging *Januses* in bronze, *Labyrinthine Tower,* and *The Destruction of the Father.*

Bourgeois begins teaching at the School of Visual Arts in New York City where she will teach until 1977. She also teaches at Columbia University, Cooper Union, and Goddard College in Vermont, and has visiting artist assignments at Pratt Institute, the Philadelphia College of Art, Woodstock Artists Association, Rutgers University, New York Studio School, and Yale University.

1975
Lynn Blumenthal and Kate Horsfield produce a videotaped interview with Louise Bourgeois for the Video Data Bank.

1976
Bourgeois is featured in *200 Years of American Sculpture at the Whitney Museum of American Art* (March 16 to September 26). She exhibits *The Blind Leading The Blind.*

1977
Bourgeois receives an Honorary Doctor of Fine Arts degree from Yale University.

1978
Bourgeois exhibits new work in a solo show that takes place at the Hamilton Gallery of Contemporary Art in New York City (September 16 to October 21). In conjunction with her exhibition of the painted wood, latex, and fabric piece *Confrontation* (1978), she presents the performance *A Banquet: A Fashion Show of Body Parts.* One of the performers, Suzanne Cooper, sings "She Abandoned Me" – a song written by Bourgeois that makes reference to Bourgeois' mother.

Robbi Tillison and art historian Gert Schiff also participate in the performance. Museum people William Lieberman, Ann d'Harnoncourt, and Patrice Marandel; art writers Peter Frank and Paul Gardner; as well as collectors Dorothy and Herbert Vogel, and Lita Hornick are members of the audience.

Louise Bourgeois: Triangles: New Sculpture and Drawings, 1978 is shown at Xavier Fourcade Gallery (September 26 to October 21). Included in the show are *Maisons Fragiles, Lair of Seven, Radar,* and *Structures I–V.*

The University of California at Berkeley Art Museum mounts *Louise Bourgeois: Matrix / Berkeley 17* (December to February, 1979) in which *Maisons Fragiles* is shown.

The Blind Leading the Blind (1947–1949) is purchased by the Detroit Institute of Art.

1979

In September, Xavier Fourcade Gallery exhibits thirty-three wood personages and the recent sculpture *Partial Recall* (1979) in *Louise Bourgeois, Sculpture 1941–1953. Plus One New Piece* (September 18 to October 13).

1980

Bourgeois travels to New Orleans to receive the Award for Outstanding Achievement in the Visual Arts at the National Women's Caucus for Art conference.

Bourgeois acquires her Brooklyn studio at 475 Dean Street on May 10. Originally a garment factory, it is a poured concrete building reminiscent of the buildings designed by architect August Perret. She inherits the contents (e.g., sewing machines, furniture, doors, and shelving) and incorporates some of these into her future work. The architectural space of the studio is like a labyrinth, with five entrances and a spiral staircase with metal submarine stairs that lead to the basement. The studio's enormous size allows her to begin working on an unprecedented scale.

Jerry Gorovoy curates *10 Abstract Sculptures: American and European 1940–1980* (March 18 to April 19) at the Max Hutchinson Gallery in New York. The exhibition includes works by Ronald Bladen, Alexander Calder, Eduardo Chillida, Charles Ginnever, Joan Miró, Mark di Suvero, George Sugarman, James Surls, and Alan Saret. From the exhibition, James Mollison of the

Australian National Gallery in Canberra acquires Bourgeois' *C.O.Y.O.T.E.* (1947–48), a variant of *The Blind Leading the Blind*. Renamed *C.O.Y.O.T.E.* after being repainted in 1979 in a lurid flesh pink, the new title stands for *Call Off Your Old Tired Ethics* and is dedicated to Margo St. James, the leader of the group C.O.Y.O.T.E.

Jerry Gorovoy organizes *The Iconography of Louise Bourgeois* (September 6 to October 11) at Max Hutchinson Gallery in New York City. The exhibition includes more than thirty early paintings, including *Reparation, Connecticutiana, Fallen Woman, Red Room, Roof Song,* and four called *Femme Maison*. Also on view are over thirty-five drawings from 1942–1974 as well as twelve prints from the late 1940s.

Bourgeois' exhibition at Xavier Fourcade Gallery in New York (September 20 to October 25), *Louise Bourgeois Sculpture: The Middle Years 1955–1970* is made up of ten marbles (including *Eye to Eye, Colonnata, Baroque, Sleep II, Clamart, Femme Couteau, Systems, Fountain*); three bronzes (*Torso, Self Portrait,* and *Janus*), and the granite version of *Trani Episode.*

Bourgeois' older sister, Henriette, dies on July 9.

1981

Louise Bourgeois acquires an abandoned house ca. 1860 in Staten Island for her son Michel. Michel never occupies the house. Bourgeois keeps it empty, turning it into a sculpture called *Maison Vide*. *Maison Vide* was also the title for one of Bourgeois' *Personnages* from the 1940s.

Patrice Marandel organizes the exhibition *Louise Bourgeois: Femme Maison* for the Renaissance Society at the University of Chicago (May 3 to June 6).

Bourgeois returns to Italy with her assistant Jerry Gorovoy during the summer. In Carrara, she creates more than twenty new marbles. Bourgeois also drapes and pins seams on a white T-shirt owned by Jerry Gorovoy and creates a figure shrouded in drapery which is gessoed for rigidity. On the top of the figure she places a geometric shape representing a house. This form becomes the model for the white marble *Femme Maison*.

Bourgeois also conceives a *Femme Maison* in black colonnata marble. It combines the long house shape of her Easton home with a cluster of black bulbous cumul forms reminiscent of her works of the 1960s, and the house on the "hill" seen in her early paintings. Bourgeois and Gorovoy also visit the artist Gonzales Fonseca, who has stored plasters that Bourgeois had left in Italy fourteen years ago. Rediscovering *Labyrinthine Tower*, *Portrait of Robert*, *Clutching*, and *Seven Mounds*, Bourgeois begins to translate them into marble.

1982
Bourgeois' retrospective at the Museum of Modern Art in New York opens on November 3 and runs until February 8, 1983. The exhibition, curated by Deborah Wye and Alicia Legg, is the first retrospective given to a woman artist at MoMA. The show travels to the Contemporary Arts Museum in Houston (March 12 to May 8, 1983), the Museum of Contemporary Art in Chicago (September 3 to October 30, 1983), and the Akron Art Museum in Ohio (November 2, 1983 to January 5, 1984).

Bourgeois makes a slide presentation for the exhibition recounting the story of her early family life, titled *Partial Recall*.

Bourgeois Truth, an exhibition of sculpture and drawings, is shown at the Robert Miller Gallery (November 23 to December 31). Bourgeois will exhibit regularly at the Robert Miller Gallery through the '80s and '90s.

1983
Bourgeois travels to Tangier, Morocco to teach at the summer program of the School of Visual Arts in New York City.

Bourgeois is elected a Member of the American Academy and the Institute of Arts and Letters in New York City, and receives an Honorary Doctor of Fine Arts Degree from the Massachusetts College of Art in Boston.

On December 5, Jack Lang, the French Minister of Culture, awards the distinction of Officier de L'Ordre des Arts et des Lettres to Bourgeois.

1984
William Rubin includes *Pregnant Woman* (1947–49) in his exhibition *Primitivism in XXth Century Art* at the Museum of Modern Art in New York (September 19, 1984 to January 15, 1985).

1985
Maeght-Lelong in Paris exhibits *Louise Bourgeois: Retrospective 1947–1984* (February to March), which then travels to Maeght-Lelong in Zurich (April and May).

The Serpentine Gallery in London exhibits *Louise Bourgeois,* organized by Stuart Morgan (May 18 to June 23).

1987
The Taft Museum in Cincinnati puts on the exhibition *Louise Bourgeois* (May 5 to June 28), which then travels to The Art Museum at Florida International University in Miami (October 23 to January 18), the Laguna Gloria Art Museum in Austin (July 1 to August 28, 1988), the Gallery of Art at Washington University in St. Louis (September 18 to October 30, 1988), and the Everson Museum of Art in Syracuse, New York (September 27 to November 26, 1989).

1988
The Museum Overholland in Amsterdam puts on an extensive exhibition of drawings (approximately 170) in *Louise Bourgeois: Works on Paper 1939–1988* (October 22 to December 31).

In October, Louise and Jerry Gorovoy travel again to Carrara, Italy. Bourgeois begins a series of works in pink marble with inscriptions that wrap around the rough-hewn marble bases. *Untitled (With Hand)* is inscribed with "I Love You"; *Untitled (With Hands)* is inscribed with "We Love You"; *Untitled (With Foot)* is inscribed "Do You Love Me?"

1989
In *Louise Bourgeois: Progressions and Regressions* (March 28 to April 22), Galerie Lelong in New York exhibits the metal-and-wood sculpture *Clouds and Caverns* (1982–1989); an alabaster and electric light version of *Le Trani Episode* (1989); *Untitled No. 7* (1989); and the mixed-media pieces *Cells: No Escape* (1989) and *No Exit* (1989).

The Centre Georges Pompidou in Paris exhibits *Articulated Lair* (1986) and *Henriette* (1985) in the

FIGURE 96. Louise Bourgeois inside *Articulated Lair,* 1986

exhibition *Magiciens de la Terre* (May 16 to August 15) at the Grande Halle de La Villette.

Henry Geldzahler curates *Louise Bourgeois: Works from the Sixties* at the Dia Art Foundation in Bridgehampton, New York (May 25 to June 25).

Bourgeois participates in *El Surrealismo entre Viejo y Nuevo Mundo* curated by Juan Manuel Bonet at the Centro Atlantico de Arte Moderno in Las Palmas de Gran Canaria, Spain (December 1989 to January 1990). It travels to the Fundación Cultural Mapfre Vida in Madrid (February to April, 1990).

Bourgeois has her first European retrospective, *Louise Bourgeois: A Retrospective Exhibition*, at the Frankfurter Kunstverein (December 2 to January 28). Organized by Peter Weiermair, it is accompanied by a major publication. The show travels to the Städtische Galerie im Lenbachhaus in Munich (February 14 to March 25, 1990); the Musée d'Art Contemporain in Lyon (July 5 to August 20, 1990); the Fundación Tapies in Barcelona (November 6 to January 6, 1991); the Kunstmuseum in Bern (March 7 to May 5, 1991); and the Kröller-Muller Museum in Otterlo (May 25 to July 8, 1991).

Louise and Jerry Gorovoy attend the opening at the Frankfurter Kunstverein on December 12th. They then travel to Carrara where Bourgeois continues working in marble.

1990

Bourgeois is honored as a MacDowell Medalist by the MacDowell Colony in New Hampshire, and she receives *The Sculpture Center Award for Distinction in Sculpture 1990* from The Sculpture Center in New York.

Her son Michel passes away.

1991

Bourgeois participates in the exhibition *Pulsió* at the Fundación Caixa de Pensions in Barcelona (May 23 to July 14).

The large piece *Twosome*, 1991, is shown in the exhibition *Dislocations* organized by Robert Storr at the Museum of Modern Art in New York (October 16 to January 7, 1992). The doors and windows on the cylindrical oil tanks are derived from the Bourgeois house in Easton, Connecticut.

Bourgeois exhibits six *Cells (Cell I–Cell VI)* at the Carnegie International in Pittsburgh (October 19 to February 16, 1992). The exhibition is organized by Lynne Cooke and Mark Francis.

Bourgeois is the first recipient of the Lifetime Achievement Award from the International Sculpture Center in Washington, D.C.

Bourgeois is awarded the Grand Prix in sculpture by the French Ministry of Culture.

1992

The National Gallery of Art in Washington, D.C., acquires *Spring* (1948), *Mortise* (1950), and *Untitled* (1952) for its permanent collection.

Bourgeois exhibits *Precious Liquids* at Documenta IX (June 13 to September 20). *Precious Liquids* is subsequently purchased by the Centre Georges Pompidou in Paris.

The Solomon R. Guggenheim Museum in New York City inaugurates its new SoHo space with the exhibition *From Brancusi to Bourgeois: Aspects of the Guggenheim Collection* (July 1 to August 27) where Bourgeois' works are paired with works by Joseph Beuys. Simultaneously, the Guggenheim Museum uptown shows *Masterpieces From the Guggenheim Collection* (June 28 to August 27), with *Dagger Child* (1947–49), *Femme Volage* (1951), *Fée Couturière* (1963), *Rabbit* (1970), *Confrontation* (1978), *Le Défi* (1991), *Cell V* (1991), and ten drawings.

Bourgeois' work is chosen as the inaugural exhition of Galerie Karsten Greve in Paris (October 24, 1992 to January 13, 1993). She exhibits a series of sculptures called *Poids*.

Bourgeois presents an installation at the Fabric Workshop in Philadelphia titled *She Lost It*. It includes a performance piece (December 5) which incorporates the wrapping of a 5½-meter-long silk-screened text "A Man and Woman Lived Together."

Peter Blum Editions publishes *Homely Girl, A Life*, a collaboration between Arthur Miller and Louise Bourgeois. His text on a blind girl who finds love and Bourgeois' etchings of images of a broken tree branch that regenerates were combined with a set of medical plates of diseased eyes.

1993

Bourgeois represents the United States at the American Pavilion of the Venice Biennale (June 9 to October 10). An expanded version of the exhibition, *The Locus of Memory*, organized by Charlotta Kotik of the Brooklyn Museum, opens at the Brooklyn Museum of Art (April 22 to July 31, 1994), and travels to The Corcoran Gallery of Art, Washington, D.C. (September 23, 1994 to January 15, 1995); the Galerie Rudolfinum in Prague (March 15 to May 28, 1995); the Musée d'Art Moderne de la Ville de Paris (June 23 to October 8, 1995), the Deichtorhallen in Hamburg (January 18 to March 17, 1996), and the Musée d'Art Contemporain de Montréal (April 25 to September 22, 1996).

The Venice Biennale exhibition consists of recent works of Bourgeois' from the 1980s and 1990s, including a new series of *Cells* that are made of wire-mesh cages. These are a departure from the *Cells* constructed out of closed wooden doors exhibited at the 1991 Carnegie International. This series includes *Cell (Choisy)* (1990–1993). Carved out of pink marble, the Choisy house is transformed into flesh. Hovering above it is a steel guillotine.

Bourgeois exhibits the first large-scale spider at the Brooklyn Museum. Made out of steel, *Spider* (1994) is shown at a 1996 exhibition of Bourgeois' work at Galería Soledad Lorenzo in Madrid and is then acquired by the Museo Nacional Centro de Arte Reina Sofía in Madrid.

Bourgeois exhibits *Cell (You Better Grow Up)* (1993) at the Tony Garnier Hall at the IIème Biennale d'art contemporain in Lyon (September 3 to October). The exhibition is organized by Thierry Prat, Thierry Raspail, and Marc Dachy.

The City of Chicago, the Art Institute of Chicago and Hull House select Bourgeois as the artist to make a sculpture park in honor of Jane Addams, the social and political activist who founded Hull House. Hull House is an educational institution for immigrants, particularly for women and children. In collaboration with Mary Jane Jacob and the architect Miriam Busevich, Bourgeois conceives six black granite sculptures consisting of hand poses on plinths.

Bourgeois receives an Honorary Doctorate in Fine Arts from Pratt Institute in Brooklyn.

Mayor David Dinkins of New York City presents Bourgeois with the "Mayor's Awards for Art & Culture" in a ceremony at Gracie Mansion.

Terra Luna Films and Centre Pompidou in Paris coproduce an hour-long documentary on Bourgeois, directed by Camille Guichard, for French television.

1994

Galerie Karsten Greve in Cologne exhibits *Louise Bourgeois: Sculptures and Installations* (January 29 to May 14).

Jeremy Strick of the Saint Louis Art Museum organizes *The Sublime is Now: The Early Work of Barnett Newman and Louise Bourgeois: The Personages* (June 30 to August 28).

Carl Haenlein of the Kestner-Gesellschaft in Hannover mounts the exhibition *Louise Bourgeois Skulpturen* (September 3 to October 30). Bourgeois exhibits *Cell Bullet Hole* (1992), which consists of three wooden balls enclosed in metal doors and two secret panels with the inscriptions "Fear Makes the World Go Round" and "What Makes Your World Go Round." Bourgeois receives the NORD/LB art prize.

Louise Bourgeois: Print Retrospective takes place at the Museum of Modern Art in New York (September 13 to January 3, 1995). The show travels to the Bibliothèque Nationale in Paris (February 9 to April 12, 1995); the Musée du Dessin et de l' Estampe Originale in Gravelines, France (May 28 to September 1, 1995); The Museum of Modern Art in Oxford (October 14 to December 31, 1995); and the Bonnefanten Museum in Maastricht (January 20 to April 13, 1996). The publication of the first volume of Bourgeois' print catalogue raisonné by Deborah Wye and Carol Smith accompanies the show.

Peter Blum Gallery in New York exhibits *Louise Bourgeois: The Red Rooms* (September 17 to December 10).

The Archives of American Art in New York City puts on the show *The Louise Bourgeois Papers: A Promised Gift to the Archives of American Art* (November 17 to December 11).

Nigel Finch directs a one-hour documentary on Louise Bourgeois for Arena Films of the BBC in London.

FIGURE 98. Louise Bourgeois in her Brooklyn studio, 1991

Marion Cajori begins working on another documentary on Bourgeois for Christian Blackwood Productions in New York. The project is still in progress.

1995
Marie-Laure Bernadac organizes *Louise Bourgeois: Pensées-Plumes* at the Musée National d'Art Moderne, Centre Georges Pompidou in Paris (February 1 to April 10) which travels to the Helsinki City Art Museum in Finland (April 28 to July 16).

With the help of Yann Andrea, the Théatre du Vieux-Colombier in Paris exhibits *Louise Bourgeois: Dessins pour Duras* (March 9 to April 23), for which Bourgeois creates eleven wood and mixed-media plaques in honor of Marguerite Duras. Two short plays by Duras, *Le Square* and *Le Shaga*, are performed during the exhibition. The work is presented again at Galerie Karsten Greve in Cologne as *Louise Bourgeois: Hommage à Duras* (September 27 to November 4).

The Tate Gallery in London organizes *Rites of Passage* (June 15 to September 3), curated by Stuart Morgan and Frances Morris. Bourgeois is represented by *J'y Suis, J'y Reste* (1990), *Red Room (Parents)* (1994), *Nature Study #5* (1995), and *Cell (Hands and Mirror)* (1995).

The MARCO in Monterrey, Mexico, mounts *Louise Bourgeois* (June 15 to January 5, 1996), curated by Richard Marshall; travels to the Centro Andaluz de Arte Contemporaneo in Seville (February 5 to May 31, 1996), and to the Museo Rufino Tamayo in Mexico City (June 4 to August 15, 1996).

The Musée d'Art Moderne de la Ville de Paris presents the travelling exhibition *Louise Bourgeois: Exposition Retrospective: Sculptures, Environnements, Dessins, 1944–1994* (June 23 to August 10).

Bourgeois receives the "1995 Biennial Award" from the Royal Museum in Tokyo and the Hakone Open-Air Museum, Kanagawa-ken, Japan. She is also awarded an Honorary Doctorate of Fine Arts from the Art Institute of Chicago.

Precious Liquids is shown in *Féminin-Masculin: Le sexe de l'art* (October 17 to January 11, 1996) at the Centre Georges Pompidou, organized by Marie-Laure Bernadac and Bernard Marcadé.

The National Gallery of Victoria in Melbourne, Australia, which owns *Cell (Glass Spheres and Hands)* (1990–1993) mounts *Louise Bourgeois*, curated by Jason Smith (October 19 to November 27). The exhibition travels to the Museum of Contemporary Art in Sydney (December 21, 1995 to April 14, 1996).

Bourgeois makes the CD *Otte*, produced by Brigitte Cornand, who also directed *Chère Louise*, a video on Bourgeois by Les Films Du Siamois in Paris for Canal +.

1996
Bourgeois receives the First Annual Urban Glass Awards for Innovative Use of Glass by a Non-Glass Artist.

Larry Rinder organizes for the University Art Museum and Pacific Film Archive of the University of California at Berkeley *Louise Bourgeois: Drawings* (January 24 to March 24), which travels to The Drawing Center in New York (April 17 to June 8).

Bourgeois' work is included in an exhibition organized by Catherine de Zegher entitled *Inside the Visible* at the Institute of Contemporary Art in Boston (January 30 to May 12). The show travels to the National Museum of Women in the Arts, Washington, D.C. (June 15 to September 15) and the Whitechapel Gallery, London (October 11 to December 8).

Headed by Alfred Pacquement, the French Government Delegation working with Olivier Kaepplin and Aude Bodet commissions Bourgeois to create a sculpture in Choisy-le-Roi. The original site of the Paul Eluard Théatre is changed to the old mayor's town hall and park. Bourgeois conceives of two hanging nests made out of aluminum (one male and one female), which will hang from a tree. On April 10, Bourgeois' *Les Bienvenus* is inaugurated at the Parc de la Mairie.

Bourgeois is commissioned by the Battery Park City Authority of New York City to create an outdoor sculpture for the new Robert F. Wagner, Jr. Park in lower Manhattan. The park faces the Statue of Liberty and Ellis Island. Six bronze hand poses titled *The Welcoming Hands* are installed but later removed due to a controversy surrounding their proximity to the Holocaust Museum. Bourgeois then exchanges the suite of bronzes for the large granite piece *Eyes* (1995).

FIGURE 99. Louise Bourgeois inside *Cell IV*, 1991   *Chronology* | 303

The Rupertinum in Salzburg, Austria mounts *Louise Bourgeois* (July 27 to October 27).

Bourgeois is included in the São Paulo Bienal (September 14 to December 15), in the exhibition curated by Paulo Herkenhoff and Jerry Gorovoy. She is represented by a selection of images about women. She also designs the exhibition posters for the show.

The Institute of International Visual Arts exhibits *The Visible & The Invisible: Re-presenting the Body in Contemporary Art and Society* (September 21 to October 26) at St. Pancras Church in London. Four fabric pieces–*Single I, Single II, Couple I* and *Couple II*–are exhibited in the bell tower.

Galerie Hauser and Wirth in Zurich exhibits *Louise Bourgeois: Red Room Installation / Drawings* (November 23 to January 25).

Galeria Soledad Lorenzo in Madrid organizes the exhibition *Louise Bourgeois* (December).

Pouran Esrafily begins collaborating with Louise Bourgeois on a feature-length experimental film whose intent is to express Bourgeois' creative process. It is currently a work in progress.

1997

Bourgeois is commissioned by the French Government to make a large-scale work, *Toi et Moi*, in cast and polished aluminum for the new Bibliothèque Nationale de France in Paris, by architect Dominique Perrault.

The Fondazione Prada in Milan exhibits *Louise Bourgeois: Blue Days and Pink Days* (May 15 to July 20), organized by Jerry Gorovoy and Pandora Tabatabai Asbaghi.

The National Medal of Arts is presented to Bourgeois by President Clinton at the White House. Her son Jean-Louis Bourgeois accepts the award on her behalf.

The National Gallery of Art in Washington, D.C., acquires the large-scale *Spider* (1997) for its outdoor sculpture garden scheduled to open in May 1999.

The Yokohama Museum in Tokyo mounts *Louise Bourgeois* (November 2 to January 15), curated by Taro Amano.

The Arts Club of Chicago mounts *Louise Bourgeois* (November 12 to January 13), which is composed of recent sculptures as well as *The Insomnia Series* (1994–1995).

1998

Bourgeois is commissioned by the Pittsburgh Cultural Trust to make a sculpture for Agnes R. Katz Plaza at the corner of Seventh Street and Penn Avenue. The project is a collaboration with the architect Michael Graves (who designed the adjacent O'Reilly Theater), and Dan Kiley, the landscape architect for Katz Plaza. Bourgeois conceives of two twenty-five-foot-high intersecting cones in bronze. Water emanates out of the top two points of each cone, intersecting into one stream, which winds its way like an unbroken thread down to the bottom basin. Black granite benches in the shape of eyeballs are situated around the park.

The Musée d'Art Contemporain in Bordeaux mounts *Louise Bourgeois*, curated by Marie-Laure Bernadac (January 30 to April 26). The show travels to the Foundation Belem in Lisbon (June 20 to August 23, 1998), the Malmö Konsthall in Sweden (September 11 to November 1, 1998), and the Serpentine Gallery in London (November 18, 1998 to January 10, 1999).

The Moderna Museet in Stockholm exhibits *Passage Dangereux* (1997) in *Wounds: Between Democracy and Redemption in Contemporary Art* (February 14 to April 19), organized by David Elliot and Pier Luigi Tazzi. It is installed in a room with works by Yannis Kounellis and Ed Kienholz.

The North Carolina Museum of Art in Raleigh mounts *Sacred and Fatal: The Art of Louise Bourgeois*, curated by Lucy Daniels (March 7 to May 31).

The Kunsthalle Wien in Austria exhibits *Bourgeois-Holzer-Lang* (October 9 to January 10, 1999), which includes a suite of eight holograms.

Passage Dangereux is subsequently shown at the Solomon R. Guggenheim Museum in SoHo in *Premises: Invested Spaces in Visual Arts & Architecture from France 1958–1998*, organized by Bernard Blistène of the Centre Pompidou (October 13 to January 11).

Cheim & Read Gallery in New York City organizes *Bacon, Bourgeois, Messerschmidt*, curated by Jean Clair (November 18 to December 31).

Bourgeois becomes an Academician of the National Academy in New York in the Sculpture Class.

1999

The Tate Gallery in London commissions a project from Bourgeois for the inauguration of the Bankside Power Station in May 2000. For the Turbine Hall Bourgeois conceives of a thirty-foot *Spider* and three steel architectural towers employing the use of staircases and mirrors.

The Kunsthalle Bielefeld mounts *Louise Bourgeois* (February 30 to May 2), organized by Thomas Kellein.

Bourgeois is awarded the Wexner Prize from the Wexner Center for the Arts at Ohio State University.

Bourgeois receives the 1999 Praemium Imperiale Award in the sculpture category from the Japan Art Association.

Bourgeois participates in the 48th International Exhibition of Contemporary Art, La Biennale di Venezia, Venice, Italy (June 13 to November 7), curated by Harald Szeemann. Included are five recent fabric works: *Untitled* (1998), *Topiary* (1998), *Three Horizontals* (1998), *Why Have You Run So Far Away* (1999), and *Quilting* (1999). She is awarded The Golden Lion for a living master of contemporary art.

Bourgeois' *Cell (The Runaway)* (1998–99), *Fillette (Sweeter Version)* (1968; cast 1999), *Double Negative* (1963) and six untitled *Personnages* from the 1950s are included in *The American Century: Art and Culture, 1950–2000* (September 23, 1999 to January, 23, 2000) at the Whitney Museum of American Art in New York.

The Museo Nacional Centro de Arte Reina Sofía in Madrid mounts the retrospective exhibition *Louise Bourgeois: Memory and Architecture* (November 16, 1999 to February 14, 2000) curated by Jerry Gorovoy and Danielle Tilkin.

Solo Exhibitions

1945
Paintings by Louise Bourgeois, Bertha Schaefer Gallery, New York

1947
Louise Bourgeois: Paintings, Norlyst Gallery, New York

1949
Louise Bourgeois, Recent Work 1947–1949: Seventeen Standing Figures in Wood, Peridot Gallery, New York

1950
Louise Bourgeois: Sculptures, Peridot Gallery, New York

1953
Louise Bourgeois: Drawings for Sculpture and Sculpture, Peridot Gallery, New York
Louise Bourgeois, Allan Frumkin Gallery, Chicago, Illinois

1959
Sculpture by Louise Bourgeois, Andrew D. White Art Museum, Cornell University, Ithaca, New York (one of five exhibitions associated with "Festival of Contemporary Arts")

1964
Louise Bourgeois: Recent Sculpture, Stable Gallery, New York
Recent Drawings by Louise Bourgeois, Rose Fried Gallery, New York

1974
Sculpture 1970–1974, 112 Greene Street, New York

1978
Louise Bourgeois: New Work (includes a performance "A Banquet/A Fashion Show of Body Parts" in conjunction with the piece *Confrontation*), Hamilton Gallery of Contemporary Art, New York
Triangles: New Sculpture and Drawings, 1978, Xavier Fourcade Gallery, New York
Louise Bourgeois: Matrix/Berkeley 17, University of California, Berkeley Art Museum, Berkeley, California

1979
Louise Bourgeois, Sculpture 1941–1953. Plus One New Piece, Xavier Fourcade Gallery, New York

1980
The Iconography of Louise Bourgeois, Max Hutchinson Gallery, New York
Louise Bourgeois Sculpture: The Middle Years 1955–1970, Xavier Fourcade Gallery, New York

1981
Louise Bourgeois: Femme Maison, Renaissance Society, University of Chicago, Illinois

1982
Bourgeois Truth, Robert Miller Gallery, New York

1982–84
Louise Bourgeois: Retrospective, The Museum of Modern Art, New York; traveled to Contemporary Arts Museum, Houston, Texas ; Museum of Contemporary Art, Chicago, Illinois; Akron Art Museum, Akron, Ohio

1983
Louise Bourgeois, Daniel Weinberg Gallery, San Francisco, California

1984
Louise Bourgeois Sculpture, Robert Miller Gallery, New York
Louise Bourgeois, Daniel Weinberg Gallery, Los Angeles, California

1985
Louise Bourgeois: Retrospective 1947–1984, Maeght-Lelong, Paris, France; traveled to Maeght-Lelong, Zurich, Switzerland
Louise Bourgeois, Serpentine Gallery, London, England

1986
Louise Bourgeois, Robert Miller Gallery, New York
Eyes, installed at the Doris Freedman Plaza, Fifth Avenue at 60th Street, New York; sponsored by the Public Art Fund and New York City Department of Parks and Recreation
Louise Bourgeois: Sculptures and Drawings, Texas Gallery, Houston, Texas

1987
Paintings from the 1940's, Robert Miller Gallery, New York
Louise Bourgeois, Riva Yares Gallery, Scottsdale, Arizona
Louise Bourgeois: Sculpture 1947–1955, Gallery Paule Anglim, San Francisco, California
Paintings & Drawings, Janet Steinberg Gallery, San Francisco, California

1987–89
Louise Bourgeois, The Taft Museum, Cincinnati, Ohio; traveled to The Art Museum at Florida International University, Miami, Florida; Laguna Gloria Art Museum, Austin, Texas; Gallery of Art, Washington University, St. Louis, Missouri; Everson Museum of Art, Syracuse, New York

1988
Louise Bourgeois: Drawings 1939–1987, Robert Miller Gallery, New York
Louise Bourgeois: Works on Paper 1939–1988, Museum Overholland, Amsterdam, The Netherlands
Louise Bourgeois: Works from 1943–1987, Henry Art Gallery, University of Washington, Seattle, Washington

1989
Louise Bourgeois: Drawings 1940–1986, Galerie Lelong, Paris, France
Louise Bourgeois: Sculpture, Robert Miller Gallery, New York

Louise Bourgeois: Progressions and Regressions, Galerie Lelong, New York
Louise Bourgeois: Works from the 50's, Sperone-Westwater Gallery, New York
Louise Bourgeois Sculpture, American Academy and Institute of Arts and Letters, New York
Louise Bourgeois: Works from the Sixties, Dia Art Foundation, Bridgehampton, New York
Louise Bourgeois: Legs, Ydessa Hendeles Art Foundation, Toronto, Canada
Louise Bourgeois: 100 Drawings 1939–1989, Galerie Lelong, Zurich, Switzerland
Louise Bourgeois: Selected Works 1946–1989, Rhona Hoffman Gallery, Chicago, Illinois
Recent Sculpture by Louise Bourgeois, Art Gallery of York University, North York, Ontario, Canada

1989–91
Louise Bourgeois: A Retrospective Exhibition, Frankfurter Kunstverein, Frankfurt, West Germany; traveled to Städtische Galerie im Lenbachhaus, Munich, West Germany; Musée d'art Contemporain, Lyon, France; Fundación Tapies, Barcelona, Spain; Kunstmuseum Berne, Switzerland; and Kröller-Muller Museum, Otterlo, The Netherlands

1990
Louise Bourgeois: Drawings and Sculpture, Barbara Gross Galerie, Munich, Germany
Louise Bourgeois: Bronze Sculpture and Drawings, Linda Cathcart Gallery, Santa Monica, California
Louise Bourgeois: Drawings, Karsten Schubert Ltd., London, England
Louise Bourgeois: 1984–1989, Riverside Studios, London, England
Louise Bourgeois 1939–89 Sculptures and Drawings, Galerie Krinzinger, Vienna, Austria
Louise Bourgeois: Bronzes of the 1940s and 1950s, Galerie Karsten Greve, Cologne, West Germany
Bourgeois Four Decades, Ginny Williams Gallery, Denver, Colorado
Louise Bourgeois: Sculptures and Drawings, Monika Sprüth Galerie, Cologne, Germany

1991
Louise Bourgeois, Ydessa Hendeles Art Foundation,
Toronto, Canada
Louise Bourgeois: Prints, Galerie Lelong, Zurich,
Switzerland
Louise Bourgeois: Recent Sculpture, Robert Miller
Gallery, New York

1992
Louise Bourgeois, Ydessa Hendeles Art Foundation,
Toronto, Canada
Louise Bourgeois: C.O.Y.O.T.E., Parrish Art Museum,
Southampton, NY
Currents 21: Louise Bourgeois, Milwaukee Art Museum,
Milwaukee, Wisconsin
Louise Bourgeois: Drawings, Second Floor, Reykjavik,
Iceland
Louise Bourgeois: Prints 1947–1991, Barbara Krakow
Gallery, Boston, Massachusetts
Louise Bourgeois, Galerie Karsten Greve, Paris, France
Recent Acquisitions, East Wing, National Gallery of Art,
Washington, D.C.
*The Fabric Workshop's 15th Anniversary Annual Benefit
Honoring Louise Bourgeois and Anne d'Harnoncourt,* The
Fabric Workshop, Philadelphia, Pennsylvania (opened
with a new performance by Louise Bourgeois titled
She Lost It, created in collaboration with The Fabric
Workshop)

1993
Louise Bourgeois, Linda Cathcart Gallery, Santa
Monica, California
Louise Bourgeois: Personages, 1940s / Installations, 1990s,
Laura Carpenter Fine Art, Santa Fe, New Mexico
Louise Bourgeois, Ginny Williams Family Foundation,
Denver, Colorado
Louise Bourgeois: Etchings, Jan Weiner Gallery, Topeka,
Kansas
Louise Bourgeois, Galerie Ramis Barquet, Monterrey,
Mexico

1993–96
American Pavilion, Venice Biennale, Italy, with an
expanded exhibition titled *The Locus of Memory*;
traveled to the Brooklyn Museum of Art, New York; the

Corcoran Gallery of Art, Washington, D.C.; Galerie
Rudolfinum, Prague, Czech Republic; Musée d'Art
Moderne de la Ville de Paris, France; Deichtorhallen,
Hamburg, Germany; Musée d'Art Contemporain de
Montreal, Canada

1994
Louise Bourgeois (etchings), Galerie Espace, Amsterdam,
The Netherlands
*Louise Bourgeois: Drawings and Early Sculptures;
Sculptures and Installations,* Galerie Karsten Greve,
Cologne, Germany
Louise Bourgeois, Galeria Karsten Greve, Milan, Italy
Louise Bourgeois: The Personages, The St. Louis Art
Museum, St. Louis, Missouri
Louise Bourgeois, Nelson-Atkins Museum of Art,
Kansas City, Missouri
Louise Bourgeois: Sculptures, Kestner-Gesellschaft,
Hannover, Germany
Louise Bourgeois: The Red Rooms, Peter Blum, New York
Louise Bourgeois, Locks Gallery, Philadelphia,
Pennsylvania
*The Louise Bourgeois Papers: A Promised Gift to the
Archives of American Art,* Archives of American Art,
New York

1994–96
Louise Bourgeois: Print Retrospective, The Museum of
Modern Art, New York; traveled to the Bibliothèque
Nationale, Paris, France; Musée du Dessin et de
l'Estampe Originale, Gravelines, France; The Museum
of Modern Art, Oxford, England; Bonnefanten
Museum, Maastricht, The Netherlands

1995
Louise Bourgeois: Drawings, Ecole Nationale des Beaux-
Arts de Bourges, France
Louise Bourgeois: Pensées-Plumes, Musée National d'Art
Moderne, Centre Georges Pompidou, Paris, France;
traveled to Helsinki City Art Museum, Finland
Louise Bourgeois: Drawings, Galerie Karsten Greve, Paris
Louise Bourgeois: Drawings for Duras, Théâtre du Vieux-
Colombier, Paris, France

Louise Bourgeois, Mitsubishi-Jisho Artium, Fukuoka City, Japan; traveled to Walker Hill Art Center, Seoul, Korea
Louise Bourgeois: Homage to Duras, Galerie Karsten Greve, Cologne, Germany
Louise Bourgeois, Galerie Pièce Unique, Paris, France

1995–96
Louise Bourgeois, MARCO, Monterrey, Mexico; traveled to Centro Andaluz de Arte Contemporaneo, Seville, Spain; Museo Rufino Tamayo, Mexico City
Louise Bourgeois, The Museum of Modern Art, Oxford, England (an exhibition of sculpture to accompany The Museum of Modern Art print retrospective); traveled to ORIEL, The Arts Council of Wales' Gallery, The Friary, Cardiff, Wales
Louise Bourgeois, National Gallery of Victoria, Melbourne, and The Museum of Contemporary Art, Sydney, Australia

1996
Louise Bourgeois: Drawings, University Art Museum, University of California, Berkeley, California; traveled to The Drawing Center, New York; The List Visual Art Center, Massachusetts Institute of Technology, Cambridge, Massachusetts
Louise Bourgeois, Gallery Paule Anglim, San Francisco, California
Les Bienvenus, permanent installation of a commission for the city of Choisy-le-Roi, France, accompanied by a solo exhibition in the Ville de Choisy-le-Roi, Service Municipal d'Arts Plastiques
Louise Bourgeois: Works on Paper, Galerie Karsten Greve, Cologne, Germany
Louise Bourgeois: Spiders Baumgartner Galleries, Inc., Washington, D.C.
Louise Bourgeois: Sculptures and Objects, Rupertinum, Salzburg, Austria
XIth Mostra da Gravura de Curitaba/Mostra América, a special room dedicated in honor of Louise Bourgeois, The Fundacão Cultural de Curitaba, through the Museu da Gravura, Curitaba, Brazil
Louise Bourgeois: The Forties and Fifties, Gallery Joseloff, Harry Jack Gray Center, University of Hartford, Westford, Connecticut

Louise Bourgeois, Galería Soledad Lorenzo, Madrid, Spain
Louise Bourgeois: Red Room Installation / Drawings, Galerie Hauser and Wirth, Zurich, Switzerland
Louise Bourgeois, Xavier Hufkens Gallery, Brussels, Belgium

1997
Toi et Moi, commissioned by the French Government, is installed in the new Bibliothèque Nationale de Paris
Louise Bourgeois: Sculpture, Centro Cultural Banco Cultural do Brasil, Rio de Janeiro, Brazil
Louise Bourgeois, Locks Gallery, Philadelphia, Pennsylvania
The Drawings of Louise Bourgeois, Centro Cultural da Light, Rio de Janeiro, Brazil
Louise Bourgeois: Ode à ma mère, The Contemporary Arts Center, Cincinnati, Ohio
Louise Bourgeois: Recent Drawings, Galerie Karsten Greve, Paris, France
Louise Bourgeois, Galerie Karsten Greve, Cologne, Germany
Louise Bourgeois: Blue Days and Pink Days, Fondazione Prada, Milan, Italy
Louise Bourgeois, Yokohama Museum, Tokyo, Japan
Louise Bourgeois: Drawings, Rhona Hoffman Gallery, Chicago, Illinois
Louise Bourgeois, The Arts Club of Chicago, Chicago, Illinois

1998
Carte Blanche à Annee Djion: The Drawings of Louise Bourgeois, Espace Saint-François, Lausanne, Switzerland
Sacred and Fatal: The Art of Louise Bourgeois, North Carolina Museum of Art, Raleigh, North Carolina
Topiary, Whitney Museum of American Art, New York
Present Tense: Louise Bourgeois, The Art Gallery of Ontario, Toronto, Canada
Louise Bourgeois: New Work, Galerie Lars Bohman, Stockholm, Sweden
Louise Bourgeois: Art is a Guarantee of Sanity, Wood St. Galleries, Pittsburgh, Pennsylvania
Louise Bourgeois: Geometry of Pleasure, Barbara Krakow Gallery, Boston, Massachusetts

1998–99
Louise Bourgeois, capcMusée d'Art Contemporain, Bordeaux, France; traveled to Fondation Belem, Lisbon, Portugal; Malmö Konsthall, Malmö, Sweden; Serpentine Gallery, London, England

1999
Louise Bourgeois Prints: 1989–1998, Maier Museum of Art, Randolph-Macon Women's College, Lynchburg, Virginia
Louise Bourgeois, Galerie Karsten Greve, Cologne, Germany
Louise Bourgeois, Dartmouth College, Jaffe-Friede & Strauss Galleries, Hanover, New Hampshire

Louise Bourgeois, Kunsthalle Bielefeld, Bielefeld, Germany
Louise Bourgeois: Topiary, Galerie Pièce Unique, Paris, France
Wexner Prize Wall, Wexner Center for the Visual Arts, Columbus, Ohio
Louise Bourgeois, Grafiska Sallskapet, Stockholm, Sweden
Louise Bourgeois: Graphic Works, Remba Gallery, West Hollywood, California

1999–2000
Louise Bourgeois: Memory and Architecture, Museo Nacional Centro de Arte Reina Sofía, Madrid, Spain

Selected Bibliography

BOOKS AND CATALOGUES

1978
Wye, Deborah. Matrix/Berkeley 17: *Louise Bourgeois* (exhibition catalogue). Berkeley: University Art Museum, University of California.

1980
Gorovoy, Jerry. *The Iconography of Louise Bourgeois* (exhibition catalogue). New York: Max Hutchinson Gallery.

1981
Marandel, Patrice J. "Louise Bourgeois: From the Inside," in *Louise Bourgeois: Femme Maison* (exhibition catalogue). Chicago: The Renaissance Society at the University of Chicago.

1982
Bourgeois, Louise. "He Disappeared into Complete Silence," (her poem and drawings), p. 17–36, *The Harvard Advocate Special Translation Issue,* Summer.
Pincus-Witten, Robert. *Bourgeois Truth* (exhibition catalogue). New York: Robert Miller Gallery.
Wye, Deborah. *Louise Bourgeois* (exhibition catalogue for her retrospective). New York: Museum of Modern Art.

1985
Frémon, Jean. *Louise Bourgeois: Rétrospective 1947–1984* (exhibition catalogue). Paris: Galerie Maeght-Lelong.
Frémon, Jean and Robert Storr. *Louise Bourgeois: Rétrospective 1947–1984* (exhibition catalogue). Zurich: Galerie Maeght-Lelong.
Morgan, Stuart. *Louise Bourgeois* (exhibition catalogue). London: Serpentine Gallery.

1986
Gorovoy, Jerry. *Louise Bourgeois* (exhibition catalogue). New York: Robert Miller Gallery.

1987
Morgan, Stuart. *Louise Bourgeois* (exhibition catalogue). Cincinnati, Ohio: The Taft Museum.

1988
Cheim, John and Jerry Gorovoy, eds. *Louise Bourgeois Drawings,* with introduction by Robert Storr. New York: Robert Miller Gallery; Paris: Daniel Lelong.
Kuspit, Donald. *Bourgeois* (an interview with Louise Bourgeois). New York: Elizabeth Avedon Editions/Vintage Contemporary Artists (a division of Random House).
———. *Louise Bourgeois Works on Paper* (exhibition leaflet/catalogue). Amsterdam: Museum Overholland.

1989
Geldzahler, Henry. *Louise Bourgeois* (exhibition catalogue). Bridgehampton, New York: Dia Art Foundation.
Weiermair, Peter with Lucy Lippard, Rosalind Kraus et.al. *Louise Bourgeois* (European retrospective catalogue). Frankfurt: Frankfurter Kunstverein. [subsequent versions published by exhibition locations: Lyon: Musée d'Art Contemporain, Lyon in French; London: Riverside Studios; Barcelona: Fundación Tapies in Spanish, Catalan and English.]

1990
Morgan, Stuart. *Louise Bourgeois: Recent Work 1984–1989* (exhibition catalogue). London: Riverside Studios.

1992
Meyer-Thoss, Christiane. *Louise Bourgeois: Designing For Free Fall.* Zurich: Ammann Verlag.
Miller, Arthur and Louise Bourgeois. *Homely Girl, A Life.* New York: Peter Blum Edition.
Sobel, Dean. *Louise Bourgeois* (exhibition pamphlet). Milwaukee, Wisconsin: Milwaukee Art Museum.

1993

Garcia Murillo, Jorge. *Louise Bourgeois* (exhibition catalogue). Mexico City: Galeria Ramis Barquet.

Kotik, Charlotta. *Louise Bourgeois Recent Work* (exhibition brochure for United States Pavilion), published by the United States Information Agency with copyright by The Brooklyn Museum, New York.

1994

Louise Bourgeois: *Album*. New York: Peter Blum Edition.

Gardner, Paul. *Louise Bourgeois*. New York: Universe Publishing.

Haenlein, Carl. ed. with Carsten Ahrens, Barbara Catoir, et.al. *Louise Bourgeois Sculptures and Installations*. Hannover, Germany: Kestner-Gesellschaf

Kotik, Charlotta with Terrie Sultan and Christian Leigh. *Louise Bourgeois: The Locus of Memory, 1982–1993*. New York: Harry N. Abrams & The Brooklyn Museum.

Strick, Jeremy. *Louise Bourgeois: The Personages*. St. Louis: St. Louis Museum of Art.

Wye, Deborah and Carol Smith. *The Prints of Louise Bourgeois*. New York: The Museum of Modern Art.

1995

Bernadac, Marie-Laure. *Louise Bourgeois Pensées-Plumes*. Paris: Cabinet d'art graphique, Centre Georges Pompidou.

Bernadac, Marie-Laure. *Louise Bourgeois*. Paris: Flammarion, Collection La Création Contemporaine.

Bourgeois, Louise and Larry Rinder. *Louise Bourgeois: Drawings & Observations*. Berkeley, California: University Art Museum and Boston: Bulfinch Press, Little, Brown & Company.

Bréerette, Geneviève. *Louise Bourgeois* (exhibition catalogue). Bourges: Ecole Nationale des Beaux-Arts.

Cole, Ian. *Louise Bourgeois Sculpture/The Prints of Louise Bourgeois*. Oxford: The Museum of Modern Art Oxford (exhibition brochure).

Edition Stemmle, 1989/1995. An English reprint of *Louise Bourgeois* (European retrospective catalogue). Frankfurt: Frankfurter Kunstverein, 1989.

Karjalainen, Tuula with Maija Tanninen-Mattila, and Marie-Laure Bernadac. *Louise Bourgeois*. Helsinki, Finland: Helsinki City Art Museum

Marshall, Richard D. and Paulo Herkenhoff. *Escultura de Louise Bourgeois: La Eleganca de la Ironia*. Monterrey, Mexico: Museo de Arte Contemporaneo de Monterrey (MARCO).

Murayama, Atsuko. *Louise Bourgeois*. Fukuoka City, Japan: Mitsubishi-Jisho Artium with the cooperation of MOMA Contemporary Co., Ltd.

Pagé, Suzanne and Béatrice Parent. *Louise Bourgeois: Sculptures, environments, dessins 1938–1995*. Paris: Musée d'Art Moderne de la Ville de Paris and Editions de la Tempête.

Pernoud, Emmanuel. *Louise Bourgeois: estampes*. Paris: Bibliothèque Nationale de France.

Smith, Jason, with essay by Robert Storr. *Louise Bourgeois*. Melbourne, Australia: National Gallery of Victoria.

1996

De Diego, Estrella. "Asomarse hacia dentro," *Louise Bourgeois* (exhibition catalogue). Madrid: Galería Soledad Lorenzo.

Zdenek, Felix. *Louise Bourgeois: Der Ort des Gedächtnisses: Skulpturen, Environments und Zeichnungen 1946–1995*. Hamburg: Deichtorhallen and Editions de la Tempête, Paris.

———. *Louise Bourgeois: The Forties and Fifties* (exhibition catalogue). West Hartford, Connecticut: Joseloff Gallery, Harry Jack Gray Center, University of Hartford.

1997

Amano, Taro, with essays by Jerry Gorovoy, Robert Storr and Louise Neri. *Louise Bourgeois: Homesickness* (exhibition catalogue). Tokyo: Yokohama Museum of Art.

Asbaghi, Pandora Tabatabai and Gorovoy, Jerry with essay by Paulo Herkenhoff. *Louise Bourgeois: Blue Days and Pink Days*. Milan, Italy: Fondazione Prada. English version also published with additional photographs.

Cottong, Kathy with essay by Paulo Herkenhoff. *Louise Bourgeois* (exhibition catalogue). Chicago: Arts Club of Chicago.

Herkenhoff, Paulo. *Louise Bourgeois*. Rio de Janeiro, Brazil: Centro Cultural Banco do Brasil.

Herkenhoff, Paulo and de Moraes, Angelica. *Louise Bourgeois: desenhos/drawings*. Rio de Janeiro, Brazil: Centro Cultural Light.

1998
Bernadac, Marie-Laure with essays by Louise Neri, Paulo Herkenhoff. *Louise Bourgeois* (exhibition catalogue). Bordeaux: capcMusée d'Art Contemporain and London: Serpentine Gallery.

Bourgeois, Louise, *Destruction of the Father, Reconstruction of the Father. Writings and Interviews 1923–1997*, edited and with texts by Marie-Laure Bernadac and Hans-Ulrich Obrist. London: Violette Editions.

Crone, Rainer. *Louise Bourgeois: The Secret of the Cells.* Munich: Prestel-Verlag.

Darrieussecq, Marie. "Dans la maison de Louise," *Louise Bourgeois* (hors exhibition catalogue). Bordeaux: capcMusée d'Art Contemporain; London: Serpentine Gallery.

Zenakis, Mâkhi. *The Blind Leading the Blind* (Lycée Fénelon). Galerie Lelong and Actes Sud, Paris.

1999
Kellein, Thomas. *Louise Bourgeois* (exhibition catalogue). Bielefeld, Germany: Kunsthalle Bielefeld.

Gorovoy, Jerry and Tilkin, Danielle with essays Joseph Helfenstein; Beatriz Colomina; Christiane Terrisse; Lynne Cooke; Mieke Bal; Jennifer Bloomer. *Louise Bourgeois: Memory and Architecture* (exhibition catalogue). Madrid: Museo Nacional Centro de Arte Reina Sofía.

Videotapes and Others

1975   *Louise Bourgeois*
Directed by Lynn Blumenthal and Kate
Horsfield
Chicago: Video Data Bank, School of the Art
Institute of Chicago
30 minutes, black and white

1983   *Louise Bourgeois: Partial Recall*
New York: The Museum of Modern Art/
The Easton Foundation
18 minutes

1987   *ART/new york, Louise Bourgeois*
Directed by Paul Tschinkel
Inner-Tube Video, New York City
28 minutes

1991   *Sculpture of the 1980's*
Business Arts, Inc.
30 minutes

1995   *Louise Bourgeois At Close Quarters*
Directed by Rosamund Bernier
Metropolitan Museum of Art, New York
60 minutes

FILMS

1993   *Louise Bourgeois*
Directed by Camille Guichard, with interviews
by Bernard Marcadé and Jerry Gorovoy
Terra Luna Films/Centre Georges Pompidou,
Paris
52 minutes

1994   *Louise Bourgeois*
Director: Nigel Finch
The Easton Foundation/Arena Films, BBC,
London
55 minutes

1995   *Chère Louise (Portrait of the Sculptor Louise
Bourgeois)*
Directed by Brigitte Cornand; produced by
Canal +
Les Films Du Siamois, Paris
60 minutes

1996   *ART CITY*
Produced and directed by Chris Maybach
& Paul Gardner
Twelve Films, New York
50 minutes

1998   *Louise Bourgeois: Mes travaux en cours 1*
(My Works in Progress, Chapter I)
Directed by Brigitte Cornand
Les Films du Siamois, Paris
35mm

Louise Bourgeois: Mes travaux en cours 2
(My Works in Progress, Chapter II)
Directed by Brigitte Cornand
Les Films du Siamois, Paris
35 mm.

AUDIOCASSETTES

1989   Louise Bourgeois at Robert Miller Gallery for
Independent Curators Incorporated, New York

COMPACT DISCS

1995   *Otte*
Directed by Louise Bourgeois; produced by
Brigitte Cornand, Paris

MINISTERIO DE EDUCACIÓN Y CULTURA   Con la colaboración de **IBERIA**